Canadian Writers and Their Works

CANADIAN WRITERS AND THEIR WORKS

FICTION SERIES • VOLUME ONE

 EDITED BY

ROBERT LECKER, JACK DAVID, ELLEN QUIGLEY

INTRODUCED BY GEORGE WOODCOCK

ECW PRESS, 1983

CANADIAN CATALOGUING IN PUBLICATION DATA

Main entry under title:

Canadian writers and their works : essays on form,
    context, and development : fiction

Bibliography: p. 272

ISBN 0-920802-43-5 (set).—ISBN 0-920802-45-1 (v.1)

1. Canadian fiction (English) - History and
criticism - Addresses, essays, lectures.*
2. Authors, Canadian (English) - Biography.*
I. Lecker, Robert, 1951- II. David, Jack,
1946- III. Quigley, Ellen, 1955-

PS8187.C36 C813'.009 C82-094801-2
PR9192.2.C36

V.1
C.2

49,461

Copyright © ECW PRESS, 1983.

The publication of this series has been assisted by grants from the
Ontario Arts Council and The Canada Council.

This volume was typeset in Sabon by Howarth & Smith.
Printed and bound in Canada.

Published by ECW PRESS, Stong College, York University,
Downsview, Ontario M3J 1P3.

The illustrations are by Isaac Bickerstaff.

CONTENTS

PREFACE

Canadian Writers and Their Works (CWTW) is a unique, twenty-volume collection of critical essays covering the development of Canadian fiction and poetry over the last two centuries. Ten volumes are devoted to fiction, and ten to poetry. Each volume contains a unifying Introduction by George Woodcock and five discrete critical essays on specific writers. Moreover, each critical essay includes a brief biography of the author, a discussion of the tradition and milieu influencing his/her work, a critical overview section which reviews published criticism on the author, a long section analyzing the author's works, and a selected bibliography listing primary and secondary material. The essays in each volume are arranged alphabetically according to the last names of the writers under study.

This is Volume One in the Fiction Series of *Canadian Writers and Their Works*. Other volumes in the series will be published as research is completed. The projected completion date for the entire series is 1987.

The editors wish to acknowledge the contributions of many people who have played an important part in creating this series. First, we wish to thank the critics who prepared the essays for this volume: Carl P. A. Ballstadt, Dennis Duffy, Carole Gerson, Lorraine McMullen, Michael Peterman, and George Woodcock. We are also indebted to the Production and Design teams at both The Porcupine's Quill and Howarth & Smith, and to Debra Burke, who keyboarded the manuscript in its initial typesetting phase. Our sincere thanks also go to Ken Lewis, and his assistant Graham Carr, for their excellent technical editing.

RL/JD/EQ

Introduction

GEORGE WOODCOCK

THERE IS SOMETHING of the fascination of a Darwinian exercise about tracing the origins of a national culture or a national litera-ture. When does a variation become so distinctive and enduring that we must call it a new species? Or, to transfer this idea into the spatial-temporal terms of a culture emerging in a young country, when does a new place create a new voice?

One can put the question in another way by asking whether American literature begins with Captain John Smith's *True Rela-tion of . . . Virginia* (1608), a vigorously written account of the first settlement in what is now the United States, or with, say, Charles Brockden Brown's *Wieland*, which was written at the end of the eighteenth century and is the ancestor of a notable Gothic strain in American fiction running through Poe and Hawthorne down to Faulkner and other Southern novelists in our own day. (It is also, incidentally, something of an ancestor of at least one of the writers discussed in this volume, for John Richardson, when he wrote *Wacousta*, can hardly have been unaware of *Wieland* or of Brown's powerful and horrific novel of Indian wars in the American wilder-ness, *Edgar Huntly*.)

I think we would have to take Brown as our benchmark, for Smith was writing for English people the narrative of an English venture in the Americas which did not survive to become part of the fabric of American society, while Brown, though he was working in a literary mode derived from Europe and particularly from the English Gothic strain represented by William Godwin, was using an American setting and American people (natives and immigrants) and, above all, writing for a developing American literary public. Yet the selection of Brown does not mean the rejection of Smith; for, though it is impossible to describe Smith as an American writer in the sense of his having helped to develop an American literary consciousness, the *True Relation of . . . Virginia* is a contribution to our knowledge of what America *was*. In the same way, the narratives of the early attempts to navigate the North West Passage or of early Hudson's Bay Company wanderers like Kelsey and Henday are contributions to our knowledge of what the land that became Canada was, without being legitimately part of Canadian literature as it eventually emerged.

In other words, there is literature that is *about* a country without being *of* it (D. H. Lawrence's splendid travel books on Mexico and Italy spring to mind as brilliant examples); and there is literature that — whatever its setting may be — is beyond doubt *of* its author's country (and, in this case, Margaret Laurence's *The Prophet's Camel Bell* and her African fictions are equally good examples).

In the writers discussed in the present volume, it seems to me, we have an interesting progression, from literature about a country but not of it, through pioneer literature that is of the country in the sense of having found its place without finding its true voice, to the critical point when, to use a chemical analogy, the new voice is about to liquefy and become perceptible.

Carole Gerson, writing in this collection on the mid-nineteenth-century trio of Leprohon, Machar, and De Mille, remarks that they "had little sense of belonging to a national literary movement" and that until the 1890s "... nearly all Canadian poets and novelists ... suffered the absence of a stimulating, self-critical artistic community transcending civil and provincial boundaries." One might even go further and say that such a "self-critical artistic community" has really emerged in Canada — at least in a literary context — only during the past half-century, beginning with the emergence of the *New Provinces* poets in the 1930s, with their critical acuity and their historical intuitions.

Yet, as Gerson adds, "In the case of Leprohon, De Mille, and Machar, a combination of choice and chance shaped their literary fortunes, destining them to support their country's conservative cultural values and to refrain from challenging the limits of their own talents." And it is here, it seems to me, in recognizing limitations, both personal and cultural, that the kind of consciousness which creates a "national literary movement" begins to emerge, for limitations define, and out of self-definition emerges an awareness of possibilities and their creative development. In other words, we have reached with novelists like these three the point when writers are about to speak in the new voice of a culture defining itself, as their immediate successors like Isabella Valancy Crawford and Sara Jeannette Duncan certainly do.

Frances Brooke, in *The History of Emily Montague*, clearly wrote about Canada but is not of Canada; she is the first of a brilliant series of birds of passage and as such belongs to Canada's literary history rather than to the Canadian literary tradition. This does not mean that she is without interest to us; on the contrary, she is of great interest since she represents a kind of literary intelligence that has often appeared among us — observing, providing data, congealing perceptions into images that remain and affect our culture even when the writer, who is never quite one of us, has departed. In a largely immigrant culture in the process of formation, the temporarily resident wanderer plays a much more welcome role than he does in the established cultures, where he always remains the outsider, a kind of itinerant trader who will carry back to his homeland the treasures of observation he has gathered but leave nothing the natives value behind him. One can compare Canadians like Mavis Gallant and Norman Levine, living out their writing lives expatriately without arousing much awareness or wielding much influence in the countries they have chosen (France and England respectively), with the long succession of writers from Frances Brooke, through Anna Jameson and Patrick Anderson, down to Brian Moore in our own day, who have lived for a few years or months among us and revealed us in the mirrors of their consciousnesses; such writers have influenced not only our views of ourselves but also our ways of expressing them, and their place in our cultural history is unassailable, even if it would be foolish to lay claim to them as Canadian writers.

Frances Brooke's *The History of Emily Montague* shows the special influence of its Canadian ambiance by being, as James Talman and Ruth Talman pointed out in *Literary History of Canada*, much less dominated by violent action than most of the eighteenth-century English novels of sensibility among which it belongs:

> Its sensation is provided by its setting: Canadian forests and rivers, Indians and habitants, waterfalls and snows. Is it a novel only, or might it be classed also with description and travel literature?[1]

9

The last sentence contains a very interesting suggestion, which I shall take up later. In the meantime, it is worth remarking on the ambivalence of Frances Brooke's attitude — or that of her characters — to the setting in which their relationships frustratingly entangle. The splendours of scenery are described in terms of conventional pre-Romantic admiration; the rigours of winter are seen in harsher terms, so that there are times when *Roughing It in the Garrison* would seem an appropriate enough alternative title for *The History of Emily Montague*. Consider a passage like this:

> I must venture to Quebec to-morrow, or have company at home: amusements are here necessary to life; we must be jovial, or the blood will freeze in our veins.
>
> I no longer wonder the elegant arts are unknown here; the rigour of the climate suspends the very powers of the understanding; what then must become of those of the imagination? Those who expect to see
>
> "A new Athens rising near the pole,"
>
> will find themselves extremely disappointed. Genius will never mount high, where the faculties of the mind are benumbed half the year.[2]

A worthy predecessor of Susanna Moodie speaks here. And *Emily Montague*, for all its occasional toying with the idea of a Canada transformed by "every elegant art" into something like an English landscape designed by Humphry Repton, with neat gardens and "enamelled meadows," ends in a note of rejection — and specifically rejection of the setting — when the bright and coquettish Bell half flippantly and half sadly remarks as she prepares to depart for England:

> Not but this is a divine country, and our farm a terrestrial paradise; but we have lived in it almost a year, and one grows tired of every thing in time, you know. . . . (III, 143)

Emily Montague is indeed virtually unique among the English eighteenth-century novels of sensibility in the way it gives depth to its rendering of a little garrison society in a provincial capital by a vivid use of the physical setting as something much more than background; yet, in doing this, it reminds me of the work of a woman writer of the preceding century who also visited a British colony and wrote a novel about it. The novel is Aphra Behn's *Oroonoko; or, The Royal Slave* (1688), set in Surinam, where Behn lived for a while as Brooke did in Quebec, and resembling *Emily Montague* in the way its vivid descriptions of an exotic environment are used to set and maintain a tone. But *Oroonoko*, with its presentation of the cruelties of slavery and the corruptness of colonial systems, is a far darker novel than *Emily Montague*, and if there is a point at which Behn's acerbic tone finds an echo among the writers discussed in this volume, it is in the sharper prose and the mordant character sketches of Susanna Moodie, whose pre-Victorian evangelical Christianity would, of course, have been deeply offended by Behn's Restoration amoralism.

But perhaps the most valid reason for evoking the ghost of Aphra Behn, the first woman to become a professional writer, is that of the seven authors discussed in this volume no less than five are women. All of them were perhaps not professional, in the sense of earning their entire livings from writing, but all of them were dedicated and persistent writers, and all of them, except Susanna Moodie, continued writing to the end of what were, in some cases, very long lives; Catharine Parr Traill lived to be ninety-seven and Agnes Maule Machar to be ninety.

The exceptional importance of women writers in Canada is a phenomenon that has become especially noticeable in recent decades, but it is striking to find the situation already present in the early years of our culture. True, the list of men writers might have been filled out with the inclusion of Joseph Howe, Thomas McCulloch, and similar names, but the dominance of women writers in this formative stage of the Canadian literary tradition would still have been evident.

In the case of women engaged in the pioneer settlement of the land, like Moodie and Traill, one can perhaps offer as an explanation — or a partial one — the fact that their menfolk were too rigorously bound to the toil the land demanded, and it is true that after a lifetime of hard work, Samuel Strickland, the brother of the two ladies, proved himself a member of the writing Stricklands only twenty-nine years after his arrival by publishing his memoirs of pioneer living in Upper Canada. But Frances Brooke, Rosanna

Leprohon, and Agnes Machar all belonged to cultured urban families. That they embarked on literary careers, and persisted in them with such strength of will, suggests a freedom of manners in early Canadian society, despite its Methodistical or Jansenist moralism, which encouraged such free enterprise in artistic terms among women of talent.

Of course, it would distort the picture these literary careers represent if one were to think of all of them as wholly Canadian. Frances Brooke went back to England in 1768 after five years — interrupted by a long trip home — in Canada. The memory of her North American experiences doubtless lingered; an anonymous novel about Canada, *All's Right at Last; or, The History of Miss West*, has with some plausibility been attributed to her. How widely *Emily Montague* was remembered or read in Canada during the generations following publication, it is hard to tell; ninety-eight years after it appeared, as Lorraine McMullen tells in her essay, it was noticed by Henry Morgan in his *Bibliotheca Canadensis* (1867), but it was not for another sixty years, in the 1920s, that the first serious consideration was given to the book by Canadian critics.

As for Frances Brooke, she slipped back into the London literary world like a trout returned to the water and was involved in writing and theatrical production until her death in 1789, the year when the French Revolution brought an end to her neo-Augustan world. Certainly she was a literary figure of modest standing, well known enough to earn the resentment of David Garrick, the amused acceptance of Fanny Burney, and the acquaintanceship of Samuel Johnson. Her status in the "Johnson circle" is unclear, and it would perhaps be taking things too far to talk of friendship. For there was a curious story about Brooke and Johnson. She is said to have asked him to read some of her plays, at the same time boasting of all her literary "irons in the fire." Pestered for a comment, Johnson irascibly replied: "Tell Mrs. Brooke she should put her plays where she keeps her irons!"

The Strickland sisters, Susanna Moodie and Catharine Parr Traill, belonged to a well-known English mid-nineteenth-century literary family. Along with three other of their five sisters, they had started writing in their teens as an elegant accomplishment and had kept it up for money when their father died and the family funds ran low. Catharine's first book, *The Tell Tale*, appeared when she was sixteen; Susanna, after early children's stories like *Spartacus*, which appeared when she was nineteen, published sketches and poems in *La Belle Assemblée*, a court and fashion magazine, when she was twenty-four. Both thus had modest literary careers by the time they sailed for Canada, and they went there with every intention of writing about their experiences. One of their sisters, Agnes, gained a considerable standing in the English literary world as a result of her many-volumed *Lives of the Queens of England*, and the best-known works of the two Canadian Strickland sisters, Catharine's *The Backwoods of Canada* and Susanna's *Roughing It in the Bush*, were written primarily with an eye to English readers, telling them about the strange and alien world of the Canadian pioneers. It was only when time made that world strange and alien to us also that *The Backwoods* and *Roughing It* became Canadian classics; by then, they had long been forgotten in England.

Yet — and this is one of the most important things about them — the Strickland sisters did not seek merely to be expatriates writing for English readers. They had committed their lives to Canada, sealing that commitment by years of hardship. Both endeavoured, with moderate success, to make careers as Canadian writers, involving themselves in whatever magazines appeared in the upper and lower colonies, it being too soon for Canadian publishing to offer them much opportunity to bring out their books locally.

In the case of the Strickland sisters, one sees the parallels between the pioneering life, as such, and the pioneering of a literary culture. The pioneer when he arrives in a new land has no model but the old land he left behind him. What he seeks to do, as Ed Rivers dreamed of doing in *Emily Montague*, is to create in the wilderness a kind of paradise free from the restrictions of his past world, yet retaining its essential order. The Moodies, the Traills, and their kind all sought to do this, yet the materials from which they had to make their new life, including the wilderness that would be its site, were all new and different. This was why the literary myth of Robinson Crusoe, a self-made man living a self-made life on a deserted island, so fascinated them. Traill was especially attracted to it, calling one of her Canadian novels *The Canadian Crusoes: A Tale of the Rice Lake Plains* and remarking in *The Backwoods of Canada*:

> We begin to get reconciled to our Robinson Crusoe sort of life, and the consideration that the present evils are but temporary, goes a great way towards reconciling us to them.[3]

But, as even Robinson Crusoe discovered, no wilderness is proof from intrusion, and every Canadian pioneer found the land inhabited by people of other cultures with whom conflict was possible, whether they were John Richardson's Indians, Susanna Moodie's Yankees, or the French, whose relationship with the English invaders forms part of the substance of *Emily Montague* and most of the substance of Rosanna Leprohon's *Antoinette de Mirecourt; or, Secret Marrying and Secret Sorrowing.*

One can deal with such a situation in a number of ways, and the approaches writers from Brooke to Leprohon use reveal the links between the way people lived in Canada during this formative period of our culture and the literature that emerged from it. For, as Dennis Duffy in his essay on John Richardson notes:

> We ignore at our peril the actual, as opposed to the imaginative, experiences any writer undergoes. When one of those experiences is a war fought at the impressionable age of sixteen, we must acknowledge those aspects of the conflict that reverberate throughout an author's work.

And there are other kinds of conflict than war.

Perhaps they come together most clearly in the concept of the garrison, first observed by Northrop Frye and since then, largely through the influence of Margaret Atwood's *Survival*, given what often seems a disproportionate importance in Canadian writing generally considered. Yet the garrison is, of course, central to John Richardson's Canadian novels, and especially to *Wacousta*, where the fortress of Detroit is the centre of an action based on defence and penetration; even though the garrison itself may be preserved, it provides no shelter for doomed individuals.

The garrison in *Emily Montague* is not visibly threatened, and no major disruptions occur in the lives of the characters through the contact between the conquerors and the conquered, as happens in *Antoinette de Mirecourt.* Yet both the *canadiens* and the Indians are used in such a way as to pose a criticism of English life: a criticism which centres on the comparative status of women, and here perhaps the salient factor lies in the correction of first impressions, the realization that strange things are not necessarily so fine as their unfamiliarity may make them seem at first sight. Encountering a company of wandering Indian women, Bell enthusiastically cries:

". . . they talk of French husbands, but commend me to an Indian one, who lets his wife ramble five hundred miles, without asking where she is going" (I, 102). But very soon she learns that the apparently free life of the Indian woman has its own constraints:

> I admire their talking of the liberty of savages; in the most essential point, they are slaves: the mothers marry their children without ever consulting their inclinations, and they are obliged to submit to this foolish tyranny. (I, 116)

But Brooke, a visitor rather than a resident, always puts her English characters in the position of observers when they relate to *canadiens* and Indians. In the experience of writers who committed themselves more deeply to life in Canada, the contacts became deeper, and their resolution led in one of two directions, towards reconciliation or towards conflict.

Conflict appears at its most melodramatic in *Wacousta*, even more than in John Richardson's other writings. The background to the action is the savage war waged against the whites by Pontiac and his Indians in 1763-64, and the famous massacre of the garrison at Michilimackinac is one of the book's set pieces. But within that action there is the titanic conflict between the fake Indian Wacousta and the commander of Detroit, Colonel de Haldimar, which ends in the death of both the antagonists. And within Wacousta himself there is the conflict between the English gentleman he once was, before de Haldimar stole his bride from him, and the savage — more cruel than any Indian — whom he became in his search for revenge.

Less violent, but no less real in terms of shaping *Roughing It in the Bush*, is the conflict Susanna Moodie wages with the Yankee settlers and the Canadians who imitate them. They scorn and persecute her as an English lady, and she in turn scarifies in prose the crudity of their egalitarian behaviour with such disdain that it is a little surprising to be reminded that the Moodies, despite their rejection of Mackenzie and his rebellion, were radicals of their own kind and admirers of the reforming Baldwins. The rebellion appropriately ends the book; it is the conflict that releases the Moodies from their seven years of battle against the bush and their hostile neighbours.

The recurrence of personal conflict, interspersed with periods of suffering from the intractable forces of nature, gives *Roughing It in the Bush* its restless and episodic form, in comparison with *The Backwoods of Canada*, in which the tone of mild enthusiasm and the smoothly running narrative seem the very expressions of a persistent urge towards reconciliation. That urge is evident on a human level in the almost idyllic account of Traill's relations with the local Indian bands and on a natural level in the loving intimacy with which she observes the land, its beautiful flowers, its strange and intriguing fauna. It is evident, from the few disagreeable scenes which are recorded, that Traill endured many of the difficulties and the disappointments with neighbours that form the substance of her sister's book, but the difficulties are shown to be temporary and the personal disappointments exceptional, so that instead of ending, as *Roughing It* does, with a relieved escape from the slavery of the bush and a last chapter entitled "Adieu to the Woods," *The Backwoods of Canada* nears its close with Catharine Parr Traill telling her English correspondent that,

> . . . for all its roughness, I love Canada, and am as happy in my humble log-house as if it were courtly hall or bower; habit reconciles us to many things that at first were distasteful. It has ever been my way to extract the sweet rather than the bitter in the cup of life, and surely it is best and wisest so to do.[4]

In a similar way, Rosanna Leprohon seeks in *Antoinette de Mirecourt* to exemplify the process of reconciliation which she believed must be attained between the French in Canada and the English intruders. In some ways, her own life had been an exemplification of that reconciliation; the daughter of an Irish merchant settled in Montreal, she had married a well-known French-Canadian doctor and had turned from the fiction about another country (five serialized novels set in England) that she wrote before her marriage to the series of novels sympathetically regarding French-Canadian life, of which *Antoinette de Mirecourt* was the most successful. (The others were *Armand Durand; or, A Promise Fulfilled* and "The Manor House de Villerai," which still awaits publication in volume form.)

The subtitle — "Secret Marrying and Secret Sorrowing" — sets the tone for one aspect of *Antoinette de Mirecourt*, a Victorian novel in which the author's frequent moralizing comments present the lesson that honour and honesty should govern relationships, not merely between the sexes, but between the generations. Antoinette is tricked into a secret marriage with a British officer, Major Audley Sternfield, and is then forced into a tortuous path of deception towards the world and towards her devoted father. Sternfield represents one face of the conquerors — the rapacious one; he marries Antoinette because she is an heiress, but he combines greed (and need) with a desire to dominate and humiliate, and in drawing his character Leprohon seems to be portraying the kind of men who — whether they came as soldiers or commercially minded civilians with an eye to the main chance — treated the French as a subject people to be dominated and plundered.

Fortune releases Antoinette when Sternfield is killed in a duel, and then it is that a different conqueror appears, in the person of the grave and compassionate Colonel Evelyn, a man who sympathizes with, and seeks to understand, the French Canadians, and whose goodness converts Antoinette's father from his indiscriminate hatred of the foreigners. Not only is Antoinette released from the consequences of her youthful folly, but a reconciliation of the two peoples is prefigured in her marriage to the noble colonel. The contrast between the novel of conflict and the novel of reconciliation is curiously demonstrated by the fact that Colonel Evelyn, like Wacousta, is a man who has been scarred by a betrayal in love, but the experience that turned one man into a monster has turned the other into something near to a secular saint.

Thus, in many ways, through conflict and the reconciliation of conflict, we see the early Canadian writers in English presenting the ways in which the pioneers (including the conquerors) came to terms with their new world, not only as an unfamiliar and at first apparently hostile terrain which had to be brought under cultivation, but also as the habitation of earlier human societies which had to be controlled or conciliated in order to create a new English-speaking society. In the process, attitudes had to be changed. The pride of the conqueror had to be abandoned, as Colonel Evelyn abandoned his. The very class attitudes that sustained the structure of English society had to be shed, for, as Susanna Moodie shows near the end of *Roughing It in the Bush*, the needs of the new life had elevated the practical abilities of the working man over the social virtues of the gentleman:

I have given you a faithful picture of a life in the backwoods of Canada, and I leave you to draw from it your own conclusions. To the poor, industrious working man it presents many advantages; to the poor gentleman, *none!* The former works hard, puts up with coarse, scanty fare, and submits, with a good grace, to hardships that would kill a domesticated animal at home. Thus he becomes independent, inasmuch as the land that he has cleared finds him in the common necessaries of life; but it seldom, if ever, in remote situations, accomplishes more than this. The gentleman can neither work so hard, live so coarsely, nor endure so many privations as his poorer but more fortunate neighbour. Unaccustomed to manual labour, his services in the field are not of a nature to secure for him a profitable return. The task is new to him, he knows not how to perform it well; and, conscious of his deficiency, he expends his little means in hiring labour, which his bush-farm can never repay. Difficulties increase, debts grow upon him, he struggles in vain to extricate himself, and finally sees his family sink into hopeless ruin.[5]

Yet, as Michael A. Peterman remarks, the enduring impression one gains from *Roughing It* is that "the pattern of adaptation, of learning through experience, prevails," and indeed the Moodies did eventually find their place in Canadian society, and Susanna never went home.

It is perhaps accidental that the one among these early Canadian writers in whom the theme or pattern of reconciliation never makes a significant appearance should also be the first Canadian-born writer in English of any significance, John Richardson. Yet Richardson's birth in Upper Canada, his immersion from childhood in the lore of frontier warfare, and his actual participation as a boy in the War of 1812 seem to have precipitated what Dennis Duffy terms his "lifelong preoccupation with the terror of existence." Certainly the need for conflict was burnt into Richardson's nature, so that even the fleeting alliance between whites and Indians he had seen in the cooperation of Brock and Tecumseh, and celebrated in his appalling poem *Tecumseh; or, The Warrior of the West*, was superseded by the conflict, black with brutality and treachery, between the two races in *Wacousta*.

Richardson always remained a man at war with his world;

Wacousta was projected from within. He existed in a milieu of self-created enmities and, unlike the Moodies and the Traills, never found a way of living in his own country, so that he spent years in England, fought in Spain during the Carlist wars, and became the first Canadian expatriate writer, dying in poverty in New York in 1852. Why were Richardson's fate and his writing so different from those of the other writers discussed in this volume? Was it because he remained at heart a child of the garrison and frontier warfare, locked in a world of fear that made him take so naturally to the Gothic manner and prevented him from finding a place in the changing world of the clearings and the towns?

As Richardson's choice of the Gothic suggests, there is a more than analogical link between the colonial life which was their subject matter and the search for appropriate forms that one sees among the writers discussed in this book. Like the pioneer farmers, the pioneer writers began by attempting to recreate the lost world of their childhood or their fathers in literary terms. But, again like the settlers, they found that the old approaches did not always fit the new circumstances.

It is true that one finds among the books discussed in these essays examples of most of the genres that were fashionable in Britain at the time or sometimes at a slightly earlier date. There are Richardson's Gothicisms, which remind one of Monk Lewis and Maturin, as well as of Brockden Brown; there are the boys' adventure fictions of De Mille's B.O.W.C. series (reminiscent in more than title of the tales in the B.O.P. — *Boy's Own Paper*) and the quasi utopia of his *A Strange Manuscript Found in a Copper Cylinder*; there are the romantic, yet moralistic, novels of Rosanna Leprohon and the awkward fiction of social conscience of Agnes Maule Machar; there are the Strickland sisters' narratives of imperial settlement, analogues of which can be found in other colonial literatures; and there is Frances Brooke's novel of sentiment, written in an epistolary form that was made famous by Samuel Richardson but which originated with women writers like Aphra Behn in the seventeenth century.

And yet, though all these authors follow patterns established in Britain, there are interesting ways in which their best works depart from Old World models, while their worst works — like Moodie's poems or Richardson's *Tecumseh* — are those in which they fail to realize that literature, like life, must adapt to a changed world. And thus, in a few key works of this early period of Canadian writing, one can see already the variations that in the end, to take up the metaphor with which I began this introduction, acquire the distinctness and the endurance that make us recognize a new species. One cannot yet detach the works to which I have been referring from English literature, but one can certainly recognize in them English literature with a difference and at a distance.

We return to the Talmans' question in *Literary History of Canada* about *The History of Emily Montague*:

> Is it a novel only, or might it be classed also with description and travel literature?

It is a question that must be balanced by the tendency of some critics to consider the ostensibly factual accounts of pioneer experiences by writers like Moodie and Traill as being — or at least being comparable to — novels. In his essay on Traill, Carl P. A. Ballstadt mentions the treatment by T. D. MacLulich of *The Backwoods* and *Roughing It* "as versions of the 'Crusoe' fable," and Michael A. Peterman notes how Carl F. Klinck argued of *Roughing It* that ". . . the book is best read as a novel that gains by 'concentration' upon Moodie's dramatization of herself as 'author-apprentice-heroine.' "

What these critics are really suggesting is that in the pioneer period there was a blurring of the boundaries between the various literary genres. Much of the fiction of the time not only was very didactic but also tended to be heavily descriptive of the environment and at times to resemble contemporary travel writing. For example, the earlier part of *A Strange Manuscript Found in a Copper Cylinder*, which tells of Adam More's wanderings when he is first lost in the Antarctic, reads very much like a pastiche of nineteenth-century polar-exploration narratives.

But to say that sometimes fiction resembles travel writing — and perhaps vice versa — is not to surrender to the current North American academic snobbery which elevates the "creative" genres of fiction and poetry and seeks to find elements of the novel or the poem in works written with neither fictional nor lyrical intent. Travel writing and autobiography have their own ways of dealing with the palpable difference between the merely factual and the wholly true, and it is not necessary to declare an autobiographical memoir like *Roughing It in the Bush* a novel merely because Susanna Moodie shapes her narrative with artifice, rearranges episodes, and heightens the chiaroscuro of characterization to present a story that will catch the reader's attention. Every autobiographer, every travel writer, even every historian or biographer with a pretension to being a good writer, does the same, and one might as justly call Donald Creighton's *The Empire of the St. Lawrence*, that splendid historical myth, a novel as apply the same description to *Roughing It in the Bush*. Both books are examples of the way in which the inchoate mass of facts — the crude data of experience — must be shaped by the writer to give it the feeling of truth. But that does not make them fiction in the sense we normally recognize, that of invention. And here, I think, we have to recognize a basic characteristic of emergent literatures: that they tend to be concerned with what William Godwin called "Things as They Are" and carry very little in the way of allegorical overload. Here I find particularly appropriate some sentences I have just read in a new essay on Homer:

> The allegorizing process tends to generalize every character or action into an abstraction. No poetry is less susceptible to this process than Homer's. . . . It has no hidden meanings. Everything described in it is intensely and uniquely itself.[6]

It is in this way, I suggest, that we must look at all beginning literatures. They are dealing with experiences that are new, but unassimilated into a new culture. They may use tried or traditional forms, in the same way as Homer used oral modes that had become formalized over centuries. Yet they are talking of the pristine and particular, not the accustomed and generalized. They are telling, like Homer, of something that, because it has not yet been subsumed into a settled order, is "intensely and uniquely itself." We do not have to look for layers of concealed meaning, partly because the writers with whom we are dealing are urgently concerned with what is there in pristine physical actuality or — in the case of the Richardsons — in dreadful imagined reality, but partly also because the culture itself has not yet developed the system of myths and symbols that will transform it from an almost accidental meeting of people and terrain into a distinctive cultural identity, a true species.

NOTES

[1] James J. Talman and Ruth Talman, "Settlement, Part III: The Canadas 1763-1812," in *Literary History of Canada: Canadian Literature in English*, gen. ed. and introd. Carl F. Klinck (Toronto: Univ. of Toronto Press, 1965), p. 85.

[2] Frances Brooke, *The History of Emily Montague* (1769; rpt. New York: Garland, 1974), I, 216-17. All further references to this work appear in the text.

[3] Catharine Parr Traill, *The Backwoods of Canada: Being Letters from the Wife of an Emigrant Officer, Illustrative of the Domestic Economy of British America* (London: Charles Knight, 1836), p. 123.

[4] Traill, *The Backwoods of Canada*, p. 310.

[5] Susanna Moodie, *Roughing It in the Bush; or, Life in Canada*, 2nd ed. (London: Bentley, 1852), II, 289-90.

[6] K. W. Gransden, "Homer and the Epic," in *The Legacy of Greece: A New Appraisal*, ed. M. I. Finley (London: Oxford Univ. Press, 1981), p. 80.

Frances Brooke (1724-1789)

LORRAINE MCMULLEN

Biography

FRANCES MOORE, eldest of three daughters of the Reverend Thomas Moore and Mary Knowles, was baptized 24 January 1724 at Claypole, Lincolnshire, where her father was curate. The Moores were an old Lincolnshire family. On her father's death in 1727, his widow and three small daughters moved to Peterborough to live with Mrs. Moore's mother, Mrs. Sarah Knowles. On Mrs. Moore's death in 1737, her daughters went to live with a maternal aunt, Sarah, and her husband, the Reverend Roger Steevens, rector of Tydd Saint Mary.[1]

By 1748 Frances had left this family home; by the 1750s she was writing poetry and plays. She first attracted literary attention with her editorship, under the pseudonym "Mary Singleton, Spinster," of a weekly periodical, *The Old Maid*, which appeared from 15 November 1755 to 24 July 1756. In the vein of *The Spectator* of Addison and Steele, the journal included essays and letters written in a lively style commenting on theatre, politics, and religion. In 1756 Frances published a number of poems and a play, *Virginia*, written some years earlier, which she had given up all hope of having produced. During the next few years, Frances continued to write for the theatre, working on a farce and a pastoral, neither of which she succeeded in having produced. By the summer of 1756, she was married to the Reverend John Brooke, rector of Colney, Norfolk, and of several parishes in Norwich.

In 1757 John left for America as a military chaplain. That year their only son, John Moore, was born. The Brookes also had a daughter who did not survive to adulthood. Three years later, Frances published the *Letters from Juliet, Lady Catesby, to Her Friend, Lady Henrietta Campley*, a translation of Marie-Jeanne Riccoboni's popular novel of sensibility, which had appeared only the previous year. Frances' own first novel, *The History of Lady*

Julia Mandeville, which was, like Madame Riccoboni's novel, epistolary, appeared in 1763. It was immensely popular. By this time a writer of some note, Frances was included in the literary circle of Samuel Johnson. Because of her interest in theatre, she was, already, acquainted with many theatrical figures.

In July 1763 Frances sailed for Quebec with her son, John, and her sister, Sarah, to join her husband, who had been appointed chaplain to the British forces there. She made at least one trip back to England, in 1764, returning to Quebec late in 1765. At Quebec the Brookes participated in the social life around Governor James Murray and the ruling British circle, which included such members as the following: Adame Mabane, a member of the Council of Quebec; Henry Caldwell, Murray's land agent and later Receiver General for Lower Canada; surgeon Samuel Collier and his wife, Jane, who was to remain a close friend; George Allsopp and John Taylor Bondfield, British merchants; and, after 1766, Guy Carleton and his attorney general, Francis Maseres, who was to describe Frances as "a very sensible agreeable woman, of a very improved understanding and without any pedantry or affectation."[2]

Governor Murray, who had found John Brooke irascible, with a tendency to be politically and socially meddlesome, had hoped that the presence of Frances and her sister "would have wrought a change [in John Brooke], but on the contrary they meddle more than he does."[3] While in Canada, Frances wrote *The History of Emily Montague*, which was published the year following her return to England. While Frances makes a point in her novel of indicating that politics is outside the realm of women, she was involved, as well as her husband, in the disputes at Quebec concerning political and religious affairs. The Brookes were adherents of the English party, composed largely of British merchants operating from Quebec and Montreal, who in the interests of their commerce sought to have Quebec assimilated politically, socially, and economically into the British Empire. Adam Mabane, who supported Murray in his attempt to retain for Canadians the rights they had always had, reported, writing to Murray after Carleton had been sent to replace Murray, that "particular Attention is paid to Mrs. Brookes [sic] either from fear of her bad Tongue, or from Gratitude for the good offices she rendered in retailing the Scandal of Quebec at the Tea Tables of London."[4]

In the fall of 1768, Frances was welcomed back into London's literary circle. In the twenty years following her return to England, she published two translations from the French and wrote one tragedy, two comic operas, and at least two novels. The first works to appear after *Emily Montague* were her translations. Her translation of Nicolas Framery's *Memoires de M. le Marquis de S. Forlaix*, a melodramatic and sentimental novel, was published in 1770, her translation of Abbé Millot's *Elémens de l'histoire d'Angleterre* in 1771. In 1773, with her close friend Mary Ann Yates, the great tragic actress, Frances became manager of the Haymarket Opera House, which had been bought by Mary Ann's husband, Richard, also a well-known actor, and Frances' brother-in-law, James Brooke. Here her knowledge of Italian, demonstrated in some early translations of poems, stood her in good stead. Besides directing productions, Frances took on negotiations with musicians. This venture lasted until 1778. Her tragedy, *The Siege of Sinope*, was produced by Thomas Harris at Covent Garden in 1782 with Mary Ann Yates in the title role of Thamyris. It had a run of ten nights. The following year, her comic opera *Rosina* was produced, also by Harris. It was an immediate success. Idyllically pastoral, with music by William Shield, *Rosina* continued to be one of the most popular productions of the century

In the meantime a second novel of Canada, *All's Right at Last; or, The History of Miss West*, published anonymously in 1774, may have been written by Frances Brooke. Although there are several errors in fact, the novel has themes, attitudes, and elements of style that suggest her as author. The French translation ascribes the original to her. *The Excursion*, a novel similar in theme to Fanny Burney's *Evelina*, appeared in 1777, the year before *Evelina*.

Before the production of her second comic opera, *Marian*, in 1788, Frances Brooke had moved to Sleaford to live with her son, John, who had carried on family tradition by studying at Cambridge and entering the ministry. He was at this time vicar of Helpringham and rector of Folkingham, in Lincolnshire. *Marian* was well received, although it was never as popular as the earlier *Rosina*. On 23 January 1789 Frances Brooke died at Sleaford. She had been in failing health for some years. Her last novel, *The History of Charles Mandeville*, was published the year following her death. Intended as a sequel to *Julia Mandeville*, the novel's main interest is its description of the utopian world in which Charles finds himself as sole survivor of a shipwreck.

Tradition and Milieu

Frances Brooke wrote in what we may call, for lack of a better term, the age of sensibility. Pope had died in 1744, Swift in 1745. The wit and satire which characterized the Augustan age were giving way to benevolence and sensibility as a prelude to the Romantic movement. It was an age dominated by Samuel Johnson, the age of Edmund Burke and Oliver Goldsmith, Laurence Sterne and Tobias Smollett, Horace Walpole and Richard Brinsley Sheridan, Blake, Crabbe, Cowper, and Burns, Voltaire and Rousseau. Brooke was in London when Samuel Richardson was writing his last novel. Her *Old Maid* appeared the same year as Burke's *On the Sublime and Beautiful*, her *Julia Mandeville* eight years before Henry Mackenzie's *Man of Feeling*.

Although she was better known as a novelist, Brooke's first love was theatre. Hers was an age unremarkable for its drama, and an age in which it was extremely difficult for a dramatist to have a new work produced. The fate of an aspiring London dramatist was in the hands of two men, the actor-managers of the only two theatres licensed to present plays, Drury Lane and Covent Garden. David Garrick, who ruled Drury Lane from 1747 to 1776, was for thirty years the most renowned and most powerful figure in the theatrical world.

During her early years in London, Brooke became acquainted with many theatrical figures, including dramatist Arthur Murphy, and actors James Quin, Henry Woodward, Peg Woffington, and Tate Wilkinson, later actor-manager at York. Peg's sister Mary (Polly), who married Robert Cholmondeley, second son of Lord Cholmondeley and nephew of Horace Walpole, was a member of the Johnson circle and, through her sister, close to David Garrick. As a friend over many years, she provided Brooke with an entrée to Garrick. To approach an actor-manager through his friends was one way of increasing the chances of being heard. Thus Brooke approached John Rich of Covent Garden through James Quin in her effort to have *Virginia* produced, and Garrick through Mary Cholmondeley.

By 1756, when she was writing *The Old Maid*, Brooke was a friend of Samuel Johnson. There are no clear links with Samuel Richardson, although Brooke was, in later years at least, a friend of John Duncombe and his wife, Susanna Highmore, both of whom had been among the young admirers of Richardson during the period 1753-56, when he was writing *Sir Charles Grandison*. In writing *The Old Maid*, Brooke had the collaboration of the Earl of Cork and Orrery, who was something of a *littérateur* and who had been a friend of Swift and later of Richardson and Johnson; also of Arthur Murphy, the actor and dramatist, who had earlier edited his own periodical, *Gray's Inn Journal*; and the Reverend Richard Gifford, who was to remain a close friend and confidant over many years.

The most obvious influence on Brooke's first work of fiction is Samuel Richardson. *Julia Mandeville* is a novel of sensibility in the epistolary mode. The French novel of sensibility was also an influence, most directly through Marie-Jeanne Riccoboni, whose novel *Lady Catesby* Brooke had translated three years earlier. This translation furthered Riccoboni's popularity — there were six editions of the translation by 1780 — and was an impetus to the developing cult of sensibility in England. The didacticism and sentimentality which characterized the novel of sensibility are evident both in *Lady Catesby* and in Brooke's own first novel.

With her second novel, *Emily Montague*, Brooke is more innovative. Her handling of the epistolary mode is more sophisticated. Her integration of landscape and climate with plot and character, as well as the realism of her description, break new ground in the novel form. In *The Excursion*, Brooke alters course again. Moving away from the epistolary novel to employ an intrusive and ironic narrator, Brooke wrote a female *Bildungsroman* which, in both narrative method and picaresque plot, is reminiscent of Henry Fielding.

Frances Brooke's friends included members of the musical and artistic worlds as well as the theatrical and literary. Among them was Catherine Read, the popular portrait painter, celebrated for her pastels, and in demand with royalty and ladies of fashion. Read's oil portrait of Frances Brooke was engraved by Mariano Bovi in 1771. Among English travellers to Italy whose aid Brooke enlisted with the Opera House was Ozias Humphrey, portraitist and member of the Royal Academy. During her tenure at the Opera House, she was also acquainted with the well-known musician and music historian Charles Burney; and William Shield, who was to collaborate with her, writing the music for her two comic operas, was employed at the Opera House while she was a manager.

Through Charles Burney, Brooke met his daughter Fanny. Young Fanny, only twenty at the time, described their first meeting in 1775, saying of Brooke in a not altogether flattering portrait: "Mrs. Brooke is very short and fat, and squints; but has the art of showing agreeable ugliness. She is very well bred, and expresses herself with much modesty upon all subjects; which in an *authoress*, a woman of *known* understanding, is extremely pleasing."[5]

Brooke's two tragedies are in the heroic classical mode made popular by Dryden. In form and structure, they break no new ground. Of most interest today are the strong women protagonists in both plays. Her two comic operas are pastorals, with simple plots, attractive music, idyllic settings, and happy endings. They succeeded admirably in their objective of providing entertainment.

During her last years, Brooke was well known and highly regarded in literary and theatrical circles. She figures in the letters, memoirs, and diaries of her contemporaries. Writers and dramatists such as Hannah More, Anna Seward, and Elizabeth Griffith admired her writing. On her death in 1789, a leading periodical, hailing her as "a lady as remarkable for her virtues, for her gentleness and suavity of manners, as for her great literary accomplishments," concluded: "She was esteemed by Dr. Johnson, valued by Miss Seward, and her company courted by all the first characters of her time."[6]

Critical Overview and Context

For the most part, the periodical press of her day praised Brooke's novels and dramas, and several periodicals reprinted excerpts from her novels. *The Critical Review* and *The Monthly Review* regularly reviewed her novels, usually commending their sensibility and their support of contemporary mores, and, on occasion, their wit and their lively women characters. The excessive sensibility of *Julia Mandeville*'s hero and heroine met with approval; their tragic end was the only aspect of the novel which drew serious objection. "It has been often, however, wished that the catastrophe had been less melancholy," writes John Nichols in his *Literary Anecdotes*.[7] A brief outline of Brooke's life published in 1783 captures the general note of approval of *Julia Mandeville*: "This production was universally read, and it was as universally admired. Few novels have been published with more celebrity, few have better deserved it. The language is remarkably elegant, and the story as remarkably interesting."[8]

Writing in a period of marked French anglophilia, Brooke was among the best known and most highly praised English novelists in France. Her novels were quickly translated into French and were praised by reviewers in such widely read European periodicals as *Année littéraire* and *Gazette littéraire de l'Europe*.

Frances Brooke was well received by her contemporaries. Interest in her work faded, however, in the next century, with the exception of the continued production of her comic opera *Rosina* and the inclusion of *Julia Mandeville* by Laetitia Barbauld for publication in 1810 in her British Novelist series. In later years, *Julia Mandeville* continued to be, to some degree, the Brooke novel known in England, while *Emily Montague*, with its account of life in Canada during the early years of British rule, was best known in Canada. Henry Morgan described *Emily Montague* in his *Bibliotheca Canadensis* in 1867, while James Le Moine referred to the novel and to Brooke in several of his accounts of early Quebec, including *Picturesque Québec*[9] and *Maple Leaves*.[10] In 1907 Ida Burwash published in *The Canadian Magazine* an article which consisted, for the most part, of a summary of the plot of *Emily Montague*.[11] In 1921 a more detailed essay by Charles S. Blue in the same magazine noted the novel's realistic description of Quebec and its sentimentalism and moralism. Blue provides more information than earlier critics concerning Brooke's other activities and works, and the Brookes' relationship to Governor Murray at Quebec.[12] H. R. Morgan, in a brief article in 1930, noted the novel's description of landscape and customs as its main source of interest to Canadians. He adds nothing noteworthy in terms of biography or criticism.[13] As to Brooke's life, with the exception of her sojourn in Canada, and as to her works, with the exception of *Emily Montague*, these earlier critics repeated the factual errors enshrined in the *Dictionary of National Biography*. They are not impressed with style, narrative technique, or any other aspect of Brooke's artistry. Their interest centres on *Emily Montague* as a report of life in Canada.

In the early 1930s, pointing up the narrow interest of one nation in *Emily Montague* and of the other in *Julia Mandeville*, a new edition of *Emily Montague* appeared in Canada, while a new edition of *Julia Mandeville* appeared in England. Lawrence J. Burpee, introducing *Emily Montague*, adds some details concerning the Brookes at Quebec.[14] E. Phillips Poole, introducing *Julia Mandeville*, provides some accurate information concerning Brooke's background[15] derived from an article a few years earlier by Sir Edmund Royds.[16] Royds's article consisted largely of letters he had collected relating to former owners of his estate, Stubton. Former owners included Brooke's family, the Moores. In his introduction to *Julia Mandeville*, Poole provides in addition to biographical material lengthy summaries of, and comments on, Brooke's dramas and novels. In his view, she moves in both genres from the melodrama and improbability characteristic of the story lines of her time to sensibility and verisimilitude.

In Canada, Desmond Pacey continued the interest in *Emily Montague*. Writing in the *Dalhousie Review* in 1946, Pacey, like earlier Canadian critics, saw the novel's portrayal of Canadian life as its main value, dismissing it artistically as conventional, repetitive, stilted, and monotonous in style, heavily didactic, and sentimental.[17] Pacey seems to have been unaware of the work of Royds or Poole, for he repeats the early errors concerning Brooke's life. He does, however, recognize her feminist attitude to marriage.

In 1950 B. Dufebvre included a chapter on Frances Brooke in his *Cinq Femmes et nous*.[18] Dufebvre quotes extensively from the letters which make up *Emily Montague* to demonstrate Brooke's attitude to Quebec, and he expresses annoyance at some of the remarks concerning religion and the French-Canadian inhabitants. He makes the intriguing suggestion that the letters of Arabella Fermor may have been written by Brooke's sister, Sarah, and those of Arabella's father by John Brooke, leaving Emily's observations to Brooke herself.

Current interest in *Emily Montague* stems from the increasing interest in Canadian literature in general since the 1960s and from the accessibility of the novel with the appearance of the paperback edition in 1961. Carl F. Klinck's introduction to this edition provides our first critically perceptive evaluation of *Emily Montague*.[19] Klinck comments on Brooke's skill in handling the epistolary mode and on the wit and liveliness of her writing.

In 1961, the year the paperback edition of *Emily Montague* appeared in Canada, an article on *The Old Maid* appeared in England. Gwendolyn B. Needham, writing in *Theatre Notebook*, draws attention to the drama criticism in *The Old Maid*, noting, for example, Brooke's criticism of David Garrick for playing Nahum Tate's *Lear* rather than the original.[20]

W. H. New's discerning article on *Emily Montague* in 1972 directs attention to some of the more subtle aspects of Brooke's art. He focuses on the tension between nature and society, which is never entirely resolved. Setting, New says, is used deliberately to establish the tension through which the author conveys her ideas.[21]

In a second article, marking the first Canadian criticism to move from *Emily Montague* to other of Brooke's works, New turns his attention to *The Old Maid*. He sees Brooke's editing of *The Old Maid* as an apprenticeship for her as a writer and as a feminist. In New's opinion, the periodical first reveals the tension evident throughout her works, "not directly between men and women so much as between roles that women accept for themselves, and hence between passive surrender to society and active participation in it."[22]

A second critic to discuss Brooke's feminism is Katherine M. Rogers, who directs her attention to the novels. Rogers makes the point that Brooke demonstrates her realism when she voices her feminist ideas on marriage through Ed Rivers, *Emily Montague*'s male protagonist; for it is unlikely, according to Rogers, that an eighteenth-century woman would make such comments. Rogers commends the good sense and objective tone with which *The Excursion*'s narrator recounts the difficulties of the protagonist. Unlike other novelists of her time, Brooke accepts her protagonist's indiscretion as a minor failing. In general, Rogers contends that in contrast to the sentimental novelists of her time, Brooke subjects her characters to practical problems in a realistic world.[23]

The serious interest in Brooke's writings which has developed since 1960 marks the beginning of a reassessment of her works. The realism and feminism noted variously by Klinck, New, and Rogers are among the most noteworthy aspects of her work, along with her skilful handling of her medium, a skill which has yet to receive adequate attention.

Brooke's Works

Frances Brooke first came to public attention as a periodical essayist. As New notes, *The Old Maid* provided Brooke with an apprenticeship for her fiction. As Needham notes, her observations on theatre mark her as an astute drama critic.

Taking on the persona of a fifty-year-old spinster, Mary Singleton, Brooke writes with lively wit on subjects ranging from marriage to current events, religion to theatre. She writes as a feminist who, despite her independent mind, nevertheless has a strong sense of decorum and a strong awareness of the writer's responsibility to point out the weaknesses of her society.

The variety of writing styles in *The Old Maid*, in the letters of various fictional characters to the editor and the reported conversations of her fictitious friends, provide an apprenticeship for Brooke's later dramas as well as her epistolary novels. Her satirical, witty, and clever observations on society, especially on women, which begin with *The Old Maid*, continue throughout her writing career. Miss Singleton's fictitious niece, Julia, provides the model for Julia Mandeville, a youthful heroine of marked sensibility, while Miss Singleton herself is the shrewd, ironic, and observant voice heard later in Anne Wilmot of *Julia Mandeville*, Arabella Fermor of *Emily Montague*, and the narrator of *The Excursion*. The tension between the conventional acceptance of the mores of society and the questioning of some of those values, notably those pertaining to women and between sense and sensibility, continues to develop through Brooke's career.

Frances Brooke's first novel, which established her popularity, is concerned with the ill-fated romance of Harry Mandeville with his cousin Julia. It is composed of seventy-seven letters, most of them written by Harry or by Lady Anne Wilmot, a lively, coquettish young widow and friend of the lovers. Anne, writing to her own lover, tells us of activities on the country estate of Lord Belmont, Julia's father, where Anne and Harry are guests, while Harry's letters are concerned primarily with his love for Julia. The climax occurs when, due to a breakdown in communications, Harry erroneously concludes that Julia's parents are planning her marriage to another. Harry is mortally wounded in a duel which he forces on Julia's supposed fiancé. Julia dies of a broken heart.

The epistolary method is particularly apt for the dramatist turned novelist. It resembles the dramatic method in providing an opportunity to present several points of view. In *Julia Mandeville*, the two main correspondents, Anne and Harry, present the central problem from different perspectives; while Harry is involved in the love affair, Anne is an observer. Each has different knowledge and brings a different attitude to bear on the problem.

Like the central character of Riccoboni's *Lady Catesby*, Julia and her lover suffer from excessive sensibility. Julia writes: "Born with a too tender heart, which never before found an object worthy of its attachment, the excess of my affection is unspeakable."[24] Harry writes of the ennobling effect of love: "The love of such a woman is the love of virtue itself: it raises, it refines, it ennobles every sentiment of the heart" (I, 192). The pleasure in sorrow characteristic of the person of sensibility is voiced by Anne Wilmot speaking of her grief at the death of the two lovers: "Pleased with the tender sorrow which possessed all my soul, I am determined to indulge it to the utmost ..." (II, 179). Anne's words lend Gothic overtones to the previously Edenic setting of the Belmont estate:

I ... prolonged my walk till evening had, almost unperceived, spread its gloomy horrors round; till the varied tints of the flowers were lost in the deepening shades of night.

Awaking at once from the reverie in which I had been plunged, I found myself at a distance from the house, just entering the little wood so loved by my charming friend; the every moment increasing darkness gave an awful gloom to the trees; I stopped, I looked round, not a human form was in sight; I listened, and heard not a sound but the trembling of some poplars in the wood; I called, but the echo of my own voice was the only answer I received; a dreary silence reigned around; a terror I never felt before seized me; my heart panted with timid apprehension; I breathed short, I started at every leaf that moved; my limbs were covered with a cold dew; I fancied I saw a thousand airy forms flit around me; I seemed to hear the shrieks of the dead and dying: there is no describing my horrors. (II, 178-81)

Horace Walpole's *Castle of Otranto* was published the same year as *Julia Mandeville*. The melodramatic climax, the sudden violence, the Gothic overtones distinguish Brooke's novel from that of Riccoboni which she had translated and indicate her awareness of the trend of the novel of sensibility towards the Gothic.

Anne's wit and humour counterbalance the excessive sensibility of the two young lovers and, in general, run counter to the traditional novel of sensibility. Anne herself stands in contrast to Julia, a conventional eighteenth-century heroine, didactically modelled on courtesy-book instructions to young women. *Julia Mandeville* was written at the beginning of a period of growing interest in courtesy books with their advice to young men and women on behaviour and deportment.[25] Despite the novel's title, Julia remains a shadowy figure. The more prominent Anne is Brooke's spokeswoman. With her wit, her outspoken manner, her frank admission that she enjoys using her arts as a coquette, and her flouting of convention, Anne is the antithesis of the courtesy-book woman. She is the credible creation of a woman writer who was necessarily resourceful, determined, and assertive in her own struggle for recognition in London's theatrical world. Anne's model may have been Charlotte Grandison, sister of the all-too-perfect hero of Richardson's *Sir Charles Grandison*, who is a foil for the heroine, the correct Harriet Byron, who eventually marries Sir Charles. Brooke moves beyond Richardson, for her independent-minded woman, rather than being reproved by her creator as is Charlotte by Richardson, is presented as the most attractive character in *Julia Mandeville*. Anne voices Brooke's feminist views, as did Mary Singleton earlier.

Julia Mandeville demonstrates Brooke's debt to Riccoboni and the French novel of sensibility and is itself a contribution to the growing English cult of sensibility and to the popularity of the novel of sensibility. Yet in her portrayal of life on the Belmont estate — the balls, outings, and rural festivities — Brooke is one of the earliest novelists to attempt a realistic account of everyday events rather than of melodramatic incidents. She achieved a blend of the two modes of sensibility and realism largely through the voices of her two correspondents — Harry, a creature of extreme sensibility, and Anne, an ironic observer. The contrasting images of women in Julia as eighteenth-century courtesy-book heroine and Anne as witty, astute commentator also contribute to the tension between the sensible and the realistic, the romantic and the ironic. A major concern in this novel, which distinguishes Brooke from Riccoboni and others of her time, is her creation of an intelligent and lively woman.

Frances Brooke's experience of Canada provided her with the setting of her second novel and an opportunity to enrich the novel of sensibility and manners with descriptions of the landscape, current events, and inhabitants of a very different world. She again structures her novel around courtship and its complications, but she uses environment and setting with increasing sophistication.

The 228 letters of this epistolary novel are dated during the eighteen-month period April 1766 to November 1767 — a period during which Brooke herself was in Canada. Most of them are written by Ed Rivers, Emily's suitor, and Arabella Fermor, her friend and confidante. Emily is a typical eighteenth-century heroine of decorum and sensibility. Arabella, a young woman of wit and common sense, provides a foil and contrast to Emily. Three sets of lovers are involved in the novel: Emily and Ed, Arabella and a Captain Fitzgerald in Canada, and Ed's sister Lucy and his friend John Temple in England.

Most of the letters are written from Canada to England, so that the scenery, customs, and inhabitants of the new land are naturally the topics discussed. Description is interwoven with the action, which concerns the ups and downs of the courtships of the three couples, all of which end happily with marriage.

Brooke sets up a number of oppositions, as in *Julia Mandeville*. The two central viewpoints are contrasting: Ed Rivers is a handsome, upright, generally conventional, and somewhat prosaic man of sensibility, while Arabella Fermor is not only, as her name suggests, something of a coquette but also a witty, lively, and observant woman. Emily, quiet and sensitive, is a marked contrast to her confidante, Arabella, or Bell as she usually is called. Temple, a charming pleasure-seeking rake, contrasts with the serious and virtuous Rivers. It is not only her characters that Brooke sets in opposition. The Canadian landscape contrasts with the English, and the French-Canadian population with the newly arrived English. Letters are interwoven and juxtaposed to reflect the play of these oppositions and contrasts.

Much of the originality of *Emily Montague* resides in Brooke's effective manipulation of the epistolary method to provide variety of narrative. There are no long, involved epistles similar to chapters in novels, as is characteristic of the works of such epistolary novelists as Brooke's mentors, Richardson and Riccoboni, and the later Fanny Burney. While Brooke rarely includes dialogue within the letters, some of the letters are so brief that they appear to be conversational exchanges. For example, Emily and Arabella, living in the same house, carry on the following exchange:

To Miss Fermor.

I am glad you do not see Colonel Rivers with my eyes; yet it seems to me very strange; I am almost piqued at your giving another the preference. I will say no more, it being, as you observe, impossible to avoid being absurd on such a subject.

I will go to Montmorenci; and, to shew my courage, will venture in a covered carriole with Colonel Rivers, though I should rather wish your father for my cavalier at present.

Yours,

Emily Montague.

To Miss Montague.

You are right, my dear: 'tis more prudent to go with my father. I love prudence; and will therefore send for Mademoiselle Clairaut to be Rivers's belle.

Yours,

A. Fermor.

To Miss Fermor.

You are a provoking chit, and I will go with Rivers. Your father may attend Madame Villiers, who you know will naturally take it ill if she is not of our party. We can ask Mademoiselle Clairaut another time.

Adieu! Your

Emily Montague.[26]

A brief letter from Bell to Lucy, written as Bell is on her way to Montmorency Falls, is followed by another which begins, "So, my dear, as I was saying, this same ride to Montmorenci — where was I, Lucy? I forget — . . ." (II, 73, Letter 81). This could be a conversation continuing after being interrupted by a knock at the door.

In her use of multiple points of view, Brooke skilfully exploits opportunities for dramatic irony. We are given, for example, George Clayton's view on his mother's request that he postpone his planned marriage to Emily, and also the views of Emily, Arabella, Ed, and Emily's guardian. Bell voices her own reactions and those of Emily in writing to Lucy in England, while at the same time Ed also writes to Lucy, giving his interpretation of events.

By varying the letter writers, Brooke varies the mood and tempo of the novel. Each of the main letter writers has a markedly different style and attitude. Ed Rivers, who writes the first letters, describes the landscape and people and initiates the plot. Once Arabella is introduced, she takes on most of such description, adding her wit and perception to her descriptions, while Ed turns his attention to love and marriage. Ed's attitude to this topic is revealed in two ways: his sermonizing letters to John Temple, whom he urges to give up his dissipated behaviour before he becomes too coarsened to value genuine love; and his letters concerning his own love for Emily, in which he speaks of love, friendship, and community of interests, rather than convenience, as a basis for marriage. Further variety is added by the essaylike letters concerning conditions in Canada written by Bell's father, Sir William Fermor, to the Earl of * * *. These letters, which appear at an appropriate moment during a lull in the action of the novel, are straightforward accounts of the political, religious, and social situation in Canada as seen by a conservative member of the British establishment.

Fermor is generally severe in his criticism of the inhabitants of the colony. Of the Indians he says:

> There is little reason to boast of the virtues of a people, who are such brutal slaves to their appetites as to be unable to avoid drinking brandy to an excess scarce to be conceived, whenever it falls in their way, though eternally lamenting the murders and other atrocious crimes of which they are so perpetually guilty when under its influence. (III, 107-08, Letter 152)

His opinion of Canadians is scarcely more flattering: "They are rather devout than virtuous; have religion without morality, and a sense of honor without very strict honesty" (III, 110, Letter 152). The word Fermor uses most frequently to describe the Canadian peasants is "indolent." He is especially critical of the "Romish" religion: "Sloth and superstition equally counter-work providence," he writes. "... A religion which encourages idleness, and

makes a virtue of celibacy, is particularly unfavorable to colonization" (II, 204-05, Letter 117). Fermor considers the assimilation of
the French Canadians to be essential:

> . . . these people, slaves at present to ignorance and supersti-
> tion, will in time be enlightened by a more liberal education,
> and gently led by reason to a religion which is not only prefer-
> able, as being that of the country to which they are now
> annexed, but which is so much more calculated to make them
> happy and prosperous as a people.
>
> Till that time, till their prejudices subside, it is equally just,
> humane, and wise, to leave them the free right of worshiping
> the Deity in the manner which they have been early taught to
> believe the best, and to which they are consequently attached.
> (II, 205-06, Letter 117)

The similarity of the views expressed in letters written by John
Brooke with those expressed in the Fermor letters supports the
theory that John Brooke was the source of many of Fermor's opinions. However, as the daughter and wife of Anglican clergymen,
Frances Brooke would be in accord with the views expressed by
Fermor. She was considered to have supported the English party on
her trip to England in 1765 and was warmly regarded by Murray's
successors. It does seem likely, however, that John Brooke was not
only the source of much of his wife's information about Quebec
affairs, but also the model for William Fermor. In 1766 John
Brooke was fifty, a likely age for Arabella's father, and, like
Fermor, Brooke seems to have been a somewhat severe man. Just as
Fermor was writing to the Earl of * * *, Brooke was writing reports
to Robert Cholmondeley, absentee auditor general of Quebec, for
whom Brooke was acting as deputy, a fact that may have given
Frances Brooke the idea for introducing the Fermor letters.

In *Emily Montague* Brooke uses environment and setting with
sophistication — to influence actions, to mirror events, and to indicate changes in attitude or situation. First, Ed voices the traditional
eighteenth-century reaction to wild nature on his approach to the
vast and empty land. Here, in Ed's words, is "the *great sublime* to
an amazing degree":

> On approaching the coast of America, I felt a kind of religious

veneration, on seeing rocks which almost touch'd the clouds, cover'd with tall groves of pines that seemed coeval with the world itself: to which veneration the solemn silence not a little contributed; from Cape Rosieres, up the river St. Lawrence, during a course of more than two hundred miles, there is not the least appearance of a human footstep; no objects meet the eye but mountains, woods, and numerous rivers, which seem to roll their waters in vain. (I, 8, Letter 2)

Brooke describes the alarm with which her protagonists view the coming of winter. The isolation when communication with the outside world is cut off is desolating. In November Arabella writes: "I have been seeing the last ship go out of the port, Lucy; you have no notion what a melancholy sight it is: we are now left to ourselves, and shut up from all the world for the winter: somehow we seem so forsaken, so cut off from the rest of human kind, I cannot bear the idea . . ." (I, 201-02, Letter 45). In December she sees her emotions mirrored in the setting: "The scene is a little changed for the worst," she writes. ". . . The lovely landscape is now one undistinguished waste of snow, only a little diversified by the great variety of evergreens in the woods: the romantic winding path down the side of the hill to our farm, on which we used to amuse ourselves with seeing the beaux serpentize, is now a confused, frightful, rugged precipice, which one trembles at the idea of ascending" (I, 212-13, Letter 48).

The discomfort of winter is both physical and psychological: "Adieu!" writes Arabella on December 29, "I can no more: the ink freezes as I take it from the standish to the paper, though close to a large stove. Don't expect me to write again till May; one's faculties are absolutely congealed this weather" (I, 214-15, Letter 48). And on January 1 she writes:

It is with difficulty I breathe, my dear; the cold is so amazingly intense as almost totally to stop respiration. I have business, the business of pleasure, at Quebec; but have not courage to stir from the stove.

We have had five days, the severity of which none of the natives remember to have ever seen equaled: 'tis said, the cold is beyond all the thermometers here, tho' intended for the climate.

The strongest wine freezes in a room which has a stove in it; even brandy is thickened to the consistence of oil: the largest wood fire, in a wide chimney, does not throw out it's [sic] heat a quarter of a yard.

I must venture to Quebec to-morrow, or have company at home: amusements are here necessary to life; we must be jovial, or the blood will freeze in our veins.

I no longer wonder the elegant arts are unknown here; the rigour of the climate suspends the very powers of the understanding; what then must become of those of the imagination? Those who expect to see

"A new Athens rising near the pole,"

will find themselves extremely disappointed. Genius will never mount high, where the faculties of the mind are benumbed half the year.

'Tis sufficient employment for the most lively spirit here to contrive how to preserve an existence, of which there are moments that one is hardly conscious: the cold really sometimes brings on a sort of stupefaction. (I, 215-17, Letter 49)

As she becomes accustomed to the weather, Bell begins to enjoy winter activities. Only a week after her outcry against the intense cold, she writes: "I begin not to disrelish the winter here; now I am used to the cold, I don't feel it so much: as there is no business done here in the winter, 'tis the season of general dissipation; amusement is the study of every body, and the pains people take to please themselves contribute to the general pleasure: upon the whole, I am not sure it is not a pleasanter winter than that of England" (I, 231-32, Letter 52). By February 25, Bell is enthusiastic:

Those who have heard no more of a Canadian winter than what regards the intenseness of its cold, must suppose it a very joyless season: 'tis, I assure you, quite otherwise; there are indeed some days here of the severity of which those who were never out of England can form no conception; but those days seldom exceed a dozen in a whole winter, nor do they come in succession; but at intermediate periods, as the winds set in from the North-West; which, coming some hundred leagues, from frozen lakes and rivers, over woods and mountains covered with snow, would be insupportable, were it not for the furs with which the country abounds, in such variety and plenty as to be within the reach of all its inhabitants.

Thus defended, the British belles set the winter of Canada at defiance; and the season of which you seem to entertain such terrible ideas, is that of the utmost chearfulness and festivity. (II, 68-69, Letter 80)

Her description of Montmorency Falls the same day shows us that the winter landscape has come to evoke the same response as that of summer — religious awe at its sublimity, rather than the preceding fear and apprehension:

As you gradually approach the bay, you are struck with an awe, which increases every moment, as you come nearer, from the grandeur of a scene, which is one of the noblest works of nature: the beauty, the proportion, the solemnity, the wild magnificence of which, surpassing every possible effect of art, impress one strongly with the idea of its Divine Almighty Architect. (II, 74, Letter 81)

References to the new land as an Eden appear from the beginning of the novel. As Ed sets out for Canada, he says, ". . . in . . . cultivating what is in the rudest state of nature, I shall taste one of the greatest of all pleasures, that of creation, and see order and beauty gradually rise from chaos" (I, 3, Letter 1). Later, exploring the land he proposes to settle, he writes: "I paint to myself my Emily adorning those lovely shades; I see her, like the mother of mankind, admiring a new creation which smiles around her: we appear, to my idea, like the first pair in paradise" (III, 82, Letter 145). Bell echoes this idea on learning that Ed must return to England: "Emily and I had in fancy formed a little Eden on Lake Champlain: Fitzgerald had promised me to apply for lands near them; we should have been so happy in our little new world of friendship" (III, 84-85, Letter 146). As Bell, in turn, leaves Canada, she dreams of the pastoral life that might have been:

Emily and I should have been trying who had the most lively genius at creation; who could have produced the fairest flowers; who have formed the woods and rocks into the most beautiful arbors, vistoes, grottoes; have taught the streams to flow in the most pleasing meanders; have brought into view the greatest number and variety of those lovely little falls of water with which this fairy land abounds; and shewed nature in the fairest form. (III, 101-02, Letter 151)

Bell's term "this fairy land" recalls Ed's reference to his aborted plans as his "air-built scheme of happiness" (III, 93, Letter 149). The choice of words implies that the hope of a return to Eden is a dream only, of a "fairy land" that can never be. The Brookes themselves applied for settlement lands in Canada in 1766; so they, too, like Ed and Bell, had at least tentatively planned to settle in Canada.

The interpretation of Canada as a pastoral land, idyllically free of the complications of life in a more complex society, is underlined by the link made between isolation in Canada and freedom from problems and responsibility. The coming of winter cuts off the small colony from the rest of the world. In the isolated setting, complications are resolved; Emily frees herself from her engagement to the colourless and unfeeling Clayton. Winter then takes on a more delightful aspect. Both Ed and Emily's and Fitzgerald and Bell's romances progress. An idyllic life seems possible. It is only when the link with England is resumed that the dream of a paradise in Canada is broken. Renewed communication brings news from England requiring Ed's return, causes Emily's hasty departure, and generally complicates the lovers' lives. With the end of the idyllic winter recess, the "air-built scheme of happiness" is quickly dissipated. The breakup of ice in the Saint Lawrence, vividly described, signifies the breakup of the happy little group at Sillery.

The feminism evident in Brooke's earlier writing is equally evident in *Emily Montague*. The author uses two characters, Ed Rivers and Bell Fermor, to voice her sentiments about women. Both Ed and Bell are feminists. Brooke develops her main feminist theme through Bell's behaviour as well as her words, and through Rivers' attitudes to women and marriage. Ed is attracted to women of intelligence and personality, or, as he says, "I persist in my opinion, that women are most charming when they join the attractions of the mind to those of the person, when they feel the passion they inspire; or rather, that they are never charming till then" (I, 178, Letter 36). Both Ed and Bell speak of the necessity for marriage of choice rather than convenience. Ed says: "Of all the situations this world affords, a marriage of choice gives the fairest prospect of happiness; without love, life would be a tasteless void . . ." (II, 136, Letter 99). In a letter of advice to his sister following her marriage, he says:

> Equality is the soul of friendship: marriage, to give delight, must join two minds, not devote a slave to the will of an imperious lord; whatever conveys the idea of subjection necessarily destroys that of love, of which I am so convinced, that I have always wished the word OBEY expunged from the marriage ceremony. (II, 195, Letter 116)

Bell says:

> Parents should chuse our company, but never even pretend to direct our choice; if they take care we converse with men of honor only, 'tis impossible we can chuse amiss: a conformity of taste and sentiment alone can make marriage happy, and of that none but the parties concerned can judge. (II, 34-35, Letter 65)

She expresses the same attitude more strongly later, when she compares parents who force their children into marriage with those who force their children into the convent:

> The cruelty therefore of some parents here, who sacrifice their children to avarice, in forcing or seducing them into convents, would appear more striking, if we did not see too many in England guilty of the same inhumanity, though in a different manner, by marrying them against their inclination. (III, 29, Letter 132)

In his debate with Temple about love and marriage, Rivers writes:

> But of this I am certain, that two persons at once delicate and sensible, united by friendship, by taste, by a conformity of sentiment, by that lively ardent tender inclination which alone deserves the name of love, will find happiness in marriage, which is in vain sought in any other kind of attachment. (I, 91, Letter 14)

In their observations of Indians, both Bell and Ed comment on the power and freedom of Indian women. Ed notes, "The sex we have so unjustly excluded from power in Europe have a great share in the Huron government; the chief is chose by the matrons from amongst the nearest male relations, by the female line, of him he is to succeed; and is generally an aunt's or sister's son . . ." (I, 67-68, Letter 11). Bell is impressed by the visit of a group of Indian women who land their canoe nearby and, on being questioned, explain that they decided to make a trip up the river to see the English at Montreal while their husbands are on a hunting trip. Bell's reaction is revealing: "Absolutely, Lucy, I will marry a savage, and turn squaw (a pretty soft name for an Indian princess!): never was any thing delightful as their lives; they talk of French husbands, but commend me to an Indian one, who lets his wife ramble five hundred miles, without asking where she is going" (I, 102, Letter 16).

Both Bell and Ed, as spokesmen for the English, observe that French-Canadian women lack sensibility. But Brooke introduces a Canadian woman who refutes this generalization; Ed encounters the charming Madame Des Roches, who proves the contrary, who has a sensibility equal to that of any Englishwoman, and who is so attractive to Ed that he admits he would have been captivated by her had he not met Emily earlier. Acquaintance with Madame Des Roches leads Bell to admit: ". . . when the heart is really touched, the feelings of all nations have a pretty near resemblance . . ." (III, 189, Letter 172).

Both Ed and Emily show throughout the novel the sensibility that is *de rigeur* in an eighteenth-century man or woman of breeding. Ed associates his love for Emily with his love of sensibility. ". . . she has the soul of beauty: without feminine softness and delicate sensibility, no features can give loveliness; with them, very indifferent ones can charm: that sensibility, that softness, never were so lovely as in my Emily" (I, 196, Letter 42). Explaining his love to his sister, he writes: "The same dear affections, the same tender sensibility, the most precious gift of Heaven, inform our minds, and make us peculiarly capable of exquisite happiness or misery" (II, 51, Letter 71). Emily in her turn writes to Rivers:

It was impossible I should not have loved you; the soul that spoke in those eloquent eyes told me, the first moment we met, our hearts were formed for each other; I saw in that amiable countenance a sensibility similar to my own, but which I had till then sought in vain; I saw there those benevolent smiles, which are the marks, and the emanations of virtue; those thousand graces which ever accompany a mind conscious of its own dignity, and satisfied with itself; in short, that mental beauty which is the express image of the Deity. (III, 51-52, Letter 137)

Although Brooke gives us the man and woman of sensibility in Ed and Emily, she warns against an excess of sensibility through her most realistic creation, Bell. "Take care, my dear Emily," warns Bell, "you do not fall into the common error of sensible and delicate minds, that of refining away your happiness" (I, 93, Letter 15). To Lucy she writes:

A propos to women, the estimable part of us are divided into two classes only, the tender and the lively.

The former, at the head of which I place Emily, are infinitely more capable of happiness; but, to counterbalance this advantage, they are also capable of misery in the same degree. We of the other class, who feel less keenly, are perhaps upon the whole as happy, at least I would fain think so. (II, 180, Letter 114)

The two central characters were probably modelled on persons the Brookes knew at Quebec. Anna-Marie Bondfield, daughter of merchant John Taylor Bondfield, is said to be the model for Arabella. Anna-Marie, born circa 1746, would have been about twenty-two at the time the novel was set, in 1766.[27] Henry Caldwell is said to be the model for Ed Rivers.[28] From the description of Caldwell and his career, he sounds very like Ed. At the time of Brooke's arrival in Quebec, Caldwell, having been promoted for bravery on the Plains of Abraham in 1759, was a retired major. Le Moine describes him as possessing "merit, intelligence, handsome person, and happy address," and as "a brave, intelligent and ambitious man." These are characteristics ascribed to Ed by his creator. Caldwell, born in 1738, would have been twenty-seven or twenty-eight in 1766. Ed was twenty-seven. As well, Caldwell later bought land in the Kamouraska and Lake Champlain regions, the very places Ed considered settling. When the Brookes returned to

England, Caldwell was still a bachelor. He married six years later.

With its more sophisticated handling of the epistolary mode and the complex role played by setting, *Emily Montague* is a more skilfully written novel than *Julia Mandeville*. For a while at least, the new land supersedes the English countryside as a new Eden. Its very remoteness adds to its paradisal qualities, so that while cut off from the rest of the world, its inhabitants achieve their greatest happiness.

In 1774, five years after *Emily Montague*, a second Canadian novel appeared, *All's Right at Last; or, The History of Miss West*, published anonymously by the circulating library of Francis and John Noble, London. Frances Brooke may have been its author.[29] Set first in London, later in Trois-Rivières, Quebec City, and Montreal, the novel revolves around the romantic adventures and misadventures of young Frances West, concluding with her marriage to her true love — but only after both have contracted marriages to other partners, who conveniently die, leaving their bereaved spouses to find happiness together. Like *Emily Montague*, this novel portrays the social life of upper-class Canadian society, describes the harshness of winter, and comments on the lively attractiveness of French-Canadian women. Characters include a handsome young colonel reminiscent of Ed Rivers and two lively Canadian women reminiscent of Bell Fermor. Again the heroine is a conventional eighteenth-century woman, closer to Julia Mandeville than Emily Montague in youth and naïveté. Letters, fewer and longer than in the earlier novel, skilfully interweave the plot lines, as correspondents link activities occurring simultaneously in three centres.

The Excursion (1777), while continuing to develop Brooke's main themes, breaks new ground in narrative method, moving from the epistolary mode to the use of an omniscient narrator. The novel concerns the encounter of a naïve country girl with corrupt London society. What takes the situation out of the ordinary is that the girl, Maria Villiers, is a would-be dramatist and novelist who dreams that her trip to London will bring her not only a handsome, wealthy, and aristocratic husband but also fame and fortune as a writer.

The author creates in Maria and her twin sister, Louisa, two young women of opposing personality and temperament, an opposition which is reflected in their appearances and which recalls the contrasting Julia and Anne of *Julia Mandeville*, and Emily and Bell of *Emily Montague*; however, this sisterly contrast plays little part in the novel; fair Louisa remains on the country estate, while the reader for the most part follows dark Maria as she sets out for the city. The ironic tension of opposites characteristic of earlier Brooke novels is maintained by the opposition of Maria's naïveté to the narrator's worldly wisdom. The narrator is as much a character in the novel as Maria and her acquaintances. She comments on the impracticality of Maria's dreams, her failure to understand what is going on around her, and her lack of common sense and decorum. Thus the narrator takes on the persona of a witty, ironic, and worldly-wise woman.

Maria's adventures and misadventures while she learns about the ways of the world make of this novel an early female *Bildungsroman*. Maria is an interesting creation: lacking the experience and sophistication of Anne Wilmot and the wit and perception of Bell Fermor, she is a parallel to Julia Mandeville in age, naïveté, and inexperience. But she is quite unlike Julia and the courtesy-book heroines of the time, for she quickly demonstrates that she is ambitious, self-confident, intelligent, and robust. She flaunts convention first by travelling to London accompanied only by an aging family retainer and later by inviting a young admirer to a private supper.

The intrusive and entertaining narrator and the mildly picaresque adventures of Maria indicate that Brooke has moved out from under the mantle of Richardson and towards that of his contemporary, Fielding. With the assistance of friends, the young protagonist, like Joseph Andrews and Tom Jones, extricates herself from the various difficulties in which her naïveté and enthusiasm have involved her, and all ends happily — with a suitably romantic marriage back in the country, where life remains simple and innocent.

Not only does Brooke switch her allegiance from Richardson to Fielding, she also pokes fun at the melodrama of most contemporary novels, among which we could place Richardson's *Clarissa*. The warning of Maria's uncle when she leaves home makes this clear: "He cautioned her, not against the giants of modern novel, who carry off young ladies by force in post-chaises and six with the blinds up, and confine free-born English women in their country houses, under the guardianship of monsters in the shape of fat housekeepers, from which durance they are happily released by the compassion of Robert the butler; but against worthless acquaintance, unmerited calumny, and ruinous expence."[30]

This sensible advice, proven apt by the difficulties Maria encounters, is only one of the realistic aspects of *The Excursion*. The description of the first drama and the first opera that Maria attends in London adds a note of accuracy, for both were playing in London on the dates noted. In February 1775 Maria sees Sacchini's opera *Montezuma* with tenor Rauzzini. The same month she sees *Braganza*, starring Mary Ann Yates, at Drury Lane. Brooke's comments on theatre audiences recall her criticism in *The Old Maid* twenty years earlier. The description of Maria's reaction to the play is, appropriately, similar to that recorded of audiences of the time.

The most celebrated of the realistic incidents in *The Excursion* involves a lampoon of David Garrick. The pretext for the attack on the actor-manager is Maria's submission to him of her tragedy. A conversation between Garrick and Maria's advocate reveals Garrick's evasiveness as we learn that he has not opened the manuscript of the play he purports to have assessed. Brooke's own experience with Garrick is no doubt the basis of her lampoon. Garrick's angry reaction is revealed in letters to his friends. What is not generally known is that Garrick wrote, anonymously, the scathing review of *The Excursion* in *The Monthly Review* (August 1777), which not only attacks the novel but also devotes most of its space to defence and praise of Garrick: ". . . it is not because Mr. Garrick is the best actor in the world, but because we think him a worthy man too, that we take the pains to inquire into the grounds of the charge brought against him."[31]

The Excursion is the shortest of Brooke's novels. Chapters extend from a few lines to several pages and are so spaced as to give the illusion that the novel is longer than it is. Here once again Brooke's theatrical interests have influenced her narrative technique. Chapters are often dramatic, brief, and acted out in dialogue. The scene often shifts quickly. At one point, for example, the scene shifts from Maria in her apartment, to her would-be seducer with his father, to one of Maria's erstwhile London friends with her gossiping cronies, and finally to her uncle in his garden. Again, Brooke exploits opportunities for dramatic irony as the reader can thus be made aware of the seducer's motives, the pseudofriend's opinion of Maria, and the uncle's lack of concern for his niece as he worries about his roses — of all of which Maria remains blissfully ignorant.

The tone of the novel remains light despite the difficulties Maria finds herself in and the author's criticism of the London world of *bon ton*. The narrator's cool, ironic voice sustains this tone even in scenes which could be fraught with emotion. Control of voice is one of the major accomplishments of the novel.

There is an obvious parallel between *The Excursion* and Fanny Burney's better-known *Evelina*, published the next year. Both recount the adventures and misadventures of a young woman entering London society. Both young women survive their mishaps to marry an ideal young man at the end of the novel. In style, however, the novels are very different. Burney follows the epistolary mode of Richardson with long letters recounting incidents in detail. The point of view is almost entirely Evelina's. Burney is not an innovator, nor does her protagonist step out of the conventional mould but rather corrects any minor errors in conduct, so that, in the words of Hemlow, she may "attain perfection in the courtesy-book virtues."[32]

The Excursion is a didactic novel although not, like *Evelina*, concerned with showing us the virtues of adhering to the eighteenth-century standard of decorum for young women. *Emily Montague* has its romantic overlay in its romantic courtship, while the reader is given a realistic portrait of Quebec in the late eighteenth century; so, in *The Excursion*, Brooke and her ironic commentator take a look at the corrupt world of *bon ton*, the dangers to young women who seek to bring their intelligence, wit, and warmth into such a world, and the unhappy theatrical situation caused by the monopolies of London's two theatres. Brooke recounted experiences which were undoubtedly very like her own and which undoubtedly she shared with other London playwrights of the day. It is most likely that the young Frances Moore, having come to the city as does Maria — and like Maria, bright, ambitious, and hopeful — encountered many of the same problems. *The Excursion* may give us the best picture we shall ever have of Brooke's early London experiences.

Brooke's last novel, *The History of Charles Mandeville*, was published the year following her death. With this novel, Brooke returns to the epistolary mode, but, unlike her earlier works, *Charles Mandeville* is composed almost entirely of the letters of one character, an observer of events. Possibilities for dramatic irony, so well exploited in earlier works, are thus obviated. Structurally, the novel recalls Riccoboni's *Lady Catesby*, which Brooke had translated many years earlier: like *Lady Catesby*, in which the only change from the letters of one character is the intrusion midway of two lengthy memoirs by the two protagonists, in *Charles Mandeville* about half the novel is taken up by two long accounts of past events — the hero's account of the fantastic eastern land where he spent his youth, and his late wife's account of his exploits in this land. Extensive reporting of conversations places the novel closer to the style of Fanny Burney than to that of Brooke's earlier novels.

Of most interest to the reader in this otherwise unremarkable novel is the fantastic land where Charles found himself at the age of eleven, the sole survivor of a shipwreck. This is a utopian land with a communal society, an advanced system of justice, and an antimaterialistic outlook. The only reward for contributions to the nation is honour; gold, jewels, and other forms of wealth are meaningless. This novel of a utopian world demonstrates Brooke's transference of her Eden from pastoral England and primitive Canada to a fantasy futuristic world.

Though the novel lacks the wit and sparkle and the feminist stance of her earlier novels, *Charles Mandeville* was designed to be a sequel to *Julia Mandeville*. The narrative picks up where *Julia Mandeville* left off, with family and friends in mourning for Julia and Harry. The return of Harry's long-lost brother Charles and his marriage to Julia's friend, Emily Howard, who has become a surrogate daughter to Julia's parents, provide the happy ending which so many readers had so sorely missed in the earlier novel. The characters are lifted fully conceived from *Julia Mandeville*, with no further development. The newcomer, Charles, is all too perfect. The novel lacks tension and, despite the presence of Anne Wilmot, has little humour. It may be that Brooke never completed the novel to her own satisfaction or had considered it unworthy of publication. Her son, as her executor, finding the manuscript among his mother's papers, is responsible for publishing it.

Brooke's dramatic output consisted of four plays: two tragedies and two comic operas. Three of these reached the stage; one was an overwhelming success, and the other two were well received. The protagonists of all four were women. As one would expect, the central characters of the two tragedies were women of strength and courage.

Brooke's first play, *Virginia*, is based on an incident in Livy's *Early History of Rome*. As was to be expected at the time, the play is classical in form, adhering to the heroic play as popularized by Dryden. It conforms to the classical unities of time, place, and action. Except for rhyming couplets or alternate rhyme to conclude the acts, speech is in blank verse. The language has a formality and stateliness in keeping with its tragic theme. Much of the action occurs offstage, in the classical tradition, and is narrated in lengthy speeches.

Brooke alters the central incident, Virginia's death at her father's hand — the only alternative to surrender to the lustful tyrant Appius — by having Virginia herself, rather than her father, choose death before dishonour. The play focuses on Virginia rather than, as in Livy, on Appius and adds to the original characters a young woman friend of Virginia through whom the theme of friendship, so dear to Brooke, is developed. Several themes develop through the conflict of Appius and Virginia, among them that power corrupts and that good can come from suffering and evil.

There is absolutely no humour in this drama. The emotional rhythm varies, however, as the situation appears hopeful or hopeless. The play ends on a note of victory as it becomes apparent that Virginia's death will lead to the overthrow of the tyrant. Brooke's weaving together of several themes within the single incident and her alternating of the emotional rhythm suggest the dramatic skills later developed in her novels. The play's high moral tone is in keeping with the age and consistent with Brooke's later works. There were few women dramatists at this time, or indeed at any time, and even fewer women tragedians. With *Virginia*, as with *The Old Maid*, Brooke broke new ground as a woman writer.

Like *Virginia*, *The Siege of Sinope* is based on a historical event in the classical world. Brooke's direct source is Giuseppe Sarti's opera *Mitridate a Sinope*, first produced at Florence in 1779. A pseudo-classical tragedy, the play is written in blank verse and adheres to the unities of time, place, and action. The protagonist, Thamyris, queen of Sinope, is faced with a conflict of loyalty to her husband, ruler of Sinope, and her father, besieger of the city, and is torn between love for father, husband, and the young son she strives to save. The most interesting aspect of the drama is Thamyris' strength and courage as she refuses to betray either husband, father, or son. An officer's description of her highlights her combination of qualities traditionally held to be feminine and masculine:

> ... All the strength
> Of manly wisdom, mix'd with woman's sweetness,
> In her fair soul in bright assembly meet;
> Soft as the dove's in Cytherea's car,
> Yet lofty as th' imperial eagle's flight.[33]

Brooke's greatest dramatic success was her comic opera *Rosina*. The music, by William Shield, included many traditional airs, among them a version of "Auld lang syne."[34] The music did much to enhance the drama. While Brooke mentions as sources of her plot the Book of Ruth, the episode of Palaemon and Lavinia in Thomson's *Seasons*, and an opera by a Monsieur Favart, it is in fact Favart's opera which is the proximate source. Charles Simon Favart's *Les Moissoneurs* was first played on 27 January 1768 and was published in 1770.[35] Although an English version entitled *The Reapers; or, The Englishman Out of Paris* was published the same year, a comparison of texts makes it obvious that the original opera in French is Brooke's source.

Rosina is delightful escapist entertainment. Set in a village of the north of England at harvest time, a Cinderella-like plot involving Rosina and the local squire unfolds between sunrise and sunset of one day. The attempt of the squire's dissolute brother, attracted by Rosina's beauty, to seduce her and, failing that, to kidnap her provides the excitement. Rosina's rustic friends, Phoebe and William, act as foils for the serious lovers and provide the comic relief. When Rosina, brought up among the peasants by an old family servant, is discovered to be the daughter of a gentleman, she is a suitable bride for the squire, his equal in class if not in fortune.

The scenes are short, the dialogue is brief, the action is lively. Rosina is a young girl of spirit who replies to her would-be seducer, when he finally offers marriage, "This, sir, is a second insult. Whoever offends the object of his love, is unworthy of obtaining her."[36] A general naturalness of dialogue adds a note of realism. The idyllic setting, the lively plot, the attractive music, and the humour provided by the comic couple combine to produce a highly successful comic opera — in terms of popularity as entertainment, the *My Fair Lady* of the eighteenth century.

Brooke's last theatrical production, *Marian*, was a second comic opera. *Marian* is similar to *Rosina* in its pastoral setting and its happy resolution of a problem of courtship and marriage within the space of one day. The plot is even slighter than *Rosina*'s: Marian, engaged to marry a penniless young man, inherits a small sum of money. Her father then wishes her to marry someone of slightly more consequence. Happily, news of her lover's recent inheritance of an estate makes him more than her equal, so that the marriage meets once more with parental approval.

Again, Shield's music enhances Brooke's opera, which was given an excellent reception. While one reviewer objects that "the story and dialogue are so little raised above common occurrences and conversation,"[37] this remark points up the fact that in her plays, as in her novels, Brooke is moving towards realism. The pastoral settings in both operas also suggest, as do the novels, that the simpler virtues and the simpler pleasures are to be found in the countryside.

There is a certain irony in the fact that Frances Brooke's most enduring works are her novels, while her plays, except for *Rosina*, are long forgotten. Nevertheless, her theatrical interests contributed to the development of her novelistic technique. Her use of the epistolary mode and her exploitation of opportunities for dramatic irony owe much to her theatrical bent. With her skilful interweaving of a complex of voices in *Emily Montague* and her manipulation of setting to echo the actions and emotions of her protagonists, she takes the novel in new directions. With her use of an ironic and intrusive narrator in *The Excursion*, she shows yet another side of her artistry. At a time when most novelists were excessively sentimental, Brooke combines wit with sensibility as she moves towards realism in plot, dialogue, and characterization. An astute and witty observer of a woman's world, in balancing sense and sensibility, she moves the novel in the direction of Jane Austen.

NOTES

I am happy to acknowledge the financial support of The Canada Council and the Social Sciences and Humanities Research Council of Canada which enabled me to conduct the research for this essay.

[1] See Lorraine McMullen, "Moore, Frances (Brooke)," *Dictionary of Canadian Biography*, IV (1979). Unless otherwise noted, biographical facts are from this source.

[2] [Francis Maseres], *The Maseres Letters 1766-1768*, ed. W. Stewart Wallace (Toronto: Univ. of Toronto Press, 1919), p. 46.

[3] Public Archives of Canada, Murray Papers, MG23, GII, Series 1, 2:184.

[4] Public Archives of Canada, Shelburne MSS. MG23, A4, 16:117.

[5] [Fanny Burney], *The Early Diary of Fanny Burney*, ed. A. R. Ellis (1889; rpt. Freeport: Books for Libraries, 1971), I, 283.

[6] "Biographical Anecdotes and Births of Eminent Persons," *The Gentleman's Magazine*, 59 (Feb. 1789), 176.

[7] John Nichols, *Literary Anecdotes of the Eighteenth Century* (London: Nichols, Son and Bentley, 1812-15), II, 346.

[8] "Mrs. Brooke," *The British Magazine and Review*, 2 (Feb. 1783), 102.

[9] James Le Moine, *Picturesque Québec* (Montreal: Dawson Brothers, 1882), pp. 375-78.

[10] James Le Moine, "The First Canadian Novelist, 1769," in *Maple Leaves* (Quebec: Frank Carrel, 1906), VII, 239-45.

[11] Ida Burwash, "An Old-Time Novel," *The Canadian Magazine*, 28 (Jan. 1907), 252-56.

[12] Charles S. Blue, "Canada's First Novelist," *The Canadian Magazine*, 58 (Nov. 1921), 3-12.

[13] H. R. Morgan, "Frances Brooke: A Canadian Pioneer," *Supplement to the McGill News*, June 1930, pp. 1-5.

[14] Lawrence J. Burpee, Introd., *The History of Emily Montague*, by Frances Brooke (Ottawa: Graphic, 1931), n. pag.

[15] E. Phillips Poole, Introd., *Lady Julia Mandeville*, by Frances Brooke (London: Eric Partridge, Scholartis, 1930), pp. 11-37.

[16] Edmund Royds, "Stubton Strong-Room — Stray Notes (2nd Series) Moore and Knowles Families — Two Sisters," *Reports and Papers of the Architectural Societies of the County of Lincoln, County of York* (Lincoln: n.p., 1926-27), pp. 97-99, 213-312.

[17] Desmond Pacey, "The First Canadian Novel," *Dalhousie Review*, 26 (July 1946), 143-50.

[18] B. Dufebvre [Emile Castonguay], "Mrs. Frances Brooke ou la femme de lettres," in *Cinq Femmes et nous* (Québec: Bélisle, 1950), pp. 9-57.

[19] Carl F. Klinck, Introd., *The History of Emily Montague*, by Frances Brooke, New Canadian Library, No. 27 (Toronto: McClelland and Stewart, 1961), pp. v-xiv.

[20] Gwendolyn B. Needham, "Mrs. Frances Brooke: Dramatic Critic,"

Theatre Notebook, No. 15 (Winter 1960-61), pp. 47-52.

[21] W. H. New, "Frances Brooke's Chequered Gardens," *Canadian Literature*, No. 52 (Spring 1972), pp. 24-38.

[22] W. H. New, "*The Old Maid*: Frances Brooke's Apprentice Feminism," *Journal of Canadian Fiction*, 2, No. 3 (Summer 1973), 9.

[23] Katherine M. Rogers, "Sensibility and Feminism: The Novels of Frances Brooke," *Genre*, 11, No. 2 (Summer 1978), 159-71.

[24] Frances Brooke, *The History of Lady Julia Mandeville*, 7th ed. (London: J. Dodsley, 1782), I, 201. All further references to this work in two volumes appear in the text.

[25] See Joyce Hemlow, "Fanny Burney and the Courtesy Books," *PMLA*, 65 (Sept. 1950), 732-61.

[26] Frances Brooke, *The History of Emily Montague* (1769; rpt., facs. ed., New York: Garland, 1974), II, 66-67 (Letters 77, 78, and 79). All further references to this work in four volumes appear in the text. The letter numbers cited are those of the corrected numbering given in McClelland and Stewart's New Canadian Library edition of 1961.

[27] Allusions to Anna-Marie as the model for Arabella are found in the travel journals of British officers who met her as Mrs. Allsopp in later years. See, for example, *The American Journals of Lt. John Enys*, ed. Elizabeth Cometti (Syracuse: Syracuse Univ. Press, 1976), p. 84.

[28] Le Moine, *Maple Leaves*, VII, 77.

[29] See Lorraine McMullen, "*All's Right at Last*: An Eighteenth-Century Canadian Novel," *Journal of Canadian Fiction*, No. 21 (1977-78), pp. 95-104.

[30] Frances Brooke, *The Excursion* (London: T. Cadell, 1777), I, 22. All further references to this work in two volumes appear in the text.

[31] Rev. of *The Excursion*, *The Monthly Review*, 57 (Aug. 1777), 141. See B. C. Nangle, *The Monthly Review, First Series, 1749-1789* (Oxford: Clarendon, 1934), p. 47.

[32] Hemlow, p. 756.

[33] Frances Brooke, *The Siege of Sinope* (London: T. Cadell, 1781), II,i.

[34] Roger Fiske, *English Theatre Music in the Eighteenth Century* (London: Oxford Univ. Press, 1973), p. 100.

[35] Charles Simon Favart, *Les Moissoneurs* (Paris: La veuve Duchesne, 1770).

[36] Frances Brooke, *Rosina* (London: T. Cadell, 1783), II,ii.

[37] "Theatrical Journal," *The European Magazine and London Review*, 13 (May 1788), 372.

SELECTED BIBLIOGRAPHY

Primary Sources

Brooke, Frances. *The Old Maid by Mary Singleton, Spinster*. London: A. Millar, 1764.

————, trans. *Letters from Juliet, Lady Catesby, to Her Friend, Lady Henrietta Campley*. By Marie-Jeanne Riccoboni. 4th ed. London: R. and J. Dodsley, 1764.

————. *The History of Lady Julia Mandeville*. 7th ed. 2 vols. London: J. Dodsley, 1782.

————. *The History of Emily Montague*. 1769; rpt. New York: Garland, 1974.

————. *The Excursion*. 2 vols. London: T. Cadell, 1777.

————. *The Siege of Sinope: A Tragedy as It Is Acted at the Theatre Royal in Covent Garden*. London: T. Cadell, 1781.

————. *Rosina: A Comic Opera in Two Acts, Performed at the Theatre Royal in Covent Garden*. London: T. Cadell, 1783.

————. *Marian: A Comic Opera in Two Acts*. London: T. M. Longman and O. Rees, 1800.

————. *The History of Charles Mandeville*. Dublin: Chamberlain and Rice, 1790.

————. *All's Right at Last; or, The History of Miss West*. 2 vols. London: F. and J. Noble, 1774.

Secondary Sources

"Biographical Anecdotes and Births of Eminent Persons." *The Gentleman's Magazine*, 59 (Feb. 1789), 176.

Blue, Charles S. "Canada's First Novelist." *The Canadian Magazine*, 58 (Nov. 1921), 3-12.

Burpee, Lawrence J., introd. *The History of Emily Montague*. By Frances Brooke. Ottawa: Graphic, 1931.

Burwash, Ida. "An Old-Time Novel." *The Canadian Magazine*, 28 (Jan. 1907), 252-56.

Cometti, Elizabeth, ed. *The American Journals of Lt. John Enys*. Syracuse: Syracuse Univ. Press, 1976.

Dufebvre, B. [Emile Castonguay]. "Mrs. Frances Brooke ou la femme de lettres." In *Cinq Femmes et nous*. Québec: Bélisle, 1950, pp. 9-57.

Ellis, A. R., ed. *The Early Diary of Fanny Burney*. 1889; rpt. Freeport: Books for Libraries, 1971.

Favart, Charles Simon. *Les Moissoneurs*. Paris: La veuve Duchesne, 1770.

Fiske, Roger. *English Theatre Music in the Eighteenth Century*. London: Oxford Univ. Press, 1973.

Hemlow, Joyce. "Fanny Burney and the Courtesy Books." *PMLA*, 65 (Sept. 1950), 732-61.

Klinck, Carl F., introd. *The History of Emily Montague*. By Frances Brooke. New Canadian Library, No. 27. Toronto: McClelland and Stewart, 1961.

Le Moine, James. *Picturesque Québec*. Montreal: Dawson Brothers, 1882.

———. "The First Canadian Novelist, 1769." In *Maple Leaves*. Quebec: Frank Carrel, 1906. Vol. VII, 239-45.

Mabane, Adam. MG23, A4, 16: 117. Shelburne MSS. Public Archives of Canada.

McMullen, Lorraine. "*All's Right at Last*: An Eighteenth-Century Canadian Novel." *Journal of Canadian Fiction*, No. 21 (1977-78), pp. 95-104.

———. "Moore, Frances (Brooke)." *Dictionary of Canadian Biography*, IV (1979).

Morgan, H. R. "Frances Brooke: A Canadian Pioneer." *Supplement to the McGill News*, June 1930, pp. 1-5.

"Mrs. Brooke." *The British Magazine and Review*, 2 (Feb. 1783), 101-03.

Murray, James. MG23, GII, Series 1, 2:184. Murray Papers. Public Archives of Canada.

Nangle, B. C. *The Monthly Review, First Series, 1749-1789*. Oxford: Clarendon, 1934.

Needham, Gwendolyn B. "Mrs. Frances Brooke: Dramatic Critic." *Theatre Notebook*, No. 15 (Winter 1960-61), pp. 47-52.

New, W. H. "Frances Brooke's Chequered Gardens." *Canadian Literature*, No. 52 (Spring 1972), pp. 24-38.

———. "*The Old Maid*: Frances Brooke's Apprentice Feminism." *Journal of Canadian Fiction*, 2, No. 3 (Summer 1973), 9-12.

Nichols, John. *Literary Anecdotes of the Eighteenth Century; Comprizing*

Biographical Memoirs of William Bowyer. London: Nichols, Son and Bentley, 1812-15. Vol. II.

Pacey, Desmond. "The First Canadian Novel." *Dalhousie Review*, 26 (July 1946), 143-50.

Poole, E. Phillips, introd. *Lady Julia Mandeville*. By Frances Brooke. London: Eric Partridge, Scholartis, 1930.

Rev. of *The Excursion*, by Frances Brooke. *The Monthly Review*, 57 (Aug. 1777), 141-45.

Rogers, Katherine M. "Sensibility and Feminism: The Novels of Frances Brooke." *Genre*, 11, No. 2 (Summer 1978), 159-71.

Royds, Edmund. "Stubton Strong-Room — Stray Notes (2nd Series) Moore and Knowles Families — Two Sisters." *Reports and Papers of the Architectural Societies of the County of Lincoln, County of York*. Lincoln: n.p., 1926-27, pp. 213-312, 97-99.

Wallace, W. Stewart, ed. *The Maseres Letters 1776-1768.* Toronto: Univ. of Toronto Press, 1919.

Susanna Moodie (1803-1885)

MICHAEL A. PETERMAN

Biography

OF ALL the Canadian pioneering figures who found time to devote to literary interests, Susanna Moodie is undoubtedly the best known among contemporary readers. Indeed, one can postulate that over the past decade Moodie has undergone a sort of literary and cultural canonization; she has become a central foundation figure in both critical and creative attempts to define the condition of the imagination in Canada.

Given the interest that Moodie and her most famous work, *Roughing It in the Bush* (1852), have aroused, it is surprising to note that so little attention has been paid to the formative years of her life. She was nearly thirty when she left the Suffolk countryside for the bush farms of Upper Canada. Hence, as is the case with her older sister Catharine Parr Traill, hers is a tale of two worlds. Any attempt to examine her work or to understand her view of literature and sense of values must locate itself firmly in the experiences of her English years.

The salient biographical details are as follows. Susanna Strickland was born in 1803 near Bungay, the sixth daughter of Thomas and Elizabeth Strickland, Thomas Strickland having recently retired from a London docks-management position and come to Suffolk in search of a gentler climate and a residence suitable to the rising status of his large family. That goal he realized in 1808 in buying Reydon Hall. A gloomy, deteriorating Elizabethan mansion on the outskirts of the village of Reydon near Southwold, it was to be Susanna's home until she married in 1831.

Reydon Hall seems to have been the summit of Thomas Strickland's ambitions and good fortune, a testament, on the one hand, to his independent, enlightened thinking and a symbol of his overreaching, on the other. It gave him status and visible proof of his achievement; moreover, it gave him a rural setting in which to continue his unusual and rigorous plan to educate his daughters in academic and outdoor skills. His watchwords were discipline, self-reliance, industry, and honesty. The fact of sex alone was for him no bar to individual capability or development. However, the twenty-mile move from Bungay to Reydon had its unforeseen consequences. It further isolated the Stricklands as Suffolk newcomers. More problematically, it removed Thomas Strickland farther from his business connections in Norwich. When illness and financial reverses forced him to spend longer periods in Norwich, the younger girls and his two sons were left increasingly on their own. His death in 1818, when Susanna was fourteen, deprived her of a guide and example she greatly depended upon. In the autobiographical story "Rachel Wilde; or, Trifles from the Burthen of a Life," she remembered him as a vigorous, independent, and conscientious thinker, an excellent father whose family "regarded him with a reverence only one degree less than that which they owed to their Creator." Thinking of her own adult life, she adds, "In after-life they are proud to echo his words, and maintain his opinions."[1]

At Reydon, thereafter, the struggle under reduced circumstances to make do and keep face was a constant one. Led by the aggressive elder sisters, the businesslike Eliza and the romantic Agnes (who would later collaborate to write *Lives of the Queens of England* and other popular histories), the girls sought to find literary markets for the writing which, as children, they had found a pleasant, beguiling pastime. Initially, Agnes, Jane Margaret, Catharine, and Susanna sought outlets in the growing markets, centred in London, for writing addressed to children and adolescents.

Of the daughters, Susanna was most like Agnes in temperament. Impulsive and acutely sensitive, she was inclined to write enthusiastic poetry, tragic drama, and romantic tales of history. Like Rachel Wilde, "she fell in love with all the heroes of antiquity" (*VM*, p. 114). Catharine recalled that Susanna's first attempt at fiction, a tale of Gustavus Adolphus, was inspired by her reading of Coleridge's translations of Schiller. These tendencies Susanna modulated for the children's market in such early heroic or moralistic tales as *Spartacus: A Roman Story*, *The Little Quaker; or, The Triumph of Virtue*, *Rowland Massingham; or, I Will Be My Own Master*, and *Profession and Principle; or, The Vicar's Tales*, as well as in the stories and poems she submitted to the then-popular juvenile and gift-book annuals.[2]

Her great aim, however, was to become a famous literary figure and a recognized force in the London world. To this end, two paternal friends proved crucial. One was the poet James Bird of nearby Yoxford; the other Thomas Harral, whose daughter Susanna knew well. Bird encouraged her writing and helped her establish literary connections in remote London, while Harral, as editor of *La Belle Assemblée*, a court and fashion magazine, began publishing her poems and sketches in May 1827.[3] She was later to find outlets in other London magazines — *The Athenaeum* (through the fatherly influence of her most important literary friend, Thomas Pringle) and *The Lady's Magazine* (which her sister Eliza had a hand in editing) — and in many of the prestigious literary annuals.[4] In addition, she collaborated with Agnes on a small book entitled *Patriotic Songs* (1830) and produced her own book of poetry, *Enthusiasm, and Other Poems*, in 1831.[5] She was, then, making steady, if unspectacular, progress towards the realization of her goals.

It would be unfair, however, to see the young Susanna Strickland simply in terms of worldly aspiration. Coexistent with her eagerness for fame was a spiritual desire that led her not only to mistrust her literary aims but also, in the face of strong family resistance, to convert from the Anglican Church to the Nonconformist persuasion in 1830. Under the guidance of James Ritchie of nearby Wrentham (whose wife instructed Susanna in the art of painting), she risked the severe judgements of Agnes and Eliza in seeking a more personal, less complacent approach to her religious needs. As well, through Thomas Pringle, who was both an influential literary man and Secretary of the Anti-Slavery League, she became a strong critic of the injustices and tyranny of slavery and wrote two pamphlets for the League describing the respective sufferings of Mary Prince and Ashton Warner, both of whom she met in Pringle's London home.[6]

The man who was to change and dramatically uproot her life, she also met at Thomas Pringle's. This was J. W. Dunbar Moodie, an Orkney man who had returned to England from South Africa to have a book published and to find a wife. After considerable wavering (apparently because she resisted the possibility of immigrating to South Africa), Susanna married Lieutenant Moodie in the spring of 1831. A year later, after having exhausted any chance of securing the basis for an independent life in England, the

Moodies and their young daughter immigrated to Upper Canada to take up land Dunbar had received for military services.

The major events of their Canadian life are generally well known. Their first two years were spent near Port Hope, where they decided to buy a farm "in the clearings." The unpleasant conditions of their life at "Melsetter" are amply described in the first half of *Roughing It in the Bush*. Misled by speculators, they sold that farm and moved to the shore of Lake Katchawanook near present-day Lakefield to take up Dunbar's land grant and be close to Thomas and Catharine Parr Traill and Susanna's brother Samuel, who had established himself as the area's most successful pioneer.[7] There they stayed nearly five years; during this time, upon the outbreak of the Rebellion of 1837, Dunbar served as a captain in a militia regiment, escaping from "the bush" only with his appointment as Sheriff of Hastings County late in 1839. From 1840 till his death in 1869, they lived in Belleville. Thereafter, Susanna spent her time with various of her grown children, often visiting her sister Catharine in Lakefield for extended periods. She died in Toronto in 1885, having written very little after the death of her husband. In her later years, she gave more of her time to painting.[8]

As in England, writing proved an important financial resource and personal outlet during Moodie's Canadian years. Still eager for fame and very sensitive to the opportunities she had abandoned, she was quick to seek markets for her work in North America and to encourage, as best she could, publication of her writing in England. Initially there were few solid opportunities. Though her poems began to appear in the early 1830s in *The Albion* [New York], *The Emigrant* [New York], *The Canadian Literary Magazine*, *The North American Quarterly Magazine*, and various provincial newspapers, it was not until she made contact with John Lovell, the editor of a newly established Montreal magazine, *The Literary Garland*, that she was regularly remunerated for her writing. From May 1839 to December 1851, she wrote prolifically for *The Literary Garland*, establishing herself as its steadiest and most versatile contributor. In *The Literary Garland* and *The Victoria Magazine*, which she and her husband edited during its short existence (1847-48), she produced virtually all the poems, sketches, and instalment fiction she would later rework into book form for the famous English publisher Richard Bentley. These later works included *Roughing It in the Bush; or, Life in Canada* (1852), *Mark*

Hurdlestone; or, The Gold Worshipper (1853), *Life in the Clearings versus the Bush* (1853), *Flora Lyndsay; or, Passages in an Eventful Life* (1854), *Matrimonial Speculations* (1854), and *Geoffrey Moncton; or, The Faithless Guardian* (1855). Most were reprinted in New York and proved very successful there. Her last major effort, a three-volume novel for Bentley entitled *The World before Them* (1868), effectively closed out her writing career, though she did oversee a reprinting of *Roughing It in the Bush* in its first Canadian edition in 1871.

Tradition and Milieu

Throughout her life, Susanna Moodie thought of herself, not as a Canadian, but as an Englishwoman. Indeed, the tenacity and pride with which she held to her English identity is one of the inescapable aspects of her writing, especially that writing done in Canada for an English audience. To that audience, she felt compelled to reveal "the secrets of the prison-house," the actualities of "the wilderness" experience she had endured in isolation and exile so far from the gentle Suffolk countryside and the literary energies of London.[9] Whatever value, opportunity, and humour she could locate in her Canadian experience — and she located a good deal — she was imaginatively anchored to social and literary ideals she had learned in England and which she came thereafter to idealize even more because of distance.

Moodie's formative world was rural and isolated, pre-Victorian and conservative. Like her sisters, she read widely in the books available in her father's library. Like them, as well, she was deeply attracted to the Suffolk region, to the romance of East Anglian history still manifest in the many ruins near Bungay and Southwold, and to the tales and lore she heard from servants and local residents, who were richly steeped in oral tradition. Increasingly, too, with the example of Agnes and Eliza before her, she grew infatuated with the glamour of literary London. The world of writers, artists, and personalities, so remote from the conditions of her Reydon life, came to fascinate and attract her.

Several kinds of books left their mark on her in these early years; in fact, so willingly did she accept these examples that in her later work there is little recognizable deviation from these first established patterns. Form she seems to have accepted as a given, never questioning that serious literature could have any objective more worthwhile than a forthright didactic aim. "Every good work of fiction," she was to tell her readers in *The Literary Garland*, "is a step towards the mental improvement of mankind." Clearly, her use of "good" here indicates a Christian and ameliorative, rather than an aesthetic, emphasis. The aesthetic was to her purely ornamental, "the beautiful and attractive garb" that clothes the vital truths.[10]

In the increasing early nineteenth-century interest in conduct books and moral tales for children, Susanna found models for her forays into juvenile literature. To the Rousseauian and optimistic cast of popular works like Maria Edgeworth's *Moral Tales* (1801), Thomas Day's *Sandford and Merton* (1783-89), and Sarah Trimmer's *Fabulous Histories* (1786), she brought a stern, Protestant edge, a function of her own home training, on the one hand, and of her growing interest in Nonconformism or Methodism, on the other. Her tales such as *Rowland Massingham* and *Profession and Principle* are typical didactic narratives of painful reformation, emphasizing the importance of, and difficulty in, overcoming wilfulness and self-centred passion in order to lead a dutiful, useful, and Christian life. What is striking about them is her ability to treat temptation dramatically even as she soberly insists that "life is but one perpetual scene of trial"[11] and that the wise individual must yield himself to the will of Providence.

The romance of history also had a great appeal for the age, inspired in part by the poetry and romances of Walter Scott. The Strickland girls grew up in an atmosphere in which history was passionately discussed and in a locale where its monuments were near at hand. Wolsey's bridge was close by, as was the church at Blythburgh where bullet holes made by Cromwell's men were still visible in the wooden doors. Avidly, the girls consumed available histories like Rapin's *History of England*, Plutarch's *Lives*, and Clarendon's *History of the Rebellion and Civil Wars in England*. This fascination, which led Agnes and Eliza to historical biography, inspired in Susanna an attraction to various heroic figures such as Gustavus Adolphus, Arminius, Jugurtha, and Napoleon.[12] In particular, figures whose devotion to the ideal of freedom and independence was of a high order earned heroic status in her imagination.

Spartacus, a man whose "spirit was too lofty to brook slavery," was the subject of her first published book.[13] Much that was to be typical of her later fiction is contained in this brief, theatrical novel, an overwritten evocation of heroic sensibility in action. Spartacus' "enthusiasm" (S, p. 13) and moral grandeur (of which his "more than mortal beauty" [S, p. 130] is an outward sign) is made to run the difficult course between devotion to the ideal of freedom and an unwillingness to rebel violently against the prevailing Roman order, much as Moodie would reveal her own sensibility in making her quest for independence consistent with her devotion to the English influence in Canada.

Spartacus, in fact, bridges two central preoccupations of the period, the historical and the sentimental. Both were staples of the popular women writers of the period, among them Maria Edgeworth, Jane Porter, Mrs. Felicia Hemans, Letitia Landon (L.E.L.), and Mrs. S. C. Hall. It was to be recognized among such company that the young Susanna aspired. Her tales and poems — and likely, as well, her tragedies, which, she told Richard Bentley, were the best of her early work[14] — sought to inspire admiration for higher standards of conduct and deeper kinds of feeling. "Enthusiasm" was her particular watchword. Very much a creature of her times, she named her first "adult" book *Enthusiasm* not only to indicate her belief in the sensibility's agency in surmounting human limitations and in perceiving suprahuman possibilities, but also to signal her commitment to religious seriousness and Nonconformism.[15] In *Mark Hurdlestone*, she has a good young woman, not unlike herself, enthuse over the bracing idea:

> Enthusiasm is the eternal struggling of our immortal against our mortal nature, which expands the wings of the soul towards its native heaven. Enthusiasm! Can anything great or good be achieved without it? Can a man become a poet, painter, orator, patriot, warrior, or lover, without enthusiasm? Can he become a Christian without it? In man's struggles to obtain fame, enthusiasm is a virtue. In a holy cause it is termed madness. Oh, thou divine Author of the human soul, evermore grant me the inspiration of this immortal spirit![16]

As Walter Houghton defines it, "that higher state of mind, in which the selfish desires of the ego, far from having to be conquered by the moral will, are swept aside by the selfless impulse of the 'noble' emotions, is a state of enthusiasm."[17] Moodie's early work, in fact, represents an interestingly naïve, yet stereotypical, example of the blending of the "complementary ethics" of earnestness and enthusiasm that Houghton sees as characteristic of many Victorian writers.[18] Her didactic tendency has its root in these, for her, complementary ideals, which she never ceased to serve or promote throughout her life.

Finally, among early influences, one cannot overlook the popularity of the sketch, a relatively new and flexible form, especially suitable to personal reflection and the celebration of scenes and characters of local interest. As the magazines and annuals featured sketches regularly, Susanna Strickland had numerous models available to her. Most important among these was Mary Russell Mitford (1787-1855), whose plays and sketches attracted Susanna and led her to write several admiring letters to Mitford in 1829 and 1830.[19]

Mitford's sketches of the Berkshire area, collected under the title *Our Village* (1824-32), made her one of the most popular and famous rural writers England has produced.[20] Her personal style, her "enthusiastic sensitivity,"[21] and her interest in rural types and activities must have appealed to Susanna, who fondly addressed her as one of the first of England's female writers. In an important article, Carl Ballstadt has called attention to Moodie's early debt to Mitford and to the five Suffolk sketches she herself wrote for *La Belle Assemblée* from 1827 to 1829, noting persuasively that if she had remained in England she would likely have produced a book about Suffolk "similar in many respects to *Roughing It in the Bush*."[22]

Written in familiar, personal style, the autobiographical sketch was the form that most effectively liberated Susanna Strickland from the conventions and attitudes that make her poetry and tales seem artificial, platitudinous, and often ridiculous to contemporary readers. In "Old Hannah; or, The Charm," the last of her Suffolk sketches, her own buoyant, youthful personality contrasts vividly to Hannah's without unnecessarily forcing moral judgements upon the reader.[23] An elderly servant, Hannah holds tenaciously to her countrified superstitions and faith in charms, despite Susanna's reservations and the effects of an elaborate practical joke played upon her by the Strickland boys. Moreover, Susanna was able to be more revealing of her own feelings, in particular her adolescent fascination with romantic love and her interest in spiritualism and magic, while creating an attractive picture of the crusty Hannah, life at Reydon, and certain folkways of Suffolk life. The approach developed here came to serve her well when, in Canada, she began to organize her memories of interesting or disturbing experiences around the typical subjects of local-colour sketches — eccentric personalities, regional customs, and rural outings.

It is more difficult to designate with certainty the writers who influenced Moodie after she left England. Clearly, she read as widely in books, magazines, and newspapers as her limited opportunities and financial constraints in the bush allowed. Most likely she held to her established tendencies in Canada, little influenced by the rapidly changing scene about her. The passion that had taken strongest hold was the reformist urge. Even before she left England, she wrote of Cowper in this spirit:

I think his works have little poetic merit. But his sentiments are noble, excellent, sublime! I venerate the independent spirit which pervades his works. He possesses a mind so clear and comprehensive, so divested of prejudice that I consider him as a Reformer of the vices of mankind to stand unrivalled.[24]

Among American writers, she admired Lydia Huntley Sigourney (America's most widely read poet before Longfellow's emergence), Harriet Beecher Stowe, and Margaret Fuller, all of whom were friends to good causes and enthusiasts of humanitarianism and reform. The cause of slavery that involved her in England continued to interest her, as she indicates in such later works as *Flora Lyndsay* and *Life in the Clearings*. Always in her judgements, moral priorities take precedence over artistic considerations. To Richard Bentley, for instance, she expressed her admiration of Dickens' *Bleak House* and *Oliver Twist*, the latter of which she deemed his finest achievement. Thackeray, by contrast, troubled her. While she admired his wit, she felt his satire was likely to effect no moral good.[25] For the general good of reform, then, she viewed methods of indirection in writing as ineffective or, worse still, misleading. Despairing of the coarseness and licentiousness implicit in the works of Smollett, Fielding, and even Richardson, she applauded the modern and improved conscience of her age that dwelt above all on "the instruction and improvement of mankind" (*LC*, p. 216). In particular, she cites the efforts of Dickens and Eugène Sue, "heaven-inspired teachers," bent upon exposing inequitable social conditions and discovering "kindred humanity" in the downtrodden and degraded members of society, be they thieves or prostitutes (*LC*, p. 215). Consciously addressing the genteel, female audience she considered hers, Moodie feelingly argues above all for "the great work of moral reform" (*LC*, p. 216). Only with such emphasis upon "the best feelings of humanity" (*LC*, p. 216), she believed, could the novel achieve the high purpose that made it a form to be valued, not mistrusted.

Critical Overview and Context

In 1959 Robert McDougall noted that, with the exceptions of *Roughing It in the Bush*, *Life in the Clearings*, and possibly *Flora Lyndsay*, "we can with a good conscience abandon [the rest of Moodie's work] to survive as best it may in the form in which it was originally printed" (*LC*, p. 285). If anything, the tendency of recent criticism has been more selective still, concentrating almost exclusively on *Roughing It in the Bush*. The only notable exception is Carol Shields, who in *Susanna Moodie: Voice and Vision* (1977) has considered certain unifying themes and distinctive patterns of thought in a number of Moodie's works, though her coverage is incomplete and her treatment often spotty.

There are a number of good reasons for this lack of interest in Moodie's work as a whole. Availability of texts is one. Limited and confusing bibliographical information is another. Scanty biographical information, hence insufficient awareness of Moodie's literary background and milieu, is a third. Finally, as McDougall suggests, much of the work is of but marginal interest both in subject matter and quality. Only as such work informs our sense of Moodie herself and her loosely conceived trilogy of emigration, settlement, and adaptation does it concern most students of early Canadian literature.

The British reviews of Moodie's major publications in the 1850s provide a persuasive rationale for this selective view of her work. To judge from the reactions of *The Spectator* and *The Athenaeum*, *Roughing It in the Bush* was welcomed with considerable delight.

The Spectator praised its variety, informativeness, liveliness, and domestic charm, lamenting only its excesses of description and reflection.[26] *The Athenaeum*'s reviewer admired Moodie's ability to rise above "the drudgery of her lot" and to balance privation and loneliness with pleasure and humour; he concluded that "in what may be called the light literature of colonization, her volumes will rank beside those of Mrs. Kirkland, and possibly above them. . . ."[27] Caroline Kirkland's humorous and thoughtful account of settling in backwoods Michigan, *A New Home — Who'll Follow?* (1840), had been a popular success of which Moodie had likely been aware, if only through reviews she had read.

Both periodicals, however, expressed increasing disappointment in the kind and quality of Moodie's subsequent books. Of *Matrimonial Speculations*, for instance, one reviewer wrote, "When Mrs. Moodie leaves off her 'roughings in the bush' she becomes coarse, without any spirit of fun or humour to redeem this hard quality."[28] Both periodicals found *Mark Hurdlestone* barely tolerable in its excesses of characterization and its use of clumsy romancer's devices.[29] They shared the view that, though *Flora Lyndsay* contained an interesting personal narrative and much useful information, it had been ineffectively transformed into fiction.[30] The same want of structure and direction was also criticized by the reviewers of *Life in the Clearings*; its sketches, they judged, partook too much of "the common magazine story" or annual contribution.[31] Indeed, *The Athenaeum*'s reviewer hoped "Mrs. Moodie [would] not further bring the 'sweepings' of her experience to market now that the real, valuable truths in her wallet have been all purchased, paid for, and sent home." Such dissatisfaction reached a climax in *The Athenaeum*'s review of Moodie's last novel, *The World before Them*, which was judged as containing "nothing to admire." As fiction it was naïve, dated, and stereotyped. "Everything that implies vitality and individuality and tone is missing," concluded the notice.[32]

While Moodie did enjoy a brief popularity in the United States — her works during the 1850s sold well and received favourable reviews — the important criticism of her North American work is Canadian and begins with the first Canadian publication of *Roughing It in the Bush* in 1871. Until that edition, there had been little encouraging local response; indeed, one reviewer in 1872 deemed that earlier criticism "captious and ungenerous"; Moodie's testiness in *Life in the Clearings* regarding *Roughing It*'s reception in Canada indicates her own dissatisfaction with these early notices.

The aforementioned review in *The Canadian Monthly and National Review* admonished Canadian readers against approaching *Roughing It in the Bush* with a closed or hostile mind:

> It is an extremely lively book, full of incident and character. Although its primary object was to give a warning by means of an example, it is by no means a jeremiad. On the contrary, we almost lose sight of the immigrants' troubles in the ludicrous phases of human character which present themselves to view in rapid succession.[33]

The warning marks a change. While in England and the United States Moodie's work enjoyed a brief popularity (only to be forgotten, for the most part, within a decade), in Canada, after considerable resistance, *Roughing It in the Bush* slowly achieved recognition and prominence. Today it is "a conceded classic."[34] In fact, Moodie herself has become so vivid an historical-cultural figure that she has been made a character or voice in a number of contemporary literary works, among them Robertson Davies' *At My Heart's Core*, Carol Shields's *Small Ceremonies*, Margaret Atwood's *The Journals of Susanna Moodie*, and Elizabeth Hopkins' one-woman play *Susanna*.

If the autobiographical element, the voice in response to its new environment and social conditions, has intrigued many Canadian authors, *Roughing It in the Bush* has also proved a valuable document to students of Canadian history, politics, and formative culture. Indeed, few books — one would include here its inevitable counterpart, Catharine Parr Traill's *The Backwoods of Canada* — have provided so rich a picture of, and response to, early conditions and social patterns in rural Upper Canada. Lloyd M. Scott in "The English Gentlefolk in the Backwoods of Canada" accurately describes the "courage" and "naïveté" with which the Moodies and Traills responded to the hardships and radical deculturation of bush life; in particular, he analyses their English middle-class responses to disorienting situations and the sustaining assumptions that governed their "seemingly hypocritical views."[35] Valuable historical perspective is also the subject of Robert McDougall's introduction to *Life in the Clearings*, in which he argues that Moodie's sense of cultural evolution, especially "her willingness and her ability to find a new position between opposing influences" (*LC*, p. xix), "can help us to form a correct notion of our national identity" (*LC*, p. xi). Robin Mathews also gives this political dimension special treatment in arguing that Moodie was "a pink tory, historical precursor of the Red Tory in Canada."[36] That students of history, politics, Canadian studies, and women's studies turn to Moodie's books so regularly is testament not only to their usefulness but to the pertinency of their views.

The growing body of critical writing about Susanna Moodie and *Roughing It in the Bush* includes biographical, bibliographical, literary-historical, and thematic studies. Audrey Morris' *Gentle Pioneers: Five Nineteenth-Century Canadians* provides useful detail about the Canadian lives of the Moodies, Stricklands, and Traills, and assimilates much of the earlier work of Trent Valley historians like G. H. Needler and Edwin Guillet.[37] Clara Thomas' "The Strickland Sisters" in *The Clear Spirit* is the most concise and reliable biographical sketch that is readily available.[38] Not to be overlooked, however, is Carl Ballstadt's unpublished thesis (University of London, 1965), "The Literary History of the Strickland Family," which is still the best record of the English literary environment that produced Susanna Moodie and Catharine Parr Traill.

For bibliographical information, there are several notable sources, though, as George Parker has pointed out, a comprehensive bibliography has been long overdue.[39] As to Moodie's English work, the Ballstadt thesis is a valuable aid. Mary Markham Brown's *An Index to* The Literary Garland (1962), Reg Watters' *A Checklist of Canadian Literature* (1972), and Alec Lucas' pamphlet *The Otonabee School* (1977) are also important resources. A forthcoming bibliography in the multivolume *The Annotated Bibliography of Canada's Major Authors* will bring together much of the disparate information concerning Moodie's wide-ranging publishing history.

Studies of a literary-historical nature are perhaps the most important resources available to current scholars, for it is only with a firm sense of the author at work in her own time that we can begin to understand the complexities and purposes of a particular work. *Roughing It in the Bush* is a case in point. Very little work has been done in investigating its evolution and textual history. Contemporary critics have, in fact, been inclined to extrapolate theories from flawed, often abridged texts and to relate them more to present concerns than to the times and audience to which they were addressed. Our sense of history, thus, often suffers in the light of contemporary cultural preoccupations.

While more of this kind of study is needed, there are several important beginnings. Carl Ballstadt's aforementioned "Susanna Moodie and the English Sketch" convincingly places Moodie in a literary tradition she effectively adapted to serve her Canadian experience. William Magee sees her as an early prototype for the local-colour school.[40] Clara Thomas' "Journey to Freedom" places the Strickland sisters' work in a tradition of women's travel writing (to which Moodie herself calls attention in her reference to Mrs. Bowdich in *Roughing It*'s first chapter).[41] A recent article by Marian Fowler has attempted to view *Roughing It in the Bush* exclusively as a sentimental novel owing much to the influence of Ann Radcliffe.[42] While the case she makes is overwrought, Fowler is certainly right in suggesting Moodie's involvement in that tradition. Finally, there is George Parker's exploratory study of *Roughing It in the Bush*'s early publishing history, in which he calls attention to the evolution of the text and certain intricacies of textual study.

Recently there has also been a variety of studies attempting to provide thematic, structural, or psychological interpretation of *Roughing It in the Bush*. Most of these have their roots in Carl Klinck's influential introduction to the New Canadian Library reprint. Here Klinck justifies his abridging of the text by arguing that the book is best read as a novel that gains by "concentration" upon Moodie's dramatization of herself as "author-apprentice-heroine."[43] From this emphasis have sprung responses such as Margaret Atwood's fascination with the Moodie personality — "divided down the middle" and expressing itself in contradictory voices — a fascination, Atwood argues, that compensates for Moodie's shapeless and disappointing books.[44] David Stouck and Sherrill Grace have followed in Atwood's myth-making wake, Stouck finding a psychological richness in Moodie's guilt-ridden imagination (the guilt, he argues ominously, is unnamed) and her preoccupation with failure and death, and Grace celebrating Atwood's interpretation of Moodie as an important instance in the contemporary creation of "a usable literary tradition."[45]

In searching for a formal pattern in *Roughing It in the Bush*, R. D. MacDonald seizes upon the movement from "romantic anticipation to disillusionment" that Susanna Moodie undergoes in learning to see nature, not as "beautiful and benevolent," but as a "dangerous taskmaster."[46] Carl Ballstadt in a later essay studies Moodie's treatment of water imagery to reach a very different conclusion — that she is conscious of adjusting to the wilderness.[47] A recent article by G. Noonan surveys *Roughing It*'s criticism (with some notable omissions) and argues that Moodie's "strategy of fiction" is to present herself deliberately as a figure who learns by experience, even as she holds to her negative views about the imprisoning bush.[48]

One other kind of critical approach, the deliberate juxtaposition of Susanna Moodie's and Catharine Parr Traill's responses to Canada, also bears mentioning here. While Clara Thomas and T. D. MacLulich see their personal adventures as contrasting applications of the Robinson Crusoe story,[49] William Gairdner develops the thesis that Moodie's subjectiveness and Traill's objectivity are an early instance of the "two realities" of the Canadian imagination, the one emotional and mythopoetic, the other rational and Puritan.[50] David Jackel maintains the comparison but argues that *Roughing It in the Bush* is a vastly overrated work, "a questionable choice for inclusion in the canon of classic Canadian literature." He perceives "the real strengths of our British inheritance" in Traill's work, not Moodie's.[51]

Moodie's Works

Because Susanna Moodie's output was large, it is impossible in this context to attempt a comprehensive study of her work. However, it is feasible to consider in some detail certain aspects of her writing that have hitherto received little attention, in particular, her work prior to 1832, the evolution of her Canadian sketches of 1847 into the English text of *Roughing It in the Bush*, and her often-overlooked autobiographical novel, *Flora Lyndsay*. Each throws light upon a writer whom we have, out of our cultural needs, made over into a variety of striking and often distorting images — a one-woman British garrison, a snobbish bluestocking, a heroic pioneer, an ill-equipped Crusoe, or a literary sort of paranoid schizophrenic.

Moodie's juvenile literature, written mostly in the 1820s, anticipates her later work in several ways. Her romantic interest in the
ideal of freedom and her middle-class emphasis upon the merits of
the humbly born are important themes from the outset. So too is
the comforting Christian fatalism that provides a rationale for long-
suffering virtue. Though she would later, in a Canadian context,
produce work of considerably greater sophistication and interest,
her early established modes of imagining and teaching remained
consistent in her writing.

Rachel Wilde's "world of poetic liberty" (*VM*, p. 214) and her
fascination with military heroes were Susanna Strickland's, as well.
One of the earliest results was her novel about Spartacus, a figure
with whom the young Susanna so identified that she congratulated
herself for rescuing him from "the oblivion with which Roman
historians have laboured to cover his name" (*S*, p. 61). But while
she gloried in linking herself to such a hero — he is a great warrior
against his will and a being "almost above humanity" (*S*, p. 11) —
it was his stature as a nobly motivated rebel that most appealed to
her. The plot she constructed makes *Spartacus: A Roman Story* a
naïve and overwritten celebration of sensibility, in which the weight
of blame for actual rebellion falls conveniently on a barbarian
named Theodoric, whose lust for battle draws the peace-loving,
high-minded hero to his ennobling death.

A somewhat different pattern is apparent in her more commonplace conduct stories. Two kinds of boys are contrasted. The one in
need of reform and control is wellborn, arrogant, selfish, and
unthinking, a forerunner of Dickens' Steerforth. For all his attractiveness and charm, he is blind to the humanity of the lower classes.
His social opposite is humbly born, generous, sometimes easily led,
but, in essence, noble of spirit. Typically, the aristocratic youth
takes advantage of his superior position to discredit or humiliate
the lower-class boy, though in the long run nemesis prevails. The
noble boy slowly but painfully learns the folly and cruelty of his
ways (*The Little Prisoner*'s Ferdinand is given a taste of incarcera-
tion by his stern, wise father, and Rowland Massingham maims his
left hand using a forbidden gun), and the humble boy's patience,
personal merit, and good works are duly recognized. There is, then,
a sharp distinction between liberty as an ideal and licence as a
dangerous pattern of behaviour, a distinction — however conven-

tional for its time — that would continue to be a central concern in Moodie's writing.

Social fables which are contradictory, but no less powerful for that, underlie these morally simplistic stories: a faith in a benevolent aristocratic paternalism (in the form of fathers, guardians, or ministers) supports a strong identification with the unappreciated worth of the humbly born youth. What results are romances of rectified order in which middle-class merit and belief in education, charitable behaviour, and the keeping of good faith slowly but surely earn social recognition and elevated status. Hugh Latimer's uncle states the case in the pious language typical of these books:

> But, Hugh Latimer, if you pursue virtue, and steadfastly adhere to the paths of truth, even if you were a beggar's brat, you would, by this course, gain the esteem of the good and sensible part of mankind, and need not fear the ridicule of those who wantonly commit crime, because they think that their rank shields them. (*HL*, pp. 9-10)

The moral rhetoric notwithstanding, the ethic of these stories is materialistic and conservative. Hugh Latimer proves himself and overcomes his envy of social position; however, he never ceases to feel "that proper diffidence which ought always to be paid to those of a superior rank" (*HL*, p. 120); nor is he blind to the ways in which rank and riches add a lustre to worth, whatever its source. Father figures like Colonel Grahame provide that lustre and temper the crimes of wilful behaviour by arguing that they result from "early prejudices" which temporarily blind the wellborn to the inner worth of people who lack "the outside show of titles" (*HL*, pp. 134-35). While these narratives generally concern the behaviour of young boys, it is clear from their distinctive pattern that they are unconscious variations on the Cinderella story, a myth of great pertinence to the longings for greater freedom and recognition of the middle class in an aristocratic society.

Despite the conservatism of the young Susanna's vision, even her conduct stories are characterized by an almost unwilling identification with the energies of a wilful and passionate sensibility. The attraction was essentially personal, as such autobiographical stories as "Rachel Wilde" reveal and as Catharine Parr Traill's memoir "A

Slight Sketch of the Early Life of Mrs. Moodie" confirms.[52] It is there inadvertently in her treatment of the young aristocrats but most obviously in such early stories as "Jane Redgrave: A Village Tale" and poems like "The Maniac."[53]

The theme of passion and its consequences seldom escaped sentimental cliché and tragic excess in Susanna Moodie's early writing. "Jane Redgrave," for instance, is the story of a much-misunderstood girl who falls in love with an errant, nobly born man. He readily deceives the romantic Jane, who is an avid reader of old-fashioned novels and a girl eager to marry a gentleman and to ignore "the cold maxims of prudence."[54] After adventures involving clandestine forest meetings, a widow dying in the snow, and supernatural coincidences, Jane has a stillborn child, goes mad (a favourite Moodie device), and, upon seeing her dead lover's corpse, realizes the true nature of existence (she "saw death stamped upon the perishing leaf") and turns her thoughts to "a better world."[55] She becomes, in short, a guardian figure, wise in the ways of the world.

But, if Moodie was inclined to tragic scenes, sensationalism, and psychological absurdities and could fill out such thin plots as that of "Jane Redgrave" to nearly novel length through the addition of digressions and various trappings, matters of passion and intuition were also of deep personal interest to her. When she turned to autobiographical fiction or fictional autobiography, she inevitably drew upon the energies and contradictions of her own temperament. Her lifelong fascination with ghosts and pseudosciences like phrenology, her "faith in the wild and wonderful" (*VM*, p. 251), is a side of her nature that coexists uneasily with her Christian piety, middle-class practicality, and Puritanism. Her love of the ridiculous and unusual often runs counter to her sober moral seriousness. As well, her romantic rebelliousness and idealizing of freedom seem at odds with her confidence in English tradition and social order. In *Roughing It in the Bush*, these contradictory personal energies find their most interesting expression.

Roughing It in the Bush; or, Life in Canada has proved both intriguing and frustrating to the numerous critics who have sought to analyse its structure. Always there are loose ends no scheme can sufficiently account for. Neither does it readily belong in any recognizable genre. Containing elements of poetry, fiction, travel writing, autobiography, and social analysis, it eludes definition. In his recent article, David Jackel takes this critical frustration to a dismissive extreme, labelling *Roughing It* "a pretentious, sentimental, self-indulgent, unstructured and derivative book" (pp. 2-3). In more detail, he writes,

> *Roughing It in the Bush* simply has no structure. The series of sketches that comprise it are "unified" only by the presence of Mrs. Moodie. Her experiences, her feelings, her opinions — her sentimental *self* — dominate the book, but they do not structure it. . . . *Roughing It* is undisciplined self-expression. (pp. 9-10)

While Jackel registers understandable disappointment that Susanna Moodie is not a better writer, his real objection is to the criticism that has elevated her to a stature superior to that of Catharine Parr Traill in the "Canadian tradition." However, in his effort to de-canonize her, he makes little attempt to see the work as it is. He quotes from Klinck's abridged text and shows but a partial awareness of available criticism and source material. Thus, inadvertently, he joins the group of critics who would hurriedly evaluate and place, often in the context of twentieth-century preoccupations and values, rather than seek to illuminate and understand, this important and unusual text.

As a collection of sketches, *Roughing It* was clearly a departure for Moodie. Most importantly, the sketch form gave her a freedom not only to range widely in mood and subject but to present material in a personal and informal way. It held her to no particular narrative unity other than that of personal voice and values. Accordingly, though a loose chronological order pertains in the book, it is entirely possible that particular sketches could have been omitted without significantly altering the overall effect. Editors like Carl Klinck have taken this view, though in the case of Klinck's edition the cuts were so major as to create imbalances.[56] On the basis of that text, David Jackel is perhaps right in arguing that *Roughing It* has no structure other than Moodie's sentimental self. His view need not, however, be the indictment he makes it. Structure as the twentieth-century critic wishes to see it can have little pertinence when applied to a book that evolved as *Roughing It* did.

And, since Moodie's sense of self was her primary literary capital, we should be careful to recognize those instances in her career when she made especially effective use of it.

Roughing It in the Bush has a complexity that results from several factors, among them the author's imaginative tensions, the book's several ostensible aims, and the fact that in pursuit of effects Moodie wrote in several distinctive styles. Another important factor is the way in which the book evolved as subject and text.

When the Moodies arrived in North America, it was Dunbar, not Susanna, who was the more acknowledged author. Not surprisingly, then, the original idea for *Roughing It* was his. Writing to his publisher, Richard Bentley, in 1834, Dunbar described the kind of project literate Englishmen of the age of empire were inclined to engage in:

> I have now been settled with my family in Canada for more than two years and having had every opportunity of becoming acquainted with the mode of life and prospects of a settler in all its details *from actual experience*, I think myself qualified to give a fair and impartial account of the country. It unfortunately generally happens that most of these writers who have given an account of Canada have either been mere "birds of passage," or influenced by interested motives. If you are inclined to treat with me for a work on Upper Canada, I shall be happy to undertake it, but my *time* is so valuable that I could not afford to sacrifice it without a fair prospect of an adequate remuneration. My plan should be to give a plain unaffected narrative of the progress and proceedings of a settler in this colony whether he settled in the cleared and improved parts of the country or went into the backwoods. I have tried both these kinds of settlement myself — hitherto successfully — and can therefore form a tolerable estimate of their respective advantages and disadvantages. My personal narrative would of course occupy a considerable portion of the work, and would be the more popular as containing not mere opinions but my actual experience in the country.[57]

As Bentley's reply was not encouraging, the idea was left to simmer. When Susanna Moodie actually began her sketches — six for *The Literary Garland* and two for *The Victoria Magazine* — is not clear. She was writing fiction and poetry in the late 1830s for *The Literary Garland* but, given the limits of her output under such difficult circumstances, not likely these sketches. It is more probable that they belong to a burst of autobiographical writing she seems to have begun in the mid-1840s.[58] Whatever the case, she had no direct contact with Richard Bentley until after the manuscript she sent him as "Canadian Life" appeared in London with its new and striking title.[59] John Bruce, a London antiquarian, negotiated on behalf of the Moodies until his illness forced Susanna herself into direct contact with her publisher.

Susanna Moodie's subsequent letters to Bentley indicate not only that *Roughing It* was a family venture but that its text was incomplete as it was first printed. "Jeanie Burns" and "Lost Children," which were sent to replace "Michael MacBride," a chapter Moodie suppressed because of the Catholic reaction in Canada (*The Literary Garland*, Feb. 1851), arrived too late for inclusion.[60] So did a long and interesting, sociological analysis of Belleville by Dunbar Moodie, which Bentley had asked for as an effective and objective means of concluding the narrative. Dunbar Moodie prefaces his comments in this chapter by noting that the "preceding sketches of Canadian life" are "truthful pictures of scenes and characters observed fifteen or twenty years ago" (*RI*, II, 295) but that conditions have altered for the better since that time.[61] While Bentley saved both "Jeanie Burns" and "Michael MacBride" for *Life in the Clearings*, he hastened to add Dunbar's "Canadian Sketches" to the second — and most complete — edition of *Roughing It*, which appeared in response to the book's popularity in late 1852.[62] Thus, its two volumes each concluded with Dunbar's analytical chapters, "The Village Hotel" and "The Land-Jobber," on the one hand, and "Canadian Sketches" (in two parts), on the other. In all, Dunbar Moodie contributed four chapters and ten poems to the project. That his considerable part in the book has been minimized by subsequent editors and perhaps even abetted by Susanna Moodie herself (in authorizing the 1871 Canadian edition) is insufficient reason to ignore the informative, objective, and generally optimistic voice he sought to bring to the book. When he writes in "The Village Hotel" that his aims include providing "a connecting link between my wife's sketches" (*RI*, I, 241) and an explanation of certain otherwise unaccountable circumstances pertaining to their situation, it is clear his sketches are meant to serve several narrative functions.

The "family" aspect of *Roughing It*'s authorship is but one element of its curious and casual evolution. A second is the transformation of the sketches themselves. Susanna Moodie's "Canadian" sketches differ in significant ways from the material she sent to Bentley. Collation reveals an attempt on her part to write for the tastes and assumptions of the particular audience she was addressing. This is not to say that the pattern of her adjustments is consistent or predictable. Indeed, in copying, she seems often to have altered phraseology according to her present mood. Nevertheless, a glance at certain conspicuous changes in material both included in, and excluded from, the much-used New Canadian Library edition rewards attention.

Generally speaking, the language is more high-toned and poetic in the English edition. "Trees" become "woods" or "groves," "around" becomes "encircled," "bite" becomes "masticate," "Indian" becomes "the wild man," "face" becomes "countenance." Euphemisms and poetic or biblical allusions increase. In "A Visit to Grosse Isle," "a fresh cargo of these lively savages" (*VM*, p. 17) is softened somewhat to read "a fresh cargo of lively savages from the Emerald Isle" (*RI*, 1, 14). Often Moodie deliberately excises material, presumably to protect the sensibilities of her English and feminine audience. In "Brian, the Still-Hunter," for instance, she describes the rough-and-ready Layton's efforts to deal with Brian after his attempted suicide at Rice Lake. With Brian "choking and growing black in the face," she writes for Bentley that "Layton then detailed some particulars of his surgical practice which it is not necessary to repeat" (*RI*, 1, 188). In *The Literary Garland* sketch, however, she shows no such delicacy. Layton turns Brian over on his "belly," not his "stomach," and proceeds as follows:

I then saw that it was a piece of the flesh of his throat that had been carried into his wind-pipe. So, what do I do, but puts in my finger and thumb, and pulls it out, and bound up his throat with my handkerchief, dipping it first in the water to stanch the blood.[63]

The lively language and vividness of the "Canadian" treatment are strong evidence of Moodie's abilities when freed of conventional restraints.

Another notable suppression affecting the Bentley text involved Moodie's first published Canadian sketch, "Old Woodruff and His Three Wives."[64] In "Adieu to the Woods," she cuts off "the history of [Woodruff's] several ventures in matrimony" with the excuse of not wishing to "trouble" her readers (RI, II, 288-89). Her verb seems deliberately chosen. The subject matter of this racy and vernacular sketch both fascinated and appalled her. The "shrewd, humorous-looking Yorkshireman," having buried three wives, is ogling the attractive friend of one of his own daughters when the Moodie family stops by on its way to Belleville. Woodruff's description of the way he treated his previous wives reveals him to be a selfish and "unfeeling wretch"; however, despite her outrage, Moodie finds irresistible delight in his deadpan comic manner.[65] Why she cut the most interesting part of this sketch is an open question. It is no more a digression than many other anecdotes and character studies she includes. Two possible reasons come to mind. First, it was a kind of realistic subject matter she may have thought inappropriate for an English audience. Secondly, as it dealt with an Englishman behaving indulgently and inhumanely and as she could locate no convenient psychological rationale (such as Mr. Malcolm's South American murder in "The Little Stumpy Man") to account for his behaviour, she may have felt it would throw an unnecessarily disagreeable light on her own countrymen, a light inconsistent with her homage to her native land.

Two other sketches provide useful glimpses into Susanna Moodie's pattern of writing, particularly the layering effect that resulted from her adaptation of material to serve the interests of a second, very different audience. "The Walk to Dummer," a sketch dropped by Carl Klinck, describes a dangerous act of charity undertaken by Moodie, her good friend Emilia S———, and Thomas Traill, what was in all a twenty-mile trek in the dead of winter through forest and cedar swamp to deliver food to a starving family. Like "A Trip to Stony Lake," also cut by Klinck, it is an important chapter evincing Moodie's ability to rise above difficult circumstances in a spirited way and to locate beauty and interest in both her "bush" relationships and the rugged landscape.

The most notable changes in "The Walk to Dummer" are embellishing alterations and additions specifically for the English audience. A "place called Dummer"[66] becomes "a place situated in the forest-depths of this far western wilderness" (*RI*, II, 222). To a simple observation about her own shyness, "I am a sad coward with strangers,"[67] Moodie adds "and I have lived so long out of the world that I am at a great loss what to do" (*RI*, II, 240). Only in the English edition does Emilia become witty and sarcastic about the lack of hospitality they encounter during one stop. A long, three-paragraph "digression" beginning "And here I would remark that it is always a rash and hazardous step for any officer to part with his half-pay" (*RI*, II, 227-29) is added to the narrative to offer practical advice to would-be gentleman emigrants. Indeed, the importance of English connections is heightened considerably throughout the sketch. Tears "burst" from Moodie's eyes more often in the English text. She also adds paragraphs that emphasize her pain at having little to give "the unhappy sufferer" and that allow her to philosophize about the trip in terms of "life's unretraceable journey" and the anguish of the traveller who, taking "the wrong track through every stage," arrives, not at "a land of blissful promise," but "the gulf of despair" (*RI*, II, 246). Whether one chooses to see the misguided-journey metaphor as a structuring device or a brief Puritan homily must depend, to some extent, on a complete study of these textual changes.

In "A Visit to Grosse Isle" there are also numerous interesting alterations. In *The Victoria Magazine* original, Moodie is very much the detached observer of the outwitting of the pretentious French doctor, the striking features of the new landscape, and the behaviour of the newly arrived emigrants. In the instance of the outwitting (*VM*, p. 14), she does not anticipate the captain's joke ("I looked hard at old Boreas, wondering all the while, what he was at"), she makes no mention of *her* Bible being mislaid (the captain says, "I don't think there's one in the ship"), and she does not emphasize that the Voltaire history is hers (it just happens to be at hand). Her own centrality in the situation and the emphasis upon her piety and literary taste belong to the English text. Similarly, while in the English text she is left alone on deck with her baby when her husband goes ashore, in the Canadian sketch he remains with her. *Her* deep disappointment at not seeing more of Grosse Isle because of the quarantine is, in the early version, *their* shared regret. In another noteworthy change, she cuts from the English text the captain's caustic joke (*VM*, p. 17) about her involuntary fasting during the day: "Well, well, I've made a good catholic of you, at any rate!"

The Canadian "Grosse Isle" is freer, more adventurous, and more colourful overall. The irascible captain, who in *Flora Lyndsay* had alienated the Moodies by making free with their servant, does not alter his rough language to warn her that "many things look well at a distance" (*RI*, 1, 10). The Frenchman actually swears (*VM*, p. 14). The sergeant, who is physically assaulted by a loud-mouthed washerwoman (the episode is glossed over in the English text), notes that "the women, sir, are the devil" (*VM*, p. 17), a remark that amuses both Moodies. Susanna Moodie herself is, overall, more open to experience and more sympathetic to what she sees. She does not moralize about the indecency of the poorer emigrants' attire, nor does she shrink disdainfully from suggestive behaviour. Of the poor emigrants whom in the English treatment she describes as "filthy beings who were sullying the purity of the air and water" (*RI*, 1, 13), she is more understanding, noting that, because they "were performing their necessary but unpoetical ablutions," they were inadvertently sullying "that enchanting spot" (*VM*, p. 16).

A consideration of the textual changes Moodie made for her English audience suggests that she was a writer who was constrained by the very conventions she admired. As Clara Thomas has astutely noted, "She never lived comfortably with her comic vision . . . or rightly estimated its potential in her writing."[68] With an English audience in mind, her inclination was to decorously harness the strongest elements of her talent — her eye for unusual detail, her love of the ridiculous, her ability to construct vivid dramatic scenes and comic encounters. A fresh personal response she was often compelled to transform into sentimental cliché or bluestocking disdain.

At the same time, it is important to note that Susanna Moodie was not blind to certain of her limitations. In a letter to Richard Bentley, she used phrenology, a pseudoscience she took very seriously, as a basis for analysis:

There is a want of *Individuality* in my writings, which I feel and lament, but cannot remedy. In the phrenological development of my head, these two organs were valleys, not lumps. A scene or picture strikes me as a whole, but I can never enter into details. A carpet must be very brilliant, the paper on the wall very remarkable before I should ever notice either, while the absurd and the extravagant make lasting impressions, and I can remember a droll speech or a caricature face for years.[69]

Moodie's overly adjectival, but conspicuously undetailed, responses to the sublime in nature perhaps owe as much to this limitation as to the Burkeian conventions she was respectfully evoking. Clearly, she was at her best in describing or dramatizing extremes and absurdities of human behaviour, though the impetus ran contrary to the sober tenets of her moral position. As her comments to Bentley suggest, her finest skills as a writer left her uncomfortable. They seemed to her somewhat frivolous, centrifugal, and lacking in essential seriousness. If Moodie, as Margaret Atwood suggests, is a divided personality, that tension lies in a romantic rebelliousness and humorous streak her Puritan consciousness always struggled to control. She was never quite in phase with the prevailing order. She was temperamentally unsuited to be for very long either a mere yea-sayer or a Mrs. Grundy.

The *Roughing It in the Bush* Susanna Moodie and her husband wrote for Richard Bentley is an intriguing and complex narrative, despite its digressiveness and hasty, haphazard construction. As T. D. MacLulich has noted, it suggests "a latent unity . . . which only just fails to be clearly realized."[70] *Roughing It*'s values as a record of experience are many, but, as literature, it succeeds because it provides a dramatized response to pioneer life, the focus of which is the author as autobiographical heroine. Her involvement and subjective responses, elements Moodie heightened in adapting her sketches for the English audience, give the book a power bordering on fiction without lessening its value as record and observation.

Moodie's peculiar blending of the sketch, travel narrative, the sentimental novel tradition, and autobiography give *Roughing It in the Bush* a forcefulness and focus unique among her work. The blending was in part accidental. It grew out of a period of intensely autobiographical writing, the reworking of much of the text to fit the imagined needs of a distant and revered audience, and a desire to write against the grain of received opinion concerning the joys and rewards of pioneering. Furthermore, while remembering in Belleville the greatest and most strenuous adventure of her life, she could see it as the failure it was, even as her imagination was aroused by the range of experiences undergone, the odd characters encountered, and the many tests endured. In effect, the bush provided Susanna Moodie with the only really interesting crucible of experience she was to know as a writer, though it is unlikely that she realized this herself.

The tensions of Moodie's imagination are many and there are several contradictory patterns at work, some explicitly and some implicitly. New World potentiality vies constantly with Old World nostalgia and felt loss. Hope and disappointment, adaptation and alienation, courage and fear, independence and imprisonment oscillate from event to event. The Puritan metaphor of the arduous journey marked by false starts and demanding tests of faith is often evoked as is an evolutionary, progressive philosophy of particular social improvement, on the one hand, and of the improvement of mankind in general, on the other.

If there is any majority agreement among those who have studied *Roughing It in the Bush* in detail, it is that the pattern of adaptation, of learning through experience, prevails. While this view is consistent with the Moodies' middle-class values, their radical politics (they named a son Robert Baldwin), and their expressed faith in both education and an evolving New World order in Canada, it is one that the emotional energy of the text seems often to contradict. At the same time, it is essential to remember that Moodie's pursuit of effects — humorous, grotesque, sentimental, melodramatic, enthusiastic, or didactic — is a consistent element of her writing. She could not resist an opportunity either to entertain or to moralize. The many occasions in which fresh or sharp observations are dulled by stylized comments suggest the frequency with which she relied upon conventions and clichés to shape her expression. Clearly, no single critical rationalization can adequately explain a book in which each sketch was meant to be entertaining in itself. As Dunbar Moodie observed in "The Village Hotel," "travellers and book-makers, like cooks, have to collect high-flavoured dishes, from far and near, the better to please the palates of their patrons" (*RI*, i, 244). *Roughing It in the Bush* is such a book.

After *Roughing It in the Bush*'s heady success, Moodie's published work followed two distinct directions. Eager to capitalize on her sudden and long-desired success, she deluged Bentley with manuscripts and proposals. The result was several unsuccessful English romances: *Mark Hurdlestone; or, The Gold Worshipper*

(1853), a study of the psychological effects of greed; *Matrimonial Speculations* (1854), a collection of three long stories; and *Geoffrey Moncton; or, The Faithless Guardian* (1855). All three expand upon material already published in *The Literary Garland* (a shorter version of *Mark Hurdlestone* had appeared even earlier in *The Lady's Magazine* in 1833). While they provide occasional biographical glimpses and attest to Moodie's preoccupation with aberrant psychological states and the grotesque, they are tedious, baggy books to contemporary readers. They constitute an object lesson in the degree to which she allowed convention and hackneyed themes to displace the fresher responses of her imagination.

The more fertile, though equally frustrating, direction Moodie pursued was to tap further her personal experiences as an emigrant and adaptive "Canadian." *Life in the Clearings versus the Bush* (1853) she hastily put together in response to Bentley's encouragement:

> If you could render your picture of the state of society in the large towns and cities of Canada, interesting to the idle reader, at the same time you make it informing to those who are looking for facts, it would be acceptable. Present them to the reader's eye as they *were* years ago and as they *are* now, and are still every year, I imagine, rapidly progressing. It might form a good work as a pendant to *Roughing It in the Bush*.[71]

Life in the Clearings suffers by contrast to *Roughing It in the Bush*. A "very civilized" (*LC*, p. viii) and generally good-humoured book, it patches together from Moodie's limited experience and knowledge an approximation of what Bentley called for, an amiable portrait of society, the kind to be found in more detail in Frances Trollope's *Domestic Manners of the Americans* and Harriet Martineau's *Society in America*. It is a book Moodie might well have taken more time to assemble and write. Too often, she compensates for lack of pertinent material by injecting old and not particularly appropriate sketches. Her ignorance of Toronto she covers with an essay on novels and their moral significance, while she devotes two chapters to an earlier published sketch, "Trials of a Travelling Musician." The three sketches properly belonging to *Roughing It* are also included. The book's initial promise as a description of social life in Canada, for which Belleville functions as a microcosm, is thus slowly undercut by the use of material inappropriate to the general subject.

The ostensible structure of the book is a trip from Belleville to Niagara Falls, a sure card, Moodie felt, for her English audience's love of the inspirational in nature. The tone of her observations is less strenuous and emotional than in *Roughing It*. Though she claims "a woman's privilege of talking of all sorts of things by the way" (*LC*, p. 4) and accepts the going idea that women cannot be philosophical or analytical, she offers a variety of interesting observations about, and thoughts upon, social practices, institutions, and the political situation in Upper Canada. These by themselves constitute a valuable and discriminating piece of social history. Her point of view — one which she implicitly shared with her husband, to whom she dedicated the book — is firmly Puritan (though not Calvinistic), open-minded, progressive, and reformist. As in *Roughing It in the Bush*, she treads a delicate and not altogether clear line between the best of English culture and tradition, on the one hand, and the opportunities of democracy, on the other, deploring mere pride and snobbery as much as untrammelled republicanism. However, her idealistic faith in education and science as the means of stimulating a morally enlightened progress balks at certain ideas. At such times, the limits of her essentially eighteenth-century sensibility are evident:

> Oh, for one hour alone with Nature, and her great master-piece Niagara! What solemn converse would the soul hold with its Creator at such a shrine — and the busy hum of practical life would not mar, with its jarring discord, this grand "thunder of the waters!" Realities are unmanageable things in some hands, and the Americans are gravely contemplating making their sublime Fall into a motive power for turning machinery.
>
> Ye gods! what next will the love of gain suggest to these gold-worshippers? The whole earth should enter into a protest against such an act of sacrilege — such a shameless desecration of one of the noblest works of God. (*LC*, pp. 257-58)

The positive views on American energy and ingenuity she had

earlier expressed proved "unmanageable realities" to an enthusiastic vision such as hers. It is worth remembering, however, that a far more complex thinker, Henry Adams, would also be deeply troubled by the dynamo he saw as symbolic of an ominous future.

Flora Lyndsay; or, Passages in an Eventful Life (1854) is also a civilized and amiable book, though unlike *Life in the Clearings* it is written as a novel. Based upon a narrative in *The Literary Garland* entitled "Trifles from the Burthen of a Life" (1851), it was filled out by Moodie to conform to expected narrative length. It should, however, be read as autobiography rather than fiction, allowing, of course, for Moodie's tendency to embellish and to heighten effects. "The book," she told Richard Bentley, "is no fiction," and certainly there is little in *Flora Lyndsay* to dispute her assertion.[72] Our "good friends, the P's," who rhapsodize about the Cape of Good Hope, are the Pringles; the visiting colonist who does much to persuade John Lyndsay to emigrate is Robert Reid of Peterborough (whose daughter Sam Strickland had married); and James Hawke is Moodie's good friend James Bird.[73]

Moreover, as Moodie explained to Bentley, the book was not meant to be a sober and moralistic tale like *Mark Hurdlestone*,

> but a bundle of droll sketches of our adventures out to Canada and preparations for our emigration and all we met and saw on our voyage. This should have been the commencement of *Roughing It*, for it was written for it, and I took a freak of cutting it out of the MS, and beginning the work at Grosse Isle.[74]

Once again, then, elements of fiction, travel narrative, autobiography, and the sketch form are blended as a means of providing dramatic continuity, lifelikeness, and light humour to a set of experiences the Moodies underwent. And again, the combination has a liberating effect upon Moodie's writing — her prose is fresher and less stylized, her fascination with eccentric characters is less circumscribed by moral priorities, and her study of her own reactions and feelings is well drawn and often revealing. The conventions, clichés, and moralistic heavy-handedness that mar *Mark Hurdlestone* and *Geoffrey Moncton* are far less apparent here.

Nevertheless, for all its merits, *Flora Lyndsay* is a thin and static book, lacking the intensity of feeling and complexity of reaction that contact with the bush inspired in Moodie's recollections. The decision to emigrate, the preparations, leave-taking rituals and mischances, a brief visit to Lyndsay's native Scotland, the tedious ocean voyage, and the trip down the Saint Lawrence make up its contents. A good part of the narrative is unfortunately given over to a tedious sentimental novella entitled "Noah Cotton," which Flora claims she wrote to pass the time during the dull ocean voyage (p. 215). Seen simply as narrative, then, *Flora Lyndsay* has many weaknesses, its leisurely additions and digressions impeding what force and impetus Moodie could locate in a story she herself recognized as partial and incomplete. Read, however, as a preface to *Roughing It in the Bush* and as a book that reveals a great deal about Moodie and her writing, *Flora Lyndsay* is an important work.

The slightly veiled Susanna Moodie of *Flora Lyndsay* may, as Marian Fowler notes,[75] burst into tears on many occasions (and thus, as character, owe something to the conventions of the sentimental novel), but she is also a woman of vitality, curiosity, and humour. Her husband, towards whom she is very affectionate and upon whose sound judgement she relies, is presented as distinctly different in temperament: rational, orderly, and practical. "I hate mystery in any shape," he tells her (p. 36). Accordingly, he functions as a foil to Flora's "besetting sin," her "love of the ridiculous" (p. 37), casting a sobering glance upon what intrigues her and warning her about the dangers that attend an indulgence of romantic curiosity.

An interesting case in point is the character study of Miss Wilhelmina Carr, a woman the Lyndsays meet before they leave England. While Miss Carr does cast doubt upon the prospects of emigration and Canada, her important role is to stir Flora's imagination. Fifty years old, wine-drinking, cigar-smoking, wearing men's hats, she is a study of a liberated woman, outspoken in her opinions and proudly independent in her movements. She asks Flora,

> ... is it not a shame that these selfish men should be tamely allowed by us foolish women to monopolise all the good things of life, and make that criminal in a female which they cannot deny themselves? You don't know how much you lose, by being frightened by their blustering into passive obedience. ... (p. 55)

John Lyndsay warns his wife against Miss Carr on several occasions, but Flora persists in her curiosity until the woman vanishes from their town like a riddle or myth (p. 59).

Wilhelmina Carr embodies something more than a stirring of Susanna Moodie's abiding interest in human folly and the ridiculous. As in *Roughing It in the Bush*, most of *Flora Lyndsay*'s character studies contain some comment upon the question of individual freedom and personal identity. In a spirited and grotesque way, Miss Carr stands for the unconventional, wilful side of Moodie herself, the side that in her autobiographical writings constantly contends with her equally strong need for assurances of familial, social, and spiritual order. Flora can no more reform Miss Carr than she can curb her own love of mystery. Yet she can only imagine being the "free agent" (p. 42) Miss Carr is. Flora is capable of rejecting bustles as "a disgusting fashion" (p. 42), but, in the eccentric woman's words, she is too much "a mental coward" (p. 57) to live as she really pleases. Hence, Flora's various attempts to reform Miss Carr, to make her more socially acceptable, fail utterly, for, as Moodie phrases it, she is no more confinable than a hurricane. Indeed, Flora's and Moodie's identification with her is so strong that no moral or social platitude applied to her significantly diminishes the idea of freedom she vividly embodies.

It has often been observed that Susanna Moodie was not an artist and that *Roughing It in the Bush* is not a work of art. To this should be added that the aesthetic (or ornamental) aspects of her writing were usually the most artificial, overwritten, and convention-bound aspects of her work. Only in those pieces in which she brought the tensions of her feelings and thoughts to the centre by blending the flexibility of the sketch with the intensifying devices of the novel did she become a writer meriting serious consideration. In such cases, "mystery" or energy vies strongly with conservative and middle-class tendencies. As with Wilhelmina Carr, whom Moodie added to "Trifles from the Burthen of a Life" to fill out that thin narrative, she was tapping myths that attracted her, even as she felt the need to harness or reform them. There was in Wilhelmina Carr a Cinderella side, albeit threateningly masculinized and resistant to given order, that held her rapt. As a writer, Moodie was at her best when she was self-revealing, not only because of her freshness and frankness but because of what she inadvertently showed about herself in the process. The wilful, romantic side of her temperament was consistently drawn to manifestations of freedom and independence, however crude or grotesque. While she idealized liberty and deplored licence, she was nevertheless attracted to the spectacle of freedom in any form. This element emerges most powerfully in her Canadian sketches.

NOTES

[1] *The Victoria Magazine, 1847-1848*, ed. Susanna Moodie and J. W. D. Moodie, introd. William H. New, facs. ed. (Vancouver: Univ. of British Columbia Press, 1968), p. 113. All further references to this work (*VM*) appear in the text.

[2] Susanna Strickland's work appeared in several of these popular annuals, then in their heyday; for example, *Ackermann's Juvenile Forget Me Not* and *Marshall's Christmas Box*.

[3] *La Belle Assemblée; or, Court and Fashion Magazine* published her work intermittently from 1827 to 1830.

[4] Her work appeared in *Friendship's Offering, The Iris, The Amulet, Emmanuel*, and *The Forget Me Not*, among others.

[5] While no known copy of *Patriotic Songs* has survived, the evidence in letters and reviews indicates it was published.

[6] Carl Ballstadt, "Susanna Moodie: Early Humanitarian Works," *Canadian Notes and Queries*, No. 8 (Nov. 1971), pp. 9-10.

[7] Samuel Strickland, who buffered the arrival of the Traills, also produced a pioneering memoir, *Twenty-Seven Years in Canada West; or, The Experience of an Early Settler* (London: Bentley, 1853).

[8] This skill Susanna passed on to her daughter Agnes, who distinguished herself in illustrating such books as *Canadian Wild Flowers*, the text of which was written by Catharine Parr Traill.

[9] Susanna Moodie, *Roughing It in the Bush; or, Life in Canada*, 2nd ed. (London: Bentley, 1852), II, 290. The second edition most closely realizes the book Susanna Moodie and her husband intended and is thus regarded here as the definitive edition. All further references to this work (*RI*) appear in the text.

[10] Susanna Moodie, "A Word for Novel Writers," *The Literary Garland*, Aug. 1851, p. 351. See also Susanna Moodie, *Life in the Clearings*, ed. Robert McDougall (Toronto: Macmillan, 1959), p. 217. All further references to this work (*LC*) appear in the text.

[11] Susanna Strickland, *Hugh Latimer; or, The School-Boy's Friendship*

(London: Dean and Munday, 1828), p. 102. All further references to this work (*HL*) appear in the text.

[12] According to Catharine Parr Traill, Jugurtha was the subject of one of her sister's early books. No evidence of the book has thus far been discovered. See "A Slight Sketch of the Early Life of Mrs. Moodie," in the Traill Family Papers, Public Archives of Canada, MG 29081, VI, 9878-90.

[13] Susanna Strickland, *Spartacus: A Roman Story* (London: Newman, 1822), p. 47. All further references to this work (*S*) appear in the text.

[14] Letter to Richard Bentley, 8 Dec. 1855, Richard Bentley Collection (R.B.C.), British Library, London. These plays she destroyed on the advice of her Nonconformist friends.

[15] Methodists and Nonconformists were often called Enthusiasts.

[16] Susanna Moodie, *Mark Hurdlestone; or, The Two Brothers* (New York: DeWitt and Davenport, n.d.), pp. 154-55.

[17] Walter Houghton, *The Victorian Frame of Mind, 1830-1870* (New Haven: Yale Univ. Press, 1957), pp. 263-64.

[18] Houghton, pp. 264-65.

[19] *The Friendships of Mary Russell Mitford as Recorded in Letters from Her Literary Correspondents*, ed. the Rev. A. G. L'Estrange (New York: Harper, 1882), I, 196-97, 204-08, 212-13, 222-24.

[20] W. J. Keith, *The Rural Tradition: A Study of the Non-Fiction Prose Writers of the English Countryside* (Toronto: Univ. of Toronto Press, 1974), p. 86.

[21] Keith, p. 89.

[22] Carl Ballstadt, "Susanna Moodie and the English Sketch," *Canadian Literature*, No. 51 (Winter 1972), p. 33.

[23] *La Belle Assemblée*, NS 9 (1829), 21-24.

[24] Letter sent from Reydon Hall to James and Emma Bird of Yoxford, Suffolk, 5 Sept. 1828, Glyde Papers, Suffolk County Register's Office, Ipswich, England.

[25] Letter to Richard Bentley, 8 Dec. 1855, R.B.C. Moodie wrote: ". . . it does you no moral good and you feel ashamed of yourself for being so much amused at the expense of others. I am angry at myself for enjoying Thackery [sic] so much. He is a literary giant but one that makes you afraid."

[26] "Mrs. Moodie's Life in Canada," *The Spectator*, 7 Feb. 1852, pp. 133-34.

[27] *The Athenaeum*, 28 Feb. 1852, pp. 247-48.

[28] *The Athenaeum*, 2 Dec. 1854, p. 1462.

[29] *The Spectator*, 8 Jan. 1853, p. 37; *The Athenaeum*, 15 Jan. 1853, pp. 73-74.

[30] *The Spectator*, 13 May 1854, p. 519; *The Athenaeum*, 6 May 1854, pp. 554-55.

[31] *The Spectator*, 13 Aug. 1853, pp. 783-84; *The Athenaeum*, 27 Aug. 1853, pp. 1012-13.

[32] *The Athenaeum*, 4 Jan. 1868, p. 16.

[33] *The Canadian Monthly and National Review*, 1 (1872), 182.

[34] David Stouck, " 'Secrets of the Prison-House': Mrs. Moodie and the Canadian Imagination," *The Dalhousie Review*, 54 (1974), 463.

[35] *Dalhousie Review*, 39 (1959), 56-69.

[36] Robin Mathews, "Susanna Moodie, Pink Toryism, and Nineteenth Century Ideas of Canadian Identity," *Journal of Canadian Studies*, 10, No. 3 (1975), 4.

[37] Audrey Morris, *Gentle Pioneers: Five Nineteenth-Century Canadians* (Toronto: Hodder and Stoughton, 1968). See also G. H. Needler, *Otonabee Pioneers: The Story of the Stewarts, the Stricklands, the Traills and the Moodies* (Toronto: Burns and MacEachern, 1953), and Edwin C. Guillet, ed., *The Valley of the Trent* (Toronto: Champlain Society, 1957).

[38] Clara Thomas, "The Strickland Sisters," in *The Clear Spirit: Twenty Canadian Women and Their Times*, ed. Mary Quayle Innis (Toronto: Univ. of Toronto Press, 1966), pp. 42-73.

[39] George Parker, "Haliburton and Moodie: The Early Publishing History of *The Clockmaker*, 1st Series, and *Roughing It in the Bush*," in *Colloquium* III, Proc. of a Conference of the Bibliographical Society of Canada, Ottawa, 19-21 Oct. 1978 (Toronto: 1979), p. 144.

[40] William H. Magee, "Local Colour in Canadian Fiction," *University of Toronto Quarterly*, 28 (1959), 176-89.

[41] Clara Thomas, "Journeys to Freedom," *Canadian Literature*, No. 51 (Winter 1972), pp. 11-19. A recent article by Janet Giltrow also explores the travel genre. See " 'Painful Experience in a Distant Land': Mrs. Moodie in Canada and Mrs. Trollope in America," *Mosaic*, 14, No. 2 (1981), 131-44.

[42] Marian Fowler, "*Roughing It in the Bush*: A Sentimental Novel," in *Beginnings*, Vol. II of *The Canadian Novel*, ed. John Moss (Toronto: NC, 1980), pp. 80-96.

[43] Carl F. Klinck, Introd., *Roughing It in the Bush; or, Forest Life in Canada*, by Susanna Moodie, New Canadian Library, No. 31 (Toronto: McClelland and Stewart, 1962), p. xiv.

[44] Margaret Atwood, *The Journals of Susanna Moodie* (Toronto: Oxford Univ. Press, 1970), p. 62.

[45] Stouck, " 'Secrets of the Prison-House': Mrs. Moodie and the Cana-

dian Imagination"; and Sherrill E. Grace, "Moodie and Atwood: Notes on a Literary Reincarnation," in *Beginnings*, ed. John Moss, pp. 73-79.

[46] R. D. MacDonald, "Design and Purpose," *Canadian Literature*, No. 51 (Winter 1972), p. 30.

[47] Carl Ballstadt, "Proficient in the Gentle Craft," *Copperfield*, 5 (1974), 99-109.

[48] G. Noonan, "Susanna and Her Critics: A Strategy of Fiction for *Roughing It in the Bush*," *Studies in Canadian Literature*, 5 (Fall 1980), 280-89.

[49] Clara Thomas, "Crusoe and the Precious Kingdom: Fables of Our Literature," *Journal of Canadian Fiction*, 1, No. 2 (1972), 58-64; T. D. MacLulich, "Crusoe in the Backwoods: A Canadian Fable?" *Mosaic*, 9, No. 2 (1976), 115-26.

[50] William Gairdner, "Traill and Moodie: The Two Realities," *Journal of Canadian Fiction*, 1, No. 2 (1972), 35-42. This essay was reprinted in improved form in a subsequent issue of the same journal: 2, No. 3 (1973), 75-81.

[51] David Jackel, "Mrs. Moodie and Mrs. Traill, and the Fabrication of a Canadian Tradition," *The Compass*, No. 6 (Spring 1979), pp. 10, 20. All further references to this work appear in the text.

[52] Public Archives of Canada, Traill Family Papers, MG29081, VI, 9878-90.

[53] "Jane Redgrave" appeared in two parts in *La Belle Assemblée* in 1829; it was published in much-expanded form in *The Literary Garland* for 1848. The poem "The Maniac" first appeared in *La Belle Assemblée* in 1829. A later version of that poem is included in *Life in the Clearings* and used in the story "The Native Village," which Moodie included in *The Victoria Magazine*.

[54] *La Belle Assemblée*, NS 10 (1829), 55.

[55] *La Belle Assemblée*, NS 10 (1829), 211.

[56] In cutting so many of the "bush" or Katchawanook chapters of *Roughing It in the Bush*, Klinck reduced the amount of material that illustrates Moodie's adaptability to the Canadian backwoods. A more dramatic Moodie is thus achieved at the expense of the rounded portrait she actually offers.

[57] J. W. D. Moodie, Letter to Richard Bentley, 9 Nov. 1834, R.B.C.

[58] This interesting shift from novels to autobiography may have owed something to Moodie's age, her distance from the great adventure and sorrow of her life — emigration, and the fact that she saw before her an inescapable "Canadian" destiny.

[59] "Memorandum of Agreement," 9 Jan. 1852, between John Bruce and Richard Bentley, R.B.C.

[60] Susanna Moodie, Letter to Richard Bentley, 16 April 1852, R.B.C.

[61] In the letter of 16 April 1852 cited above, Susanna Moodie described these late-arrived chapters as "a very useful, and almost necessary addition to the work."

[62] Richard Bentley added Dunbar Moodie's "Canadian Sketches" to the second edition because it involved no internal changes in pagination.

[63] *The Literary Garland*, NS 4 (1847), 462.

[64] "Old Woodruff and His Three Wives," *The Literary Garland*, NS 4 (1847), 13-18.

[65] "Old Woodruff and His Three Wives," pp. 17-18.

[66] "The Walk to Dummer," *The Literary Garland*, NS 4 (1847), 101.

[67] "The Walk to Dummer," p. 105.

[68] Thomas, "The Strickland Sisters," p. 58.

[69] Susanna Moodie, Letter to Richard Bentley, 1853, R.B.C. The letter is dated only 1853.

[70] MacLulich, "Crusoe in the Backwoods: A Canadian Fable?" p. 120.

[71] Richard Bentley, Letter to Susanna Moodie, 29 June 1852, R.B.C.

[72] Letter to Richard Bentley, 3 Sept. 1853, R.B.C. In "Trifles from the Burthen of a Life," the heroine is named Rachel M———, her first name corresponding to that of Rachel Wilde, Moodie's autobiographical character in her earlier story "Rachel Wilde; or, Trifles from the Burthen of a Life." Clearly, the name and the title carried special meaning for her.

[73] Susanna Moodie, *Flora Lyndsay; or, Passages in an Eventful Life* (New York: DeWitt and Davenport, [1854]), pp. 7-8, 90-91. All further references to this work appear in the text.

[74] Letter to Richard Bentley, 1853, R.B.C. The letter is dated only 1853.

[75] Fowler, "*Roughing It in the Bush*: A Sentimental Novel," p. 87.

SELECTED BIBLIOGRAPHY

Primary Sources

Books and Periodical Contributions

Strickland, Susanna. *Spartacus: A Roman Story*. London: Newman, 1822.

[Strickland, Susanna.] *The Little Quaker; or, The Triumph of Virtue.* London: Cole, n.d.

Strickland, Susanna. *The Sailor Brother; or, The History of Thomas Saville*. London: Dean and Munday, n.d.

———. *The Little Prisoner; or, Passion and Patience*. London: Dean and Munday, n.d.

———. *Hugh Latimer; or, The School-Boy's Friendship*. London: Dean and Munday, 1828.

———. *Rowland Massingham; or, I Will Be My Own Master*. London: Dean and Munday, n.d.

———. *Profession and Principle; or, The Vicar's Tales*. London: Dean and Munday, n.d.

Strickland, Agnes, and Susanna Strickland. *Patriotic Songs*. London: Green, 1830.

Strickland, Susanna. *Enthusiasm, and Other Poems*. London: Smith, Elder, 1831.

[Strickland, Susanna.] *The History of Mary Prince, a West Indian Slave.* London: Westley and Davis; Edinburgh: Waugh and Innis, 1831.

———. *Negro Slavery Described by a Negro: Being the Narrative of Ashton Warner, a Native of St. Vincent's*. London: Maunder, 1831.

Moodie, Susanna, and J. W. D. Moodie, eds. *The Victoria Magazine, 1847-1848*. Rpt. Facs. ed. Ed. and introd. W. H. New. Vancouver: Univ. of British Columbia Press, 1968.

Moodie, Susanna. *The Little Black Pony and Other Stories*. Philadelphia: Collins, 1850.

———. *Roughing It in the Bush; or, Life in Canada*. 2nd ed., enl. 2 vols. London: Bentley, 1852.

————. *Life in the Clearings versus the Bush*. London: Bentley, 1853. Rpt. *Life in the Clearings*. Ed. and introd. Robert L. McDougall. Toronto: Macmillan, 1959.

————. *Mark Hurdlestone; or, The Gold Worshipper*. 2 vols. London: Bentley, 1853.

————. *Mark Hurdlestone; or, The Two Brothers*. New York: DeWitt and Davenport, [1853].

————. *Flora Lyndsay; or, Passages in an Eventful Life*. New York: DeWitt and Davenport, [1854].

————. *Matrimonial Speculations*. London: Bentley, 1854.

————. *Geoffrey Moncton; or, The Faithless Guardian*. New York: DeWitt and Davenport, 1855.

————. *The World before Them*. 3 vols. London: Bentley, 1868.

————. *George Leatrim; or, The Mother's Test*. London: Hamilton, 1875.

Letters

Moodie, Susanna, and J. W. D. Moodie. Letters to Richard Bentley. Richard Bentley Collection. British Library, London.

Secondary Sources

Atwood, Margaret. *The Journals of Susanna Moodie*. Toronto: Oxford Univ. Press, 1970.

————. *Survival: A Thematic Guide to Canadian Literature*. Toronto: House of Anansi, 1972.

Ballstadt, Carl. "The Literary History of the Strickland Family." Diss. London 1965.

————. "Susanna Moodie: Early Humanitarian Works." *Canadian Notes and Queries*, Nov. 1971, pp. 9-10.

————. "Susanna Moodie and the English Sketch." *Canadian Literature*, No. 51 (Winter 1972), pp. 32-38.

————. "Proficient in the Gentle Craft." *Copperfield*, 5 (1974), 99-109.

Brown, Mary M. *An Index to* The Literary Garland. Toronto: Bibliographical Society of Canada, 1962.

————. "*The Literary Garland* and a Case of Literary Larceny." *Journal of Canadian Fiction*, 2, No. 3 (1973), 65-68.

Davies, Robertson. *At My Heart's Core*. Toronto: Clarke, Irwin, 1950.

Eaton, Sara. *Lady of the Backwoods: A Biography of Catharine Parr*

Traill. Toronto: McClelland and Stewart, 1969.

Edwards, Mary Jane. "Susanna Moodie." In *The Evolution of Canadian Literature in English: Beginnings to 1867.* Ed. Mary Jane Edwards. Toronto: Holt, Rinehart and Winston, 1973, pp. 163-66.

Fowler, Marian. "*Roughing It in the Bush*: A Sentimental Novel." In *Beginnings.* Vol. II of *The Canadian Novel.* Ed. John Moss. Toronto: NC, 1980, pp. 80-96.

Gairdner, William. "Traill and Moodie: The Two Realities." *Journal of Canadian Fiction*, 2, No. 3 (1973), 75-81.

Giltrow, Janet. "'Painful Experience in a Distant Land': Mrs. Moodie in Canada and Mrs. Trollope in America." *Mosaic*, 14, No. 2 (Spring 1981), 131-44.

Grace, Sherrill E. "Moodie and Atwood: Notes on a Literary Reincarnation." In *Beginnings.* Vol. II of *The Canadian Novel.* Ed. John Moss. Toronto: NC, 1980, pp. 73-79.

Guillet, Edwin C. *The Valley of the Trent.* Toronto: Champlain Society, 1957.

―――. *Early Life in Upper Canada.* Toronto: Univ. of Toronto Press, 1963.

Houghton, Walter. *The Victorian Frame of Mind, 1830-1870.* New Haven: Yale Univ. Press, 1957.

Hume, Blanche. *The Strickland Sisters.* Toronto: Ryerson, 1929.

Jackel, David. "Mrs. Moodie and Mrs. Traill, and the Fabrication of a Canadian Tradition." *The Compass*, No. 6 (Spring 1979), pp. 1-22.

Keith, W. J. *The Rural Tradition: A Study of the Non-Fiction Prose Writers of the English Countryside.* Toronto: Univ. of Toronto Press, 1974.

Kirkland, Caroline. *A New Home — Who'll Follow?* Boston, 1840; rpt. New Haven: Yale Univ. Press, 1965.

Klinck, Carl F. "A Gentlewoman of Upper Canada." *Canadian Literature*, No. 1 (Summer 1959), pp. 75-77.

―――, introd. *Roughing It in the Bush; or, Forest Life in Canada.* By Susanna Moodie. New Canadian Library, No. 31. Toronto: McClelland and Stewart, 1962.

―――, gen. ed. and introd. *Literary History of Canada: Canadian Literature in English.* 2nd ed. Toronto: Univ. of Toronto Press, 1976.

MacDonald, R. D. "Design and Purpose." *Canadian Literature*, No. 51 (Winter 1972), pp. 20-31.

MacLulich, T. D. "Crusoe in the Backwoods: A Canadian Fable?" *Mosaic*, 9, No. 2 (1976), 115-26.

Magee, William H. "Local Colour in Canadian Fiction." *University of Toronto Quarterly*, 28 (1959), 176-89.

Mathews, Robin. "Susanna Moodie, Pink Toryism, and Nineteenth Century Ideas of Canadian Identity." *Journal of Canadian Studies*, 10, No. 3 (1975), 3-15.

McCourt, Edward A. "Roughing It with the Moodies." In *Masks of Fiction: Canadian Critics on Canadian Prose*. Ed. A. J. M. Smith. New Canadian Library Original, No. O2. Toronto: McClelland and Stewart, 1961, pp. 81-92.

Mitford, Mary Russell. *Our Village: Sketches of Rural Character and Scenery*. London: George B. Whittaker, [1824-32].

———. *The Friendships of Mary Russell Mitford as Recorded in Letters from Her Literary Correspondents*. Ed. A. G. L'Estrange. 2 vols. New York: Harper, 1882.

Moodie, J. W. Dunbar. *Scenes and Adventures as a Soldier and Settler during Half a Century*. Montreal: Lovell, 1866.

Morris, Audrey. *Gentle Pioneers: Five Nineteenth-Century Canadians*. Toronto: Hodder and Stoughton, 1968.

Moss, John. *Patterns of Isolation in English Canadian Fiction*. Toronto: McClelland and Stewart, 1974.

Needler, G. H. *Otonabee Pioneers: The Story of the Stewarts, the Stricklands, the Traills and the Moodies*. Toronto: Burns and MacEachern, 1953.

Noonan, G. "Susanna and Her Critics: A Strategy of Fiction for *Roughing It in the Bush*." *Studies in Canadian Literature*, 5 (Fall 1980), 280-89.

Parker, George. "Haliburton and Moodie: The Early Publishing History of *The Clockmaker*, 1st Series, and *Roughing It in the Bush*." In *Colloquium* III. Proc. of a Conference of the Bibliographical Society of Canada. Ottawa, 19-21 Oct. 1978. Toronto: 1979, pp. 139-60.

Scott, Lloyd M. "The English Gentlefolk in the Backwoods of Canada." *Dalhousie Review*, 39 (1959), 56-69.

Shields, Carol. *Small Ceremonies*. Toronto: McGraw-Hill Ryerson, 1976.

———. *Susanna Moodie: Voice and Vision*. Ottawa: Borealis, 1977.

Stouck, David. " 'Secrets of the Prison-House': Mrs. Moodie and the Canadian Imagination." *The Dalhousie Review*, 54 (1974), 463-72.

Strickland, Jane. *Life of Agnes Strickland*. Edinburgh: Blackwood, 1887.

Strickland, Samuel. *Twenty-Seven Years in Canada West; or, The Experience of an Early Settler*. London: Bentley, 1853.

Sutherland, Ronald. "The Body-Odour of Race." *Canadian Literature*, No. 37 (Summer 1968), pp. 46-67.

Thomas, Clara. "The Strickland Sisters." In *The Clear Spirit: Twenty Canadian Women and Their Times*. Ed. Mary Quayle Innis. Toronto: Univ. of Toronto Press, 1966, pp. 42-73.

——. "Happily Ever After: Some Canadian Women in Fiction and Fact." *Canadian Literature*, No. 34 (Fall 1967), pp. 43-53.

——. "Journeys to Freedom." *Canadian Literature*, No. 51 (Winter 1972), pp. 11-19.

——. *Our Nature — Our Voices: A Guidebook to English-Canadian Literature*. Toronto: new, 1972.

——. "Crusoe and the Precious Kingdom: Fables of Our Literature." *Journal of Canadian Fiction*, 1, No. 2 (1972), 58-64.

Traill, Catharine Parr. *The Backwoods of Canada*. London: Charles Knight, 1836.

——. "A Slight Sketch of the Early Life of Mrs. Moodie." Vol. 6. Traill Family Papers. Public Archives of Canada.

John Richardson (1796-1852)

DENNIS DUFFY

Biography

BORN IN QUEENSTON, Upper Canada, in 1796, John Richardson died in 1852 in New York City, alone and poor.[1] Of United Empire Loyalist and Ottawa Indian ancestry, Richardson fled from Canada to the United States, reversing the typical Loyalist pattern. His was an unusual literary career, and this biographical section will try to display the unusual personality behind that career.

Educated in Detroit and Amherstburg, the son of a medical officer in the British army, Richardson fought beside Tecumseh in the War of 1812 as a gentleman volunteer. The ignominious disaster of Moraviantown in 1813 saw Tecumseh slain and Richardson taken eventually to a prisoner-of-war camp in Frankfort, Kentucky. The end of hostilities saw him released, given a commission in the British army, and stationed for a time in the West Indies. Placed on half pay in 1815, Richardson spent the next twenty years living the existence in London and Paris that produced his novel *Ecarté; or, The Salons of Paris* (1829). Gaming, sexual intrigue, and the efforts of the decently born hustler to live on nothing-a-year form the stuff of the novel, which Richardson notes came at least partly out of his personal experience.

His first published work had been *Tecumseh; or, The Warrior of the West* in 1828. This was a lurid, turgid epic in Byronic *ottava rima*, a verse form that the greater poet had employed for supremely comic purposes. Certainly Richardson's attempt to use it for tragic effect resulted in little beyond bathos. Yet the poem's pseudo-Miltonic horrifics, its dire prophecies, and bizarre combats presage the melodrama of *Wacousta*, Richardson's best-known work.

The unfinished *Kensington Gardens in 1830: A Satirical Trifle* was succeeded by *Wacousta; or, The Prophecy: A Tale of the Canadas* in 1832. With this remarkable work, Richardson made his mark on the English-Canadian imagination. It proved of sufficient popularity to be hacked into a touring-company melodrama soon after the author's death. It impressed itself sufficiently upon the consciousness of one of Canada's better twentieth-century poets to produce James Reaney's stage version of 1978.[2] For all its faults, *Wacousta* remains of interest still and seems virtually the sole reason for the survival of its author's name.

The Spanish civil war of 1936-39 was not the first occasion when British idealists and adventurers intervened in a Spanish internal conflict. While the twentieth-century British involvement consisted principally of figures on the left, the earlier one in which Richardson fought during 1834-37, the Carlist war, saw them on the Royalist side. The first literary evidence of the irascibility and quarrelsomeness that were to shadow Richardson's remaining years appears in a succession of Carlist war memoirs and polemics: *Journal of the Movements of the British Legion, with Strictures on the Course of Conduct Pursued by Lieutenant-General Evans* (1836); and in 1837 and 1838, two further contentious self-vindications.

In 1838, *The Times* [London] dispatched Richardson to cover the 1837 rebellions in Upper and Lower Canada, a post from which he was dismissed when his support of Lord Durham contradicted editorial policy. Richardson remained in Upper Canada, founding a newspaper in Brockville, *The New Era*. The year 1842 saw the failure of that journal, though in the meantime he had written a sequel to *Wacousta* entitled *The Canadian Brothers; or, The Prophecy Fulfilled* (1840). This latter incorporated his prisoner-of-war experience in Kentucky. During his time as an editor, Richardson also made a pet of a deer he had found. No finer index to this irascible man's complexity of character exists.

War of 1812 appeared in 1842. This was the first of a projected series of volumes which the Legislative Assembly of Upper Canada had paid him to produce. Upon completion of that volume, Richardson decided that the grant had supported the opening of the project, but nothing more would be forthcoming unless the muse grew inspired by more cash. Inspiration ceased.

So did a second newspaper, *The Canadian Loyalist and Spirit of 1812*, which ran during 1843-44. In 1845, Richardson landed a pork-barrel appointment as superintendent of the Welland Canal police, a job he lost when the post was abolished in 1846 and after he had attempted to turn a group of local patrolmen into something like a crack hussar regiment. His wife of thirteen years had died in 1845.[3] Now the years darken.

Eight Years in Canada (1847) proves to the author's satisfaction that the claims to high public office to which his merits entitled him were disregarded through a dismal succession of stupidity and ill will on the part of his rulers. *The Guards in Canada; or, The Point of Honour* (1848) defends its author against rumours of card-sharping and personal cowardice in a manner certain to extend to those charges the widest publicity. In 1850 he set out to seek his fortune in the literary underworld of New York.[4]

The strictures against his erstwhile American enemies, who now formed his audience, were carefully excised from his novel of the War of 1812, *The Canadian Brothers*, reissued in a new edition entitled *Matilda Montgomerie* (1851). A number of brief, shoddy productions followed: *Hardscrabble; or, The Fall of Chicago* (1851), *Westbrook, the Outlaw; or, The Avenging Wolf* (1851), *Wau-Nan-Gee; or, The Massacre at Chicago* (1852). Only *The Monk Knight of St. John: A Tale of the Crusades* (1850) stands out from this period, and that on account of its wildly pornographic nature.

When in 1852 he died — of poverty more than any other cause — he was working on what we would now call an exploitive spin-off, a "quickie" account of the life of the internationally famous sex object Lola Montez, former mistress to the King of Bavaria. John Richardson had come a long way from the youth who had shared the same battlefield with the noble Tecumseh.

Tradition and Milieu

No critic should write of John Richardson as if he were John Keats. To deliver exhaustive accounts of literary and aesthetic influences would serve to distort a proper view of a writer whose production betrays little evidence of forethought, reflection, or meditation on the poetical character. Yet Keats's longing for a life of sensation rather than of thoughts could serve as an acute assessment of the Richardsonian canon.

To say that Richardson wrote sensationalist novels is scarcely to assert that he wrote sensational fiction. Yet his output stems from two dominant, popular strains in the fiction of his day: the novel of sentiment, and the Gothic novel. As a sentimental novelist, Richardson structures his stories around the attempts of young lovers to remain united in the face of the obstacles presented by parents, the great world, and the sheer perversity of circumstances. Coincidence, mistaken identity, the ease with which young love yields to misunderstandings — these provide the means by which the story is told. The uniting of the young lovers proclaims a victory for sentiment, for the power of loving states of feeling, when tenaciously held, to change the world of hard fact and materialistic motivation.

Take this mode of viewing experience, darken and Satanize it, and Gothic fiction results. Now the spiritual aspects of existence assume the same priority they had in sentimental fiction, but they are powerful, negative forces seemingly beyond human control. It is more than a matter of tempestuous villains, mouldering castles, and mysterious visitations of the dead. These are the paraphernalia to a progress of perverse forces which again and again smother human visions of hope and release. In the world of Gothic fiction, the past is a grim amalgam of deceptions and betrayals, a dank breeding ground of schemes for revenge and retribution. It threatens at every moment to overwhelm the young lovers and to frustrate their unstated conviction that perfect love casteth out fear.

At this point, literary critics begin a series of name droppings as a guide to the neophyte and as a way of bestowing immortality on works few sensible people would ever willingly read. It seems more useful, however, to concentrate instead upon a single, well-known work which represents the fiction of its time and shares certain characteristics with *Wacousta*.

In 1837, five years after *Wacousta*, Charles Dickens began serial publication of *Oliver Twist*. It too combines the sentimental with the Gothic in a way revealing the sort of literary climate in which Richardson's novel appeared. The naïve, innocent Oliver, who manages to pass years in public institutions without ever becoming "street smart," moves numbly through a world badly needing to recognize the value of innocence. The saccharine lovers, Rose and Harry Maylie, and the benign Mr. Brownlow, however distressing to the modern reader, embody also that principle of loving serenity so lacking in the world of public institutions. And sure enough, the plot will wrench round events sufficiently to bring Oliver to a real home and the lovers to their own new one.

The plot must wrench the events because the novel is Gothic as well as sentimental. The most frightening embodiment of the dark forces present is not Bumble, not even Fagin, but the demented Monks. His is the face that appears out of nowhere, adding a dimension of radical evil to the perfectly explicable criminality of Fagin's gang and the institutional callousness of Bumble. Briefly then, here is a struggle with a past fierce enough to devour the present, and this is also the world of *Wacousta*. Against the cold, calculating rationality of de Haldimar ranges the fury of Wacousta's lust to avenge past misdeeds; and against the love of Frederick and Madeline stand the savageries of white and red alike that destroy the rest of the de Haldimars. And all this happens not in the rotting rat warren that is Dickens' London but in the vast loneliness of the North American frontier.

The very mention of the frontier brings up a source of the Richardsonian imagination that literary critics too easily ignore: the war that shaped his youth. We ignore at our peril the actual, as opposed to the imaginative, experiences any writer undergoes. When one of those experiences is a war fought at the impressionable age of sixteen, we must acknowledge those aspects of the conflict that reverberate throughout an author's work.

As Richardson experienced it, the War of 1812 was a frontier war. No affair of pitched battles, it was a war of raids and counter-raids disguised as campaigns, in which whites and their Indian allies sought to defend themselves through vigorous offensives and by harassments of a numerically superior enemy. Under the dashing leadership of General Brock and the great Tecumseh of the Shawnee, the small force of British regulars, Indians, and local volunteers had bluffed General Hull's American forces at Detroit into surrendering. Brock had thrown his motley force into the offensive, raised to Hull the spectre of Indian massacre should his allies grow frustrated during a lengthy siege and campaign, and brought off a coup that a more hardbitten enemy commander could have easily countered. That swift decisiveness of Brock and Tecumseh was then frittered away after Brock's departure for the Niagara front and his heroic death which followed. Tecumseh's forces, those masters of a war of ambush and disruption, were wasted in fruitless sieges, while passive British commanders attempted to wage static warfare. Finally, the command of the Great Lakes was lost to an American fleet that a bold commander would have raided and burned while it lay a-building at Sackett's Harbour. The threat of American amphibious operations compelled retreat from the western peninsula. The British commander scuttled back to the escarpment near Hamilton, leaving Tecumseh to hold together a demoralized force that was finally brought to bay by the hard-riding Kentucky mounted riflemen near Moraviantown. There Tecumseh died and Richardson was taken prisoner in a battle that was over before it began. The remainder of the war in the west was one of burnings, raids, and uneasy lulls in combat.

Richardson fought in a war in which the combatants were dwarfed by the immense, forested spaces that surrounded them. The capture of Detroit had shown the role that deception and threat could play in human affairs; while the casting away of the victory revealed that the loss of mettle, the abandonment of a reso-lute, dynamic stance, had its consequences too. What began as a painterly composition with scenes of "romantic grandeur" and as "a wild and romantic picture, in which melancholy grandeur shone principally conspicuous,"[5] ended in defeat and imprisonment.

Human affairs in *Wacousta* are ever at the mercy of chance and deception. Personal identity proves a slippery concept as poseurs and look-alikes abound within a very constricted space. Whether garbed in a scarlet officer's tunic or war paint, ruthless personalities discover at the frontier ample scope for their most savage obses-sions.

In Richardson, we find a sensibility nourished by a culture of sensationalism, a popular climate delighting in the depiction of great surges of love and terror. Here the rules of probability, and even common sense about the nature of experience, can be suspended, so that the epic hero, Wacousta, is not only nearly omnipotent in his hate but also more than willing to die for love. We know that the Romantics took Milton's Satan to be the hero of *Paradise Lost*, finding him wicked but grand, gigantic in his ruth-lessness but dauntlessly courageous. Richardson and the literary climate he worked in, so influenced by the dark heroes of Lord Byron, took this figure and made no bones about his evil. He was left clearly at the centre of the action, and his evil attributed to the force of thwarted love. The firm divisions among aspects of the human personality that conventional morality rests upon are dissolved. What is it to be fully human? The answer put by sensationalist fiction seems to be, that to be fully human is to experience even the darkest of feelings to their fullest. To be heroic is to be all things, demon and lover alike. *Wuthering Heights* (1847) was to take this sentiment and give it literary immortality in the character of Heathcliff. After Emily Brontë's novel, the demon lover that Coleridge glimpsed so oracularly in "Kubla Khan" would become a commonplace. No one would ever confuse the technical qualities of *Wacousta* with those displayed in *Wuthering Heights*, but the fact remains that in his heroic villain Richardson gave his audience a memorable exemplar of the figure grown Satanic through the denial of love. This alone would make of Richardson a writer of considerable interest to students of his time.

Yet I must repeat my hypothesis that a set of political circumstances in the Upper Canada of his day helped reinforce this moral. Richardson "works" as a Canadian writer not only because of his birthplace and choice of subjects, not only because he embodies themes some critics find peculiarly Canadian, but also because the experience of his formative years bears out the moral confusion of the world of his novels. All these features of his imaginative life that asserted the fragmentary, confused, and contradictory nature of human experience were present in his actual life, as well. That life remains part of both our imaginative and our political history. And in that sense, Richardson's milieu is in some way ours, as well.

Critical Overview and Context

To thumb through old periodical reviews of Richardson's work in the hope of thereby gauging critical opinion is to ignore a far surer method of determining the response to his best work during his era. His first novel, *Ecarté*, was blasted by a prominent critic for its true-to-life portrait of a Parisian existence untouched by British middle-class moral standards; it then sunk without trace.[6] Yet *Wacousta* went through six editions during its first eight years of existence, and it was reprinted five further times up to 1967 when the abridged paperback edition appeared.[7] No other piece of Canadian fiction of that era, or of any other (with the exception of *Anne of Green Gables*), has captured that kind of sustained attention over the years. The "whys" of that attention will be discussed later, but for the present the very fact of these reprintings testifies to an importance in our imaginative life that no succession of rave reviews could ever grant.

Richardson proved a man of one book; his other fiction appeared in small and obscure editions. His novel *Westbrook* was not really located until 1972 in a fugitive periodical, though its existence had been rumoured for years.[8] Interest in Richardson and Canadiana provided for the reprinting of such works as his history of 1812 (still currently available in a photocopied reprint) and of his *Wacousta* sequel, *The Canadian Brothers*, as well as the uncovering of a small piece of travel literature.[9] But all this remains no more than attention bestowed by an academicized literary culture upon the author of *Wacousta*.

Two more facts about the survival of that book need to be interpreted. The first is that 1906 saw a New York and Chicago publication of a deluxe edition, with illustrations and chapter headings by C. W. Jefferys. It was later reprinted. Here was a prestige popular edition, with Canada's foremost popular and historical illustrator decking the novel out in costlier ways than ever. Jefferys was no N. C. Wyeth, and the chapter headings succeed far better than the overly dramatized illustrations, but the edition itself bespeaks a publisher's confidence in the quality of the product and its sure appearance under Christmas trees and at prize-day awards. Of course, *Wacousta* is no more a "boys' book" than *Alice in Wonderland* is children's literature, but its action-packed story line obviously enabled it to reach that market.

A second fact central to ascertaining the extent of the novel's appeal is one already mentioned: its appearance as drama, both as the "mellerdrammer" of the 1850s and the more highbrow, but still melodramatic, play that James Reaney made of it in 1978. More will appear below on the last, but both indicate the power and simplicity of the novel's bare bones. The nineteenth-century production beefs up the roles of both a stage Irishman and a stage black and cuts back on the number of corpses littering the stage at the conclusion. The contemporary one cannot make up its mind as to whether it is portraying curiosa or camp. The very fact of these plays' existence, however, speaks volumes as to the power of Richardson's lone volume.

Scholarly interest in Richardson and his place in our literature can be caught in its beginnings by glancing at two works, Ray P.

Baker's *A History of English-Canadian Literature to the Confederation* (1920) and W. R. Riddell's 1923 monograph on him in the Makers of Canada series. Baker's historical survey of Canadian literature, a useful volume for its time, deals cogently with Richardson as a Romantic in a decidedly un-Romantic society. Thus he notes the author's rigid divisions of womanhood into either the insipidly virtuous or the "ardent and voluptuous." With a similar sense of the sharp dichotomizations and the categorizing of existence either as banal or enthralling, Baker notes the contrast between the Amherstburg of Richardson's youth and that of his glimpse of it during his maturity:

> The brightness of a garrison town with the scarlet coats of the soldiers, the toques of the half-breeds, and the feathers of the Indians, had been succeeded by the drab uniformity of a small provincial village.[10]

Baker caught so well Richardson's tendency to put forward black/white distinctions and to etch himself as a man born out of his time,[11] the tools of a popular romancer. He ignored, however, what was to be the hallmark of the criticism of Richardson in our own time: the concern with the way in which the Richardsonian imagination dissolved so many of those ready distinctions found in his plotting and characterization and the consequent descent into a dreamlike world of polymorphous identity.

Riddell's volume is a standard biography in the heroic mould, as befits a treatment of a "Maker of Canada." The rackety facts of Richardson's life are not ignored, but they are cast within a solemn framework that precludes any very close engagement with the depths and quirks of the subject's personality. Nonetheless, it is a substantial volume and improves upon the earlier account of Richardson's life found in A. C. Casselman's opening pages of the *War of 1812* reprint.

The most recent biography of Richardson, Beasley's *The Canadian Don Quixote*, ought to be definitive. Certainly it is thorough in its use of sources and reveals as many of the facts of his life as we shall likely ever know. It suffers from its ardent partisanship and from its exaggerated claims as to the value of even the author's worst work; but it displays the biographer's *sine qua non* — a love of his subject and a frankness about that subject's blemishes.

To glance at two contemporary critics of Richardson bears out what this essay noted previously: that the last decade has witnessed a rediscovery of the mythic power of *Wacousta* and an interest in coming to grips with the darkness and turmoil of that novel. Thus Margot Northey's account of the novel in *The Haunted Wilderness* and John Moss's in his *Patterns of Isolation in English Canadian Fiction* and *Sex and Violence in the Canadian Novel* display what appears to interest present-day critics most in *Wacousta*.

Margaret Atwood's *Survival* gave *Wacousta* a parenthetical mention as another instance of a "garrison" novel, a theme which preoccupies that influential handbook.[12] It is paradoxically fair to say that Northey's work fleshes out that comment, but in a psychological fashion. That is, her treatment deals with patterns of narrative and imagery rather than with the fluctuations of plot. Her book's larger concern — Gothicism in Canadian fiction — ensures that its treatment of *Wacousta* will emphasize whatever is there of rage, madness, and psycho-sexual disturbance.

Very briefly, the same is true of Moss's two books also. Details of these interpretations will surface in my own criticism of the novels, but the larger question that concerns this study remains. Which Richardson are we reading now? What kind of response to his work has the present critical climate engendered, and how has it reshaped the work we thought we were reading?

A split exists at present within the Canadian critical public, between psychologists and collectivists. The issue is which interpretation of the force and drift of the English-Canadian literary imagination will prevail. On the one hand, our literature gives us a plethora of instances of alienated, deranged, culturally wounded individuals, who must seek their salvation through encounters with deep, chthonic forces rather than through the immersion in communal and/or political processes. The most talked-about fiction of the 1970s — Davies' "Deptford trilogy," Atwood's *Surfacing*, Engel's *Bear* — obviously falls into this category. Hand in hand with this goes a psychologizing of our literary criticism and a broad interest in those aspects of literary experience stressing derangement and alienation.

Without getting lost in academic infighting, I would say that a "formalist" opposition to the entire psychologistic approach to Canadian literature, in general, and to *Wacousta*, in particular, lies behind the insights of Sandra Djwa and L. R. Early on the debt the novel owes to Elizabethan revenge tragedy. That same concern with literary form as a determiner of a novel's psychology powers Robert Lecker's stimulating revaluation of the meaning of the novel's many instances of deception.[13] Another angle of approach to the novel appears in Robin Mathews' combative article on its communal themes.[14] The significance of all these differing approaches lies in the fact that *Wacousta* has become a battleground for the question of whether the sweep of Canadian literature lies towards the renewal of community or the avoidance of it. Whichever direction criticism takes, the fact remains that *Wacousta* has been placed very firmly as a work which both sides have to consider. For a novel so long seen as a compelling potboiler and no more, this represents no small advance in reputation. Whatever its faults, it is we who must come to terms with them.

Nowhere can this be discerned more fully than in James Reaney's unsuccessful dramatization of the book. One of this country's finest dramatists (for who can deny that title to the creator of *The Donnellys?*) found a responsive enough chord struck in him by *Wacousta* to attempt to stage it. Had the play let the symbolic overtones of the plot bespeak themselves, it would have succeeded. It was the author's overt symbolic interventions (such as the anachronistic and dissonant use of toy cars to indicate the future awaiting Fort Detroit) which left the audience puzzled as to how it was to view the play. Yet here was Reaney taking as a given the story's appeal and relevance to a contemporary audience.

The century and a half of critical and public attention paid to *Wacousta* has not only confirmed the enduring qualities of the work, but it has made of Richardson's imagination a powerful force to be dealt with when outlining the shape of our literary experience. The contours of that imagination must now be sketched.

Richardson's Works

Because the work of Richardson remains so uneven and because only a single novel of his has endured, no scheme of criticism which treats equally his various works seems a proper one. My method, therefore, will be to describe first what I conceive to be the Richardsonian imagination, that is, the general view of experience that arises from his work as a whole. Based largely on *Wacousta*, this view will also encompass other works where they seem relevant. Secondly, the structure and style of *Wacousta* itself will be considered. Finally, brief notices of the remaining novels will at least acquaint the reader with individual titles and their place in the entire canon.

A. *Richardson's Stance*

In the dark, haunted world of John Richardson, someone is always watching. However bizarre or unsettling the spectacle, it must be witnessed. No satisfactory way exists for resolving the tension between social restraint (the garrison) and instinctual freedom (the wilderness), no mechanism works that will restore order to a political and sexual morass. Only a grim determination to endure grants any peace to the yearning psyche.

Richardson's canon mirrors forth, in a nightmarish fashion, concerns that are treated in a modulated, "waking" manner in other writers. The social order within the novels may stress civility, decorum, and deference, but a lawless and uncontrollable universe, and the terror it produces, overturn these social restraints. Man perceives that lawlessness; it forces him to erect frail barriers against it, until those defences themselves turn savage. However stoutly and rigidly defended the garrison, however intact the Eden, some force from within will always turn it inside out. If sexual and social identities lapse, so also do the political and moral distinctions between various forms of behaviour. Thus the Richardsonian world remains ultimately amorphous, a cascade of experience in which the chief meaning lies in this: the resolute observance of chaos by a party seeking to overcome it or, at least, to view it without flinching.

A very simplified version of the novel's *story* (the plot takes these events and reveals them at the most dramatic moments and through flashbacks and confessions) would begin with the rivalry between two British army subalterns for a sheltered Highland girl, Clara Beverley. The officers are stationed in the Highlands after Culloden, and Clara has been raised on an isolated estate by her fugitive Jacobite father. (Through an empathy with animals that the creator later paralleled, Clara has a pet stag.) De Haldimar not only wins Clara by a trick but frames Reginald Morton on a charge that secures his rival's court-martial and dismissal. Morton joins the French army, nearly killing de Haldimar's soldier sons on the Plains of Abraham. By the time of Pontiac's uprising in 1763, Morton has become the renegade Wacousta, bloodthirstiest of Pontiac's advisers. All this is background to the novel's actual events, set in Fort Detroit during that time of native resistance. Before the novel concludes, de Haldimar has had Morton/Wacousta's nephew (also named Reginald Morton, but appearing in disguise as Frank Halloway) judicially murdered in a court-martial, while Wacousta's scheme of revenge results in the death of de Haldimar, his younger son Charles, and daughter Clara. As Richardson solemnly puts it: "... ours is a tale of sad reality. ... Within the bounds of probability have we, therefore, confined ourselves."[15]

However elastic the author's definition of probability, we have in the work of Richardson what John Moss has termed a "resounding enthusiasm" for exploiting "a seemingly universal inclination for depravity, perversity, and bad taste."[16] Moss notes also the polymorphous/perverse aspects of sexuality in the novel: the beautiful men admiring each other rather than women, the women who in their turn display a greater interest in their own sex than in the other, the females who pair with brutal dominators, and finally the strong sexual feelings surrounding brother/sister relationships. Moss's *Sex and Violence in the Canadian Novel* enters into greater detail on this subject, discovering that in *Wacousta* there is more to sex than sex itself. The "sexual conundrum," the triangle that we often encounter, defines an "ideal condition of unity or completion, while showing it to be practically impossible or possible only on an arcane or esoteric level."[17] No need to duplicate his analysis; what other meanings emerge from sexuality in *Wacousta*?

If an erotic interest in members of one's own sex or family holds some connection with a habit of narcissism, then this mirror-gazing aspect of our sexuality pervades the novel. How clotted the story is with relatives, look-alikes, and namesakes! First, observe the de Haldimars, the sole survivor of whom marries a cousin. The de Haldimar girl attracts Wacousta's attentions not only for vengeance' sake. Her close resemblance to the mother whose name she bears interests him most of all. Second, recall Wacousta, who takes as his concubine the wife of his dead nephew. Both share the same name of Reginald Morton. Finally, when the young Clara's lover (who for some unaccountable reason is not a close relative) mourns her loss, he is struck by her resemblance to her brother, whom he also deeply admired.

Coupled with this theme of mirror gazing is that of disguise or pseudonymity. Masking, considered from the standards of realist fiction, reaches operatic extremes. For "opera," one should perhaps read "minstrel show," as when Wacousta appears before the British garrison in blackface, decked in a coffee-boy's turban. This favourite device of Richardson is repeated in *The Canadian Brothers*, where the villain, Desborough (Wacousta's son; they share superhuman strengths and *heldentenor* voices), appears in blackface. Westbrook, villain in the novel of that title, wears a mask during an attempted rape. The two Reginald Mortons appear disguised and pseudonymously, and the Morton/Wacousta is also known as the "Fleur-de-Lis" warrior. Cooper's Natty Bumppo bore a string of names (Deerslayer, Hawkeye, Leather-stocking), but nicknames, not devices for concealment. Wacousta's nephew Reginald Morton travels under the alias of Frank Halloway, since he is a gentleman-ranker seeking to evade his past. The officers of the garrison at Fort Detroit disguise themselves when in enemy country, a practice so commonplace that Colonel de Haldimar can spurn rather self-righteously Pontiac's denunciations of British espionage. In this book, two officers dashing about enemy country in disguise simply is not spying. The novel's "fifth business," an Indian woman whose love for the hero is exploited by the whites, appears as a warrior as often as she wears normal dress, while the carnival aspect of things gets truly enlivened by a young chieftain's masquerade as a beaver.

Here is a pervasive atmosphere of shaky and mistaken identities. Individuals either flow into each other or transform themselves with frightening ease into self-effigies, in the manner of the myths and legends told by both red and white peoples. Think of the procession of animist religions with their totems and metamorphoses, and then of a span of Western literature running from Ovid to Kafka. The slipperiness of individual identity has become a modernist cliché, and one cannot shunt *Wacousta* along a premodernist track. Still, among all the signs of civilization's vulnerability in the wilderness, none remains more striking than the ease with which social and sexual identities reduce themselves to masks and postures. Richardson remains a conservative humanist, rather than a modernist, since his culturally degenerative disease attains epidemic, but never universal, range. Colonel de Haldimar's civilized barbarity does him in; Wacousta's plain barbarity does the same for him. Two young, scarred lives remain, though in his sequel to *Wacousta*, *The Canadian Brothers*, Richardson can only send them off to the West Indies in a few paragraphs and let a hurricane dispose of them there. The modernist idea of moral relativism does not exist here. Though the Indians massacre their enemies in lurid enough style to have devilish epithets bestowed on them, the Redcoats are not seen to carry out similar atrocities. They kill in a "legal" fashion, and the author conveys no irony about this. Even in later novels, which deal with killers, rapists, and cannibals on the order of Desborough and Westbrook, these characters remain horrifying examples of self-willed degeneration (as when Westbrook imitates Milton's Satan in peeking at the lovemaking of a young couple), ghoulish monsters who, however powerful, exert no appeal over the younger heroes. Westbrook is killed by a wolf who has taken to nursing his grandson, so removed is he from humanity and nature alike.

The wolf-men, Desborough and Westbrook, remind us that the wilderness in which they exist bears a complementary, rather than an originative, relationship to their wickedness. They do not suddenly "go native" when exposed to the bush; they flee there because they have already become savage. Wacousta strives for a Byronic, melancholy grandeur during his lengthy flashback/confession to Clara. Like any Romantic worth his salt, he bases his story on a Miltonic myth: the paradise lost was the Edenic setting in which he first encountered Clara's mother. Her father, a rebel proscribed after the uprising of 1715, built a sexless paradise for them in which pastoral elegance blended both a library and a pet stag. Swept by bursts of emotion during his lengthy narrative (chaps. xxix-xxxii), Morton/Wacousta demonstrates that even the wilderness cannot extinguish the remnants of the man of feeling he must have been.

This motif from a sentimental novel reminds us that we cannot consistently view Richardson's wilderness in stark opposition to the garrison. We are given imaginative bursts of terror, which the resources of civilization then seek to soften and account for. Yet this sense of cosmic terror comes through recurrent symbolic and narrative motifs, rather than through overt discourse. It is as much a matter of what the novel shows as it is of what the novel says. The sexless paradise is doomed; the evil underside of the garrison's values looms no larger than the wilderness' sympathetic response to the evil, yet some moral comeuppance remains. As the killing of Westbrook by the wolf indicates, even the bush has its limits.

If the dichotomies between bush and fort are not as radical as they first appear, what mark of his awareness of this does the author provide? Margot Northey writes of the symbolic aspects of the bridge in *Wacousta* on which so much of the action takes place. Here forest and fortress meet.[18] The bridge forms an enduring link (it is still there for the sequel, half a century later) between the two polarities. It functions as the man-made avenue on which civilized man ventures into a darkness which he assumes exists only out there, rather than within himself, as well. In fact, the colonel's judicial murder of Frank Halloway happens on the bridge; the evil we see there owes nothing to the wilderness.

Some of the moral complexities of the Richardsonian universe can be caught in a name. "Frank Halloway" (Wacousta's nephew) is both frank in his admission of the dereliction of duty for which the colonel has him shot and hollow because he bears a false identity and thus is not free to explain the circumstances that would exonerate him from guilt. They are also easily glimpsed in a moment from *The Canadian Brothers* when an Arcadian picnic of officers and their ladies concludes with one of the men bitten by a rattlesnake. He is saved from death by a woman whose skills at handling snakebite make her seem "a vampire and a sorceress," and she goes on to darker deeds.[19] In a part of the forest away from this scene, the brute Desborough sits gnawing on a human arm he has cured and smoked. Can we think of these people as points along a line, or perhaps as figures standing along that bridge that links garrison with bush? The officers rest at one end, Desborough at the other. Between them stands the sorceress, practising her black arts with ease in the garrison society. Nowhere can the reader find a firm boundary; characters switch identities to suit their goals or pass easily from one realm to another.[20] All this makes the universe a haven of chaos and terror. The man of imagination responds to it by fixing what he must see into an aesthetic, distancing composition.

Richardson's regard for the picturesque carries a moral implication beyond that of a connoisseur's stance. To compose a picturesque scene serves as a way of composing oneself in the face of bewildering or terrifying events. Consider the role played by the picturesque in Richardson's characteristic modes of perception. It is there in his first novel, *Ecarté*, where the author adopts a genre painter's stance towards a slapstick tussle aboard a channel ferry: "a scene which would not have disgraced the pencil of a Hogarth."[21] One of the opening scenes in *Wacousta* is termed "picturesque" (p. 27), and the Hogarthian allusion recurs in his fiction, applied this time to a scene of comic horror in which an Indian's hand comes out of nowhere to snatch some food from some beleaguered whites. We are told that it is a scene "for some American Hogarth."[22] Even the grim Westbrook, at the age of forty-five married to his seventh wife, manages to build a cabin in the bush which "commanded a highly romantic aspect" of the Thames (p. 1). The genre scenes, the vistas of romantic grandeur, convey the author's attempts at what Keats, when he admired it in Milton, called "stationing." A small but significant detail of this skill at creating significant background occurs in *Wacousta*, where the room of Clara and Madeline de Haldimar at Fort Michilimackinac holds a collection of New World flora and fauna combined with Old World artefacts, a mark of their attempt to blend both places and live, as it were, on the bridge (chap. xix). Even when, at the end of his life, Richardson penned a pornographic romance about the Crusades, *The Monk Knight of St. John*, he displayed an almost Spenserian power to describe erotic/violent encounters within carefully evoked settings that complement the actions and freeze them into a series of *tableaux* (pp. 14-16, 27, 145-55).

Ultimately, man's hope for sanity in a world so beset with violence and confusion, a world where nature's serenity ceaselessly mocks man's disturbance,[23] lies in his adoption of a beholder's stance. This imaginative/moral gesture lets the observer view with some understanding events and forces that can never be fully sounded by him. The narrative technique of *Wacousta* has each section of the work open with mysterious occurrences which several following chapters then strive to explain. Wacousta's flashback to his days as Reginald Morton offers an individual instance of what is a larger device of explanatory recollection in the novel. This technique defines the nature of the work's imaginative/moral stance. Experience remains discontinuous and inexplicable until the beholder has distanced himself from what he has seen. He can then fit it into some larger associative pattern, historical or symbolic.

Because Richardson's work is so frequently bad, because he so exuberantly breaks every canon of taste, critics have allowed persistent motifs in his fiction to go unremarked, as if they were only formulaic devices of an unreflective imagination. Let me stress the qualifier, "only." That is, there are things to be learned even in so flawed a writer as Richardson, shoddy practices with grander implications. In the light of his concern with views and viewers, for example, one speculates upon the significance of the voyeurism that so marks his narratives. The events in *Wacousta* must form our literature's most extensive peep show. Characters are forever peered at by others, and part of Wacousta's power lies in a talent for making disconcerting stares through windows at parties gathered within. We have noticed the incidence of spying and masking in the novel, as well as its preoccupation with mistaken identity and concealment. If ambush served as the principal tactic of frontier warfare, then that very real aspect of the life he portrayed served Richardson's narrative habits well, adding another dimension to his motif of the unseen watcher. His two Fort Dearborn novels, *Hardscrabble* and *Wau-Nan-Gee*, take place within garrisons first unsuspecting of, and then terrorized by, their enemy's power to observe them from concealment. Lovers are nearly caught *in flagrante* in *Ecarté*, while one of the heroes in *The Canadian Brothers* beholds in secret a father-daughter encounter with distinct sexual overtones. Loving couples are observed at play more than once in *The Monk Knight*, where one figure even enjoys fantasizing about a friend's embrace of the daydreamer's wife. Westbrook in his novel not only watches the lovers but later rapes the woman while forcing her lover to watch. Indeed, *Westbrook* offers an even more vivid indication of the author's interest in such matters: Richardson's memoirs tell of a low hotel in Brockville where the room partitions proved rickety enough to see through.[24] In *Westbrook*, the heroine stays at that hotel, where the villain observes her while she undresses (p. 47).

At this point, the reader may wish to account for this obsession by invoking whatever similar pathology motivates Richardson's interest in cannibalism and rape. After all, one, the other, or both occur in every fictional work of Richardson with the exception of *Hardscrabble*. Yet voyeurism denotes terror as well as interest on the part of the peeper. It demonstrates not only a wish to participate in the act but a fear of the act itself, a fear of its seeming violence and brutality. Voyeurism remains a mode of setting distance, a method of detachment. Thus, when we examine the most erotic of Richardson's works, *The Monk Knight*, we find a paradox. The work frequently rhapsodizes about sex, even to the extent — daring in its time — of excusing female homosexuality on the grounds that "should not woman love as passionately as a man, what God made so perfect in another" (p. 62). Yet sex in the book intertwines with violence, deception, bondage, cannibalism, and burial. Could not the voyeuristic aspect of the Richardsonian stance be simply another instance of his attempted detachment from the horrors and confusions of the intractable universe? The observer watches events, though not primarily to participate imaginatively in what he sees (a pleasant side effect) but to place it in some kind of perspective that will distance him from its terror. Richardson remains a humanist, rather than a modernist, because he continues to believe that terror is observed by gazing upon a *tableau*, rather than into a mirror.

This detachment occurs in other less vivid ways, as in Richardson's repeated laments for a lost time of happiness and spontaneity. It runs throughout his writing, from the tamed-deer Eden of Reginald Morton and Clara Beverley's meeting place in *Wacousta* to the strident assertions of a lost emotional and sexual paradise in *The Monk Knight*.[25] The Richardsonian imaginaton, therefore, remains the artist's refuge within a world of stark horror. Always, the threat is there, with malign forces like Wacousta eagerly waiting for the garrison's defenses to slip. The artist then becomes the ultimate watcher, placing what he beholds into some sort of arrangement that grants a pattern and meaning to the experience. Recall again the bridge in *Wacousta* and the extremes of experience it seeks to connect. Richardson as an artist never gets away from that bridge, which, like the one built by Satan in *Paradise Lost*, connects earth with hell.

B. Wacousta's *Style and Structure*

The novel opens like *Hamlet*, with terrified sentries wondering what forces are stalking the fort. The first spoken words — " 'Which way did he go?' " — recall the "Who goes there?" that begins the Shakespearian drama. A current critic has pointed out that the specific form of this novel owes a great deal to Elizabethan revenge tragedy;[26] indeed, the novel's epigraph, taken from an eighteenth-century version of one such tragedy, further attests to this.

Revenge tragedy proved a very popular mode of Elizabethan drama, and the generic title requires little explanation.[27] In a typical instance, the hero suffers from some wrong that cannot be righted by any legal means, either because of his own powerlessness or the corruption of society itself. He therefore carries out a succession of vengeful acts by any means that come to hand — chiefly deception and terror. The tragedy arises when the hero's drives and the scheme itself grow so uncontrollable that they entail the death of the hero. *Hamlet* is a very great play, but it exploits to the fullest the conventions of revenge tragedy and can be treated as the most distinguished example of the genre.

The world of revenge tragedy is very much a fallen one, in which the hero's initial integrity collapses as his goals enable him to excuse the shoddiest means. So fallen is the world that even those attempting to redress its evil find themselves enmeshed in evil of their own, to such an extent that their final destruction appears appropriate. Revenge tragedy's fascination — and one cannot ignore the "playability" as well as the poetic intensity of such works as Webster's *Duchess of Malfi*, Tourneur's *Revenger's Tragedy*, and Middleton's *Women Beware Women* — lies in its exposition of flawed heroism. It takes as a given that heroism contains an admixture of villainy and that the greater the hero, the greater the flaw. No literary work bears a single source, and while in terms of the fiction of its time, *Wacousta* stands as another instance of the sentimental and the Gothic, it has also its roots in a form that itself hearkens back to the mediaeval morality play. For behind the villainous heroes of revenge tragedy are the sinful figures in mediaeval drama who tread the earth successfully until they are finally forced to pay the bill they have been running up.

To observe this aspect of *Wacousta* seems no antiquarian exercise. Rather, it tips the reader off to some of the familiar devices that occur there. The tyrannical, rigid patriarch whose public position conceals a history of fraud, the welter of events, alarums, and reversals that keeps the plot busy, the littering of the final pages with corpses: these are common enough in revenge tragedy, which may explain why the novel has been twice dramatized.

In its narrative patterns, the novel relies on an almost rigid story-telling device, which in this case is not only a formula but also a concrete manifestation of one of the novel's messages. Events appear in mysterious and dramatic fashion; they are explained in later chapters, when the reader has caught up on the story. Then it is time for another happening. Besides being a suspense-creating mechanism common to potboilers, this way of recounting events also serves to remind the reader that the world of the novel is made up largely of unexpected, bewildering events. Their meaning can be ascertained only with difficulty and after some reflection. From its fearful, nighttime opening, the book tells a story in which darkness and mystery hold sway over human affairs. No story can be told straightforwardly; nature abhors a straight line.

Fort, forest, and bridge: these are the spaces in which the story occurs. For all the unrelenting, authoritarian watchfulness of Colonel de Haldimar and despite the regularity and rigidity of the systems he embodies, leaks keep popping up in the ark he commands. Thus, Wacousta can sneak into the fort at will, and despite the colonel's harsh penalties, men continue to sneak out. If in fact the fort were the hermetically sealed vessel de Haldimar wants to make it, then it would have fallen. For, if one of his sons had not become the beloved of an Indian woman, then the garrison would never have been alerted to Pontiac's stratagem for capturing the fort. Ironically, de Haldimar can present a row of fixed bayonets to the astonished Pontiac because his less rigid son presented the hand of friendship to a woman of Pontiac's tribe.

Fort, forest, and bridge: the structure of the novel rests upon a number of contrasts that are bridged in a way that reassures some and disquiets others. To the tidy, dichotomous mind of the colonel, no bridge can ever really exist between fort and forest. To men of his stamp, the bridge should be a drawbridge, an affair of convenience to allow for forays into the forest. No greater contrast obtains in his imagination than that separating British officer from savage warrior. Yet Wacousta, once Reginald Morton, was himself a British officer. De Haldimar, now the upholder of what he conceives to be civilized values, was once a liar and cheat who betrayed a good friend.

Recall what was discussed previously: the twinnings, the sexual ambiguities, the disguises, the deceptions — what do they show but a world in which tidy distinctions and well-kept boundaries dissolve under the force of individual perception and appetite? Ultimately, the contrasts dissolve between male and female, soldier and savage, fort and forest, hero and villain. Spatial, psychological, and sexual boundaries melt. This results, however, not in some blissful, pseudo-Eastern utopia in which yin and yang keep forever swirling in the mists of cosmic consciousness. What happens instead is cruelty and slaughter. Wacousta does not play the role of introducing the de Haldimar children to a looser and more spontaneous existence away from their rigid father. No, he murders as many as he can and rejoices in his power to encompass vengeful destruction.

Shifts in identity, magical forests, supervillains, winsome heroines, prodigious feats of strength and violence: these technical devices of characterization and setting are matters we are used to finding in fairy tales. Despite Richardson's previously quoted statement about the novel's realism, any reader soon learns that the book makes sense either as romance, or not at all. In *Wacousta*, however, romance takes on a peculiar meaning. If romance's psychological analogue is dream, then there are good dreams and nightmares. The suspension of certain commonsensical patterns in *Wacousta* reproduces the condition of the mind at play, but the play is that of the nightmare. Dreams give us the world tailored to human desire. Not all these desires are altruistic and sociable, and thus *Wacousta* stands in a line of Canadian dream-fictions that includes Philip Child's *Village of Souls* and Margaret Atwood's *Surfacing*. They do not present happy dreams.

A writer more intent upon the formulas of sentimental comedy alone would have lightened the blackness of the ending. Why should so many decent people perish because one rogue long ago despoiled another? Here is where the Gothic aspect of the story holds the trumps, for no one is allowed a suspension of the laws by which grim pasts misshape what ought to be happy presents.

To appreciate the stylistic flavour of the book, one must not focus on the actual rhetoric, which is often pompous, overblown, and needlessly complex. Whether used in describing setting and emotion —

At length came that terrible and eventful day, and, as if in mockery of those who saw no beauty in its golden beams, arrayed in all the gorgeous softness of its autumnal glory. Sad and heavy were the hearts of many within that far distant and isolated fort as they rose, at the first glimmering of light above the horizon, to prepare for the several duties assigned them. (p. 179)

— or in dialogue —

"Ha! where indeed is she?" ... "Almighty God, where is she?" ... "Clara, my beloved sister, do you not know me? It is not Baynton, but your brother, who now clasps you to his breaking heart." (p. 282)

— present-day readers cannot ignore the stilted, overemphatic nature of the style. Of course, that style comes out of a different view of a work of art than ours and, therefore, need not be worse than ours, but only different. The fact that it calls attention to itself so pressingly means only that a member of Richardson's audience wanted engagement with a work that proclaimed its artistic, its full-blown, high-styled nature. All that is true, but a glance at the examples shows how these generalities must yield to actual literary experience. The adjectival overkill ("terrible and eventful," "Sad and heavy," "far distant and isolated"), the inversion-for-inversion's-sake (the sentence beginning "Sad and heavy"), the clichéd, needless ornamentation of the dialogue (" 'who now clasps you to his breaking heart' "): these attest that even those supporting a version of stylistic relativism must pale at the specifics of this or, at least, acknowledge that Richardson followed all too faithfully his Elizabethan theatrical models.

If no reader of *Wacousta* would return to it for stylistic considerations and if the general narrative mode of happening-followed-by-flashback becomes eventually monotonous (keeping in consideration the thematic benefits of this practice), then does its virtue lie only in its themes? Certainly, any student glancing at the Canadian literature that follows Richardson will recognize what a rich grab bag of recurrent themes *Wacousta* is: the fort and the forest, the eroticized landscape, the indifference of nature, the dissolution of personal identity, and the fall of Eden. Certainly these alone would compel rereading. Yet there is more to the book than this. First, the Western imagination, in a line that runs from Milton's Satan to Brontë's Heathcliff, has been haunted by the demon lover. Wacousta lacks their stature, but he still retains considerable interest. Secondly, the story itself, however mechanically told at times, bears great interest. Its tale of vengeance stretches over two continents and concludes within an historical period of considerable colour. Beyond the welter of disguises and stratagems followed by the fictional characters in the story stretches the horizon of historical fact. Pontiac's allies *did* capture Michilimackinac through the ruse of pursuing a wayward lacrosse ball into the inner reaches of the fort. Detroit *was* saved because the commander had been told by a native informer of Pontiac's plans and had prepared for just such trickery. Whether found in historical textbooks or historical novels, this is thrilling stuff. Finally, *Wacousta* contains the single *sine qua non* of any popular novelist's production: something is always happening. A man has disappeared, another has been court-martialled and shot, women are abducted, sorties are made, attacks are mounted, grim secrets revealed, tragic pasts uncovered, and so forth. Let the reader only get behind the style, and he is engaging in a good read.

Take, for example, a set piece (chap. xx) on the taking of Michilimackinac. It begins and ends with distanced perspectives. A family crisis has sent Madeline de Haldimar, who will later marry her cousin Frederick, to Michilimackinac, accompanied by Clara, Colonel de Haldimar's daughter. From their apartment in the fort, they spy through a telescope an attack by an Indian in disguise on a boat moored nearby. Clara faints at the sight, while Madeline runs to sound the alarm. Clara revives and observes that the scene outside appears far from threatening as the inhabitants of the fort are watching the Indians playing at lacrosse. It is a day of sport. She no sooner thanks God for proving her fears baseless than a war cry sounds the attack. Now she witnesses the Indians, "the yelling fiends" (p. 269), at their work of slaughter, since their trick had been to gain admittance to the fort as part of the game, and then begin the attack.[28]

Rapidly the fort succumbs, and, amid all the horror of indiscriminate killing, Richardson sounds a familiar theme in the story:

> And yet the sun shone in yellow lustre, and all nature smiled and wore an air of calm, as if the accursed deed had had the sanction of heaven and the spirits of light loved to look upon the frightful atrocities then in perpetration. (p. 271)

Clara now hears Madeline's shrieks and watches her carried off even as she hears steps approach herself. But it is the chivalrous Captain Baynton, rather than an enemy, who enters Clara's room and bears her away. A lurid touch is added when Baynton feels "his feet dabbling in the blood" (p. 275) of his fellow officers as he proceeds through a hallway but lightly partitioned from a room in which a massacre occurred. The chapter has been one of visual search from a distance — the telescope, the sight of the massacre and of Madeline's abduction — and the motif continues as Baynton now seeks to gain a boat he spies offshore.

His emotional stress leads him to crow in defiance, which in turn alerts the Indians who are now watching him. They catch up to Baynton, who throws Clara to one of the crew. Baynton is killed, but the boatman slays the Indian in turn, and the vessel then pushes off to escape. Planks have been placed across the stern as a screen against bullets, and thus again occurs a viewing device:

> A small aperture had, however, been bored [through the planks] for the purpose of observing the movements of the enemy without risk. *Through this an eye was now directed.* . . . (p. 278; emphasis added)

This seeing device allows the crew to eliminate the strongest of their swimming pursuers. The chapter began with the telescopic view of a surprised boatman braining his attacker as he is startled from sleep; it concludes with the blow of a sailor's cutlass that severs the fingers of a pursuer from the gunwale of the craft. The final view is that of those aboard, distantly watching the swimmers' heads as they appear "like so many rats upon the water, as they returned once more in disappointment from their fruitless pursuit" (p. 279).

The chapter has moved at a pell-mell pace; an internal motif of distant observation has proved a solid counterpoint to its involvement in the immediate circumstances of terror, massacre, and flight. An example of what Richardson can do at his best in *Wacousta*, it advances the narrative; holds the reader in suspense (what will be Madeline's fate in captivity; will Clara *really* escape?), and heightens the novel's preoccupation with the experience of viewing. Again, the reader easily forgives the style as he finds himself within a vivid, sensuous world which defies any comprehension beyond what the seemingly simple act of viewing can give.

C. *Other Works*
In view of this study's concerns, *The Monk Knight of St. John: A*

Tale of the Crusades proves the most interesting of Richardson's other works. In many ways, it seems a debased version of *Wacousta*, with that novel's ambiance of sexual ambiguity and violence converted into this novel's prime concern. This is scarcely the place to join the contemporary debate on the exact definition of pornography; let it be stated that by the standards of its own day, this novel was a pornographic work. The very shoddy paper and binding, plus the absence of any publisher's imprint, plus what we know of the author's desperate circumstances at this time, all bear out the textual evidence.[29] Whatever the motivations behind its production, the novel seethes with the typical Richardsonian themes.

The monk, Abdallah, once a Moor, was converted to Christianity after his capture by the Crusaders, and he eventually became a member of one of the military/monastic orders, the Knights of the Hospital of St. John of Jerusalem. The plot quite defies description, especially since it contains more than one mysterious gap in logic. Suffice it to say that the hero sins widely, loves deeply, and fights mightily. As the knight pursues his tempestuous and treacherous career, the incidents of rape, murder, cannibalism, and deviant s₂x multiply.

The charges of sodomy, bestiality, and devil worship tha' a power-hungry French monarch trumped up to justify suppression of the Knights Templar (the other military/monastic order of ,he Crusades) in 1312 provided future historical novelists with ready-made villainous characters. Thus, wicked Templars cross the pages of Sir Walter Scott. Richardson employed the same dossier but switched orders. Of course, the work is laughable as historical fiction — it is a subliterary tale of horror and violence set in a never-never mediaeval era. The temporal setting is actually the timeless era of romance, the fairyland mediaevalism of Spenser's *Faerie Queene*, in which armour, battlements, languishing females, and powerful wizards make up the trappings of a mediaeval culture in which the chief interest is its remote quaintness. Spenser not only is one of the greatest of English poets but also is one of the most sensuous and erotic, as the "Bowre of Bliss" episode in Book II of *The Faerie Queene* attests. One of Spenser's strengths is an ability to create *tableaux* of passion and combat, and Richardson provides a less poetic and more titillating version of this in at least one instance when a group of knights engage in a highly stylized combat over a Saracen female tied naked to a tree (pp. 14-16). The scene is all blood and bare breasts, with the victor attempting rape among the heads that roll about the battleground, a stock *tableau* from any manual of perversity. Yet it does indicate that Richardson's novel attempts to create a somewhat high-class pornography that exploits a culture's stock of mediaeval and pseudomediaeval images.

In a fashion familiar to readers of subliterature attempting to legitimize itself, the novel alternately pleads for what would now be termed sexual liberation and slavers over the sex it actually portrays. The reader is solemnly assured that the Crusades failed, not for the usual political, economic, and social reasons historians have posited but through the perverse nature of the Crusaders' sex lives (p. 31). Sex certainly is a force here that shakes men to their very depths, seismically disturbing even so hardened a sinner as Abdallah (p. 17). The very accidental touch of a woman's bare breast by him and his subsequent agitation becomes "a triumph . . . of a hallowed and divine sentiment, over the cold and abstract conventionalism" (p. 21) of a world in bondage. Sex, which is "divine and mystic love" and "God's holiest mystery" (pp. 27-28), becomes the way out of the fallen world. For this reason, men ogle boy pages, and women clasp other women in close embrace to the author's approval. Even heterosexuality attains a measure of aesthetic delight, as when a couple embracing form a "group . . . worthy of the chisel of the sculptor" (p. 27).

A reader may well ask why this liberating force always appears allied with blood and violence, why a sexually liberated (to use an anachronistic term) woman's final act should be that of eating the corpse of her lover and then vomiting (p. 190). The answer is that here the rationale of sexual liberation thinly covers what is, in fact, the matter of a number of barbaric fantasies. This enables writer and audience alike to experience the thrill of illicit fantasizing as a spin-off of the pursuit of sexual enlightenment.

Yet the work remains of significance for the purposes of this study in that it shows us the workings of the Richardsonian imagination when out of control. When concentrating upon the production of an "acceptable" literary work, the hero/villain is placed within a realized setting (the forest) that complements his powers and gives him — not credibility in the commonplace meaning — but resonance. The story of deception and betrayal flows out of a host of crushing misdeeds and bungled recognitions.

The atmosphere of sexual ambiguity becomes not only a matter of sensationalist exploitation but a striking aspect of the general fluidity of personality and character. The gap between social roles and personal identity, and the ease with which the personality is cut in two, loom as part of the larger fragility that civilization exhibits in the face of the threats the forest poses. Finally, the watcher's eye is not the voyeur's. The perception is not fixated but shifts from view to view in an effort to maintain the saving, composing qualities of the act of perception itself.

These virtues, when compared with a work as debased as *The Monk Knight*, demonstrate that there are degrees even of badness and that *Wacousta*, whatever its faults, flows from the pen of a writer trying to convey some facts he has grasped imaginatively about the horrifying aspects of experience. *The Monk Knight*'s stereotypical, slapdash, and prurient nature shows that what controlled imaginative power displays as genuinely horrible, can — when uncontrolled — become merely entertaining. By the time of *The Monk Knight*, the bridge in *Wacousta* has been washed away, and the forest can only be sketched distantly as a view from the fort, something to entertain and excite the bored soldiery.

The Canadian Brothers; or, The Prophecy Fulfilled interests this study in two ways — its role as a sequel to *Wacousta* and the use it makes of the author's time of imprisonment in Kentucky. The brothers, Gerald and Henry Grantham, are the offspring of Frederick and Madeline of *Wacousta*, whose lives have been disposed of early on in the sequel. Desborough, their enemy, is the son of Wacousta and Ellen Halloway, the wife of his nephew. Readers of Richardson's *War of 1812* will realize how much of his wartime experience figures in this book, with Gerald the sailor's life coming closer to the author's than does Henry the soldier's. The easy division of the brothers into land and sea forces indicates that Richardson cannot really return to the imaginative and narrative invention of *Wacousta* but must, instead, pen a war novel which drags in the plot of leftover revenge from time to time. The bridge that figured so largely in the earlier novel still stands, but the fusion of horror with the everyday experience it represents is not as apparent or powerful as in *Wacousta*.

Two exceptions to this exist: the first is the pastoral picnic mentioned above, the scene of officers and their ladies that could have come from the pen of one of the Royal Engineer draughtsmen who provide so much of the visual record of early Upper Canada. Not only does the picnic spot sport a rattlesnake, but Desborough lurks in the surrounding forest, munching on a human arm he has cured (I, 207; II, 137-39).

If this is a touch of the old Richardson, a second portion of the novel recalling earlier powers is that concerning Gerald's imprisonment after Moraviantown. There he falls under the spell of the seductive Matilda Montgomerie, the sorceress who first displayed her powers in curing the snakebite during the picnic. She is Desborough's daughter, and the villain comes to her wearing a black face mask in an incident with unmistakable sexual feeling (II, 171-73). What happens next is that Richardson incorporates into his novel the almost legendary matter of the "Kentucky" tragedy, the murder by Anna Cook Beauchamp's young lover of her former one. The murder case in 1825 has attracted American novelists from William Gilmore Simms to Robert Penn Warren, and it is interesting to see the Canadian novelist working it into his own chronicle.[30] This story of female aggression, seduction, and murder appears to have been ready-made for Richardson's use, and it is surprising that he made no more of it than he did. His failure to do so indicates how little of Wacousta resides in its sequel. What we have are echoes: Desborough's powerful voice recalls that of his father, while his killing of Henry by dragging him over a precipice at the Battle of Queenston Heights recalls the final, vengeful act of his father against the de Haldimars. Otherwise, The Canadian Brothers remains a pedestrian effort at carving a novel out of war experiences better chronicled in the author's volume of history.

Wacousta, Desborough, Abdallah the monk knight — bold, bad villains preoccupied Richardson. In the figure of Westbrook in the serialized novel that bears his name, Richardson returned from his gimcrack version of the Crusades and produced another of his frontier monsters. The seven instalments of the novel indicate that the management of the New York Sunday Mercury forced the author abruptly to terminate the novel, rather than conclude it according to any narrative plans that Richardson may have had. Seeking to flatter the nationalism of his audience, Richardson twice states with gratitude that his monster is not American but Canadian (pp. 72-73), a far cry from the impassioned Canadian who in his first work scorned the Americans for their purported flaying of Tecumseh's corpse.[31]

The work panders to its audience in another way, as well, in that it follows in the path of the widely read American shocker, Maria Monk's *Awful Disclosures* (1836). This popular, purportedly nonfictional work exploited every anti-Catholic prejudice and portrayed the monastic/conventual life as a steamy, Gothic sexual jungle.³² One might note that this very strong tradition in English letters ranges from the decadent Italy of Elizabethan drama, with its incestuous cardinals and sex-obsessed, nunlike heroines, to Matthew Gregory Lewis' eighteenth-century Gothic landmark, *The Monk* (1796). Maria Monk, *The Monk Knight* — the very names speak eloquently of the resonance of Lewis' work, and Richardson in his earlier work on Abdallah indicates what a profitable vein he found in Gothicized Catholicism. In *Westbrook, the Outlaw; or, The Avenging Wolf*, Richardson places his usual sexually compelling heroine Emily — her nose is "voluptuous in contour, and sensual in expression" (p. 25) — in the company of a lay brother, Anselmo. Her mathematics tutor cannot resist her charms, and so the pupil-teacher combination echoes Paolo and Francesca, and Eloise and Abelard. Richardson piously asserts his own freedom from any anti-Catholic prejudices (p. 33), though the reader may wonder exactly what a cleric with an Italian name is doing as a mathematics tutor in early Upper Canada. Perhaps Anselmo's name and clerical position is rooted in the eighteenth-century tradition of English Gothic, but that tradition itself springs in part from a hostile vision of Catholicism. Deliberately or unthinkingly, Richardson's version of "Maria Monk" continues an English literary tradition in which the sexual disturbance of the Roman Catholic clergy functions as a "given."

Despite Anselmo's conviction that fecund nature itself blesses the love between Emily and himself (pp. 42-43), nature in the form of Westbrook grossly intrudes upon that union. Westbrook's first attempted rape, while wearing a mask, is interrupted by Anselmo. Later, after watching the couple at amorous play, Westbrook successfully intervenes and rapes Emily while the bound Anselmo watches. He later shoots and kills her.

Westbrook embodies the larger-than-life energies of the Richardsonian hero-villain. Married at the age of forty-five to his seventh wife when the story begins, his emotions are cataclysmic in their intensity (p. 3), and both the law and his neighbours prove powerless to stop him from terrorizing the countryside at will. Despite his cabin with its romantic prospect of the river, he roams easily over the Upper Canadian wilderness and the "continuous, low and foetid extent of unwholesome-looking marsh" (p. 9). Like Wacousta, he is observer-voyeur as well as actor and easily finds his way to lookout points, whether in hotel rooms or the forest.

Only nature can curb this primitive force. Thus he is slain by an angry she-wolf who has suckled his abandoned grandson. Though Westbrook, like Desborough and Wacousta, is distinguished by a mighty voice, in this case a wolf howl, his savagery proves too extreme for the animal he imitates. He is slain by the wolf when he menaces her human suckling. A final drama of revenge is played out when we learn the baby's father had been slain by Westbrook and thus " 'the child, through the affection of the wolf, was the avenger of its parent's wrongs' " (p. 74).

This savage, nearly pornographic fantasy displays a world no less grim than *Wacousta*'s. What sort of justice exists here if it depends upon the maternal instincts of a wolf? What hope is there for man if he is capable of a savagery greater than a wolf's and if outlaw man is impervious to any challenge but that posed by nature? However slight the fiction, it reinforces the reader's sense of Richardson's lifelong preoccupation with the terror of existence.

With his two Fort Dearborn novels, Richardson sought to present an American trilogy on Wacoustan themes. Despite his broad hint to the reader in the second volume, *Wau-Nan-Gee; or, The Massacre at Chicago* (p. 125), that a third can be in the works if the earlier ones succeed, the public's lack of response sent him instead to *Westbrook*. Both *Wau-Nan-Gee* and *Hardscrabble; or, The Fall of Chicago* give us the familiar Richardsonian wilderness, in which nature smiles while massacres take place, women are sexually assaulted in underground caverns, men of the forest saunter at will in and out of the defended garrisons, a cannibal devours an enemy's heart, and always the garrison goes about its business beneath an all-seeing enemy eye (*Hardscrabble*, pp. 289-90, 349; *Wau-Nan-Gee*, pp. 10-11, 21, 36, 79, 100). The closest the novels come to humour occurs during the earlier one, in the macabre incident of a hidden enemy's hand reaching from behind to grab a piece of turkey from an unsuspecting group of whites. Just as Richardson expunged the anti-American sentiments from *The Canadian Brothers* when he turned it into *Matilda Montgomerie*, so in *Wau-Nan-Gee* he defends General Hull's needless surrender to the British and Indians at Fort Detroit, a capitulation he quite properly mocked in *The Canadian Brothers*.

Hardscrabble seems largely the wish-fulfilment fantasy of the author, whose military experience in the Carlist war — judging from his own pamphlets — consisted of brisker conflicts with his superiors than with the enemy. In the novel, a perky subordinate utterly outwits his dull superior and carries all triumphantly before him.

In themselves, the novels are uncommonly slight products of the author. Their chief interest lies in their demonstration of Richardson's attempt to work the tried-and-true wilderness vein, but this time within an American setting. With their benevolent Indian hero (Wau-Nan-Gee is a kind Wacousta) in imitation of Cooper, they lose a good deal of the bite and *bizarrerie* a reader expects from Richardson. Captain Renayne, the insubordinate junior officer who triumphs over stupidity on high, remains himself no more credible than Major Richardson's attempt to exploit a setting and theme that had already engaged his fullest imaginative powers.

The mention of wish fulfilment turns the discussion back to Richardson's first novel, *Ecarté*. Appearing in the three-decker form necessitated by the conventions of the time among publisher, reader, and circulating library, the novel contains a great deal of filler in the manner of stories-within-the-story. The principal story line concerns the adventures of Clifford Delmaine, and though "founded principally on facts," may "in some measure be accounted personal" (I, 198). Delmaine certainly resembles his creator in his impetuosity and in his gift for seeking and finding disaster. He is a man whose "generosity and feeling triumphed over every more narrow and prudential consideration" (I, 49).

A craze for gambling proves his greatest disaster, though he comes through a duel with an English bully unscathed. The *demi-monde* of courtesans, gamblers, and adventurers forms the novel's chief interest. Here is the Paris of Balzac, only as seen through the eyes of a half-pay British officer determined to live by his wits. In what will be a familiar Richardsonian occurrence, the hero catches his mistress nearly *in flagrante* with another man. Delmaine's eventual revenge comes when the woman dies from a burst blood vessel, the result of her shock at his later unfeeling treatment of her. The wish fulfilment recurs in the magical process by which Delmaine comes unharmed and free from guilt through all his experiences. The novel shows every sign of hurried writing (for example, even the author complains that he is ignorant of the explanation of a vexing detail [III, 340]) and of slavish imitation of high-society novels of its time spiced with excursions into unrespectable company. Historians of the future may remember it as a work that contains a mention of one Godot, a moneylender. The name was to return, but in a different occupation and literary genre.

Conclusion

In the face of the dreary chronicle of the last few pages, the reader may well wonder at the fluke that produced *Wacousta*. Perhaps it was inevitable that some writer would realize that there was a place on the North American frontier for the Byronic brooder, the man wronged in love who stalks the earth like Cain in search of surcease from sorrow. The popularity of Fenimore Cooper had demonstrated that the human creatures of the American forest could exert a powerful hold on the literary audience. The uprising of Pontiac and its attendant dramatic events cried out for a fictional chronicler. All this may be true, but it cannot really explain how a writer of Richardson's flaws in his previous and later fiction came to produce a work as significant as *Wacousta*.

Of course, much of its appeal can be explained by its energetic cultivation of ground already tilled: the demon lover, the forest, the Indian uprising. No doubt the marketability of these devices was never far from the author's mind. Revenge tragedy, the sentimental novel, and the Gothic novel all shaped the work, as well. But its power surely lies chiefly in its vision of a universe of terror in which not only the restraints of civilization are dissolved but personal identity cracks beneath the challenge presented by the wilderness. What enabled Richardson in *Wacousta* to express this subtext in a way that so impresses the reader remains conjectural. Certainly, to repeat an earlier argument, one cannot distort him into a would-be modernist, nor can one even be certain of calling the dissolution of identity a conscious product of the author's imagination.

This much is certain, however: Richardson, in his single memorable novel, produced a vision of life within a Canadian setting where madness stalks the defended garrison as easily as does

Wacousta. For that vision — overly lengthy, overly ornate, excessive in almost every respect — we still remember him, in our dreams, in our fictions, and in the strange blend of both that marks so much of Canadian literature.

NOTES

Portions of this study have appeared in my *Gardens, Covenants, Exiles: United Empire Loyalism in the Literature of Upper Canada/Ontario* (Toronto: Univ. of Toronto Press, 1982).

[1] All biographical information is from the following sources: A. C. Casselman, Introd., *Richardson's War of 1812*, by John Richardson (1902; rpt. Toronto: Coles, 1974), pp. xi-lviii; William Renwick Riddell, *John Richardson* (Toronto: Ryerson, 1923); David Beasley, *The Canadian Don Quixote: The Life and Works of Major John Richardson, Canada's First Novelist* (Erin, Ont.: Porcupine's Quill, 1977); and Norah Story, "Richardson, John," in *The Oxford Companion to Canadian History and Literature*, 1967 ed.

[2] The text of the early melodrama, reproduced from the working script left behind by a touring actor in London, Ontario, during the 1850s, appears in R. Jones, ed., "Wacousta or, the Curse," *Black Moss*, 2nd ser., No. 1 (Spring 1976), pp. 41-74. For Reaney, see his *Wacousta: A Melodrama* (Erin, Ont.: Porcépic, 1979).

[3] Richardson had been married in 1825 to a Jane Marsh, who had died some time before 1832. The epitaph he composed for his second wife bears repeating:

> Here reposes, Maria Caroline, the Generous-Hearted, High-Souled, Talented and Deeply-Lamented Wife of Major Richardson, Knight of the Military Order of Saint Ferdinand, First Class, and Superintendent of Police on the Welland Canal during the Administration of Lord Metcalfe. This Matchless Wife and This (illegible) Exceeding Grief of Her Faithfully Attached Husband after a few days' illness at St. Catharines on the 16th August, 1845, at the age of 37 years. (A. C. Casselman, p. xxxviii)

[4] For a glimpse of the down-at-heel, Grub Street aspects of his final days, see *The Pick* [N.Y.], 1, No. 14 (22 May 1852), quoted in Carl Ballstadt,

ed., *Major John Richardson: A Selection of Reviews and Criticism* (Montreal: L. M. Lande Foundation, 1972), p. 53.

[5] *Richardson's War of 1812*, pp. 134, 158.

[6] Beasley, p. 54. For selected contemporary reviews of Richardson's writings, see Ballstadt, *Major John Richardson*.

[7] Desmond Pacey, "A Colonial Romantic, Major John Richardson, Soldier and Novelist; Part I: The Early Years," *Canadian Literature*, No. 2 (Autumn 1959), p. 21.

[8] See David Beasley's preface to John Richardson, *Westbrook, the Outlaw; or, The Avenging Wolf: An American Border Tale* (1851; rpt. Montreal: Grant Woolmer, 1973). All further references to this work appear in the text.

[9] John Richardson, *Tecumseh and Richardson: The Story of a Trip to Walpole Island and Port Sarnia* (Toronto: Ontario Book, 1924).

[10] Ray P. Baker, *A History of English-Canadian Literature to the Confederation* (Cambridge: Harvard Univ. Press, 1920), p. 135.

[11] See *The Monk Knight of St. John: A Tale of the Crusades* (New York: n.p., 1850), p. 79. All further references to this work appear in the text.

[12] Margaret Atwood, *Survival: A Thematic Guide to Canadian Literature* (Toronto: House of Anansi, 1972), p. 94.

[13] Sandra Djwa, "Letters in Canada 1976," *University of Toronto Quarterly*, 46 (Summer 1977), 473-74; L. R. Early, "Myth and Prejudice in Kirby, Richardson, and Parker," *Canadian Literature*, No. 81 (Summer 1979), pp. 25-28; and Robert Lecker, "Patterns of Deception in *Wacousta*," *Journal of Canadian Fiction*, No. 19 (1977), pp. 77-85.

[14] Robin Mathews, "John Richardson: The Wacousta Factor," in his *Canadian Literature: Surrender or Revolution*, ed. Gail Dexter (Toronto: Steel Rail, 1978), pp. 13-25.

[15] Major [John] Richardson, *Wacousta: A Tale of the Pontiac Conspiracy* (Toronto: Historical Publishing, 1906), p. 379. All further references to this work appear in the text. Every edition of *Wacousta*, except the very first (London: T. Cadell, 1832), has been abridged, though none to the extent of the 1967 New Canadian Library edition. The text used here is a representative and widely available example of the *Wacousta* that the vast majority of readers have encountered over the past century and a half. See Douglas Cronk, "Bibliography," in James Reaney, *Wacousta*, pp. 161-63.

[16] John Moss, *Patterns of Isolation in English Canadian Fiction* (Toronto: McClelland and Stewart, 1974), p. 42.

[17] John Moss, *Sex and Violence in the Canadian Novel: The Ancestral Present* (Toronto: McClelland and Stewart, 1977), p. 86.

[18] Margot Northey, *The Haunted Wilderness: The Gothic and Grotesque in Canadian Fiction* (Toronto: Univ. of Toronto Press, 1976), pp. 24-25.

[19] John Richardson, *The Canadian Brothers; or, The Prophecy Fulfilled: A Tale of the Late American War* (1840; rpt. Toronto: Univ. of Toronto Press, 1976), I, 207, 220. All further references to this work appear in the text.

[20] I cannot agree with Robin Mathews' argument that a plausible, humane alternative to the complementary horrors of both garrison and wilderness exists in the small French-Canadian settlement that Richardson locates near the fort. Richardson simply fails to provide sufficient importance — whether narrative or symbolic — to that hamlet to give it the kind of weight Mathews discerns. It would be comforting if it did show the reader "a social order which prizes land, wealth and people, but employs them creatively for everyone's freedom and benefit," but we do not see the village often or fully enough to make that symbolic value — assuming it to exist — at all clear. Even the brightest stars cannot guide us on a cloudy night. See Mathews, p. 17.

[21] John Richardson, *Ecarté; or, The Salons of Paris* (London: Henry Colburn, 1829), I, 63. All further references to this work appear in the text.

[22] John Richardson, "Hardscrabble: A Tale of Chicago," in five instalments in *Sartain's Union Magazine*, 6 (Jan.-June 1850), 393. All further references to this work appear in the text. This novel also appeared in complete form as *Hardscrabble; or, The Fall of Chicago* (New York: DeWitt and Davenport, [1851]), but the periodical publication is far easier to obtain and I have therefore used it for purposes of citation.

[23] This commonplace of Romantic observation recurs throughout Richardson's fiction. See, for example: *Ecarté*, I, 243; *Wacousta*, pp. 172, 267; and *Wau-Nan-Gee; or, The Massacre at Chicago* (New York: H. Long and Brother, 1852), p. 79. All further references to this last work appear in the text.

[24] John Richardson, *Eight Years in Canada* (Montreal: H. H. Cunningham, 1847), p. 117.

[25] The Crusades took place during a time when the "cold and soul-annihilating conventionalisms of modern life were unknown," and "selfishness had not attained that refinement which progressive civilization has nurtured" (pp. 5-6). In such an atmosphere, where a celibate touching a woman's breasts produces a "triumph of nature over art — of truth over

falsehood — of a hallowed and divine sentiment, over the cold and abstract conventionalism of a world which, child-like, forges its own chains, fetters its own limbs, and glories in the display of its own bondage" (p. 21), sex becomes "the most exquisite proof of the boundless love of the Great God of the Universe" (p. 40). The author also links sexual repression with the acquisitive, materialist nature of the New World, noting that "we live a century too soon," since a better age must be at hand (p. 79).

[26] Djwa, pp. 473-74.

[27] See Fredson T. Bowers, *Elizabethan Revenge Tragedy, 1587-1642* (Princeton: Princeton Univ. Press, 1940).

[28] This chapter contains a number of infernal epithets about the Indians and demonstrates the gap between Richardson's rhetoric and his imagination. As I have sought to demonstrate, his imagination spins forth patterns in the novel that blur the distinction between red and white, among others. They indicate a savagery in Colonel de Haldimar no less marked than that in Wacousta. The heightening of the massacre scene requires, however, that the author turn the Indians into the Enemy, that he dehumanize them in order to set them apart from the whites. What this produces is a split in the novel between its imaginative depths and the rhetorical excess used by the author to render the scene as dramatic as possible. This is the sort of occurrence that prevents the novel from presenting an integrated experience to the reader. See Leslie Monkman, "Richardson's Indians," *Canadian Literature*, No. 81 (Summer 1979), pp. 86-94.

[29] Against this, see the exaggerated claims made for the book's seriousness in Beasley, pp. 161-64.

[30] For the "Kentucky" tragedy, see "Anna Cook Beauchamp," in *O Brave New World: American Literature from 1600 to 1840*, ed. Leslie A. Fiedler and Arthur Zeiger (New York: Dell, 1968), pp. 636-39.

[31] *Tecumseh; or, The Warrior of the West* (London: R. Glynn, 1828), pp. 134-35n.

[32] See R. A. Billington, Introd., *Awful Disclosures of the Hotel Dieu Nunnery*, by Maria Monk (1836; rpt. Hamden, Conn.: Archon, 1962).

SELECTED BIBLIOGRAPHY

Primary Sources

Richardson, John. *Tecumseh; or, The Warrior of the West*. London: R. Glynn, 1828.

———. *Ecarté; or, The Salons of Paris*. London: Henry Colburn, 1829.

———. *Kensington Gardens in 1830: A Satirical Trifle*. [1830]. Rpt. Introd. Carl F. Klinck. Toronto: Bibliographical Society of Canada, 1957.

———. *The Canadian Brothers; or, The Prophecy Fulfilled: A Tale of the Late American War*. 1840; rpt. Toronto: Univ. of Toronto Press, 1976.

———. *Eight Years in Canada*. Montreal: H. H. Cunningham, 1847.

———. *The Guards in Canada; or, The Point of Honour*. Montreal: H. H. Cunningham, 1848.

———. *The Monk Knight of St. John: A Tale of the Crusades*. New York: n.p., 1850.

———. *Hardscrabble; or, The Fall of Chicago*. New York: Dewitt and Davenport, [1851]. See also "Hardscrabble: A Tale of Chicago." *Sartain's Union Magazine*, 6 (Jan.-June 1850), 143-49, 217-26, 281-90, 348-54, 390-96.

———. *Westbrook, the Outlaw; or, The Avenging Wolf: An American Border Tale*. 1851; rpt. Montreal: Grant Woolmer, 1973.

———. *Wau-Nan-Gee; or, The Massacre at Chicago*. New York: H. Long and Brother, 1852.

———. *Richardson's War of 1812*. Introd. A. C. Casselman. 1902; rpt. Toronto: Coles, 1974.

———. *Wacousta: A Tale of the Pontiac Conspiracy*. Toronto: Historical Publishing, 1906.

———. *Tecumseh and Richardson: The Story of a Trip to Walpole Island and Port Sarnia*. Introd. A. H. U. Colquhoun. Toronto: Ontario Book, 1924.

Secondary Sources

Atwood, Margaret. *Survival: A Thematic Guide to Canadian Literature.* Toronto: House of Anansi, 1972.

Baker, Ray P. *A History of English-Canadian Literature to the Confederation.* Cambridge: Harvard Univ. Press, 1920.

Ballstadt, Carl, ed. *Major John Richardson: A Selection of Reviews and Criticism.* Montreal: L. M. Lande Foundation, 1972.

Beasley, David, introd. *Westbrook, the Outlaw; or, The Avenging Wolf.* By John Richardson. 1851; rpt. Montreal: Grant Woolmer, 1973.

————. *The Canadian Don Quixote: The Life and Works of Major John Richardson, Canada's First Novelist.* Erin, Ont.: Porcupine's Quill, 1977.

Billington, R. A., introd. *Awful Disclosures of the Hotel Dieu Nunnery.* By Maria Monk. 1836; rpt. Hamden, Conn.: Archon, 1962.

Bowers, Fredson T. *Elizabethan Revenge Tragedy, 1587-1642.* Princeton: Princeton Univ. Press, 1940.

Casselman, A. C., introd. *Richardson's War of 1812.* By John Richardson. 1902; rpt. Toronto: Coles, 1974.

Djwa, Sandra. "Letters in Canada 1976." *University of Toronto Quarterly,* 46 (Summer 1977), 473-74.

Early, L. R. "Myth and Prejudice in Kirby, Richardson, and Parker." *Canadian Literature,* No. 81 (Summer 1979), pp. 25-28.

Fiedler, Leslie A., and Arthur Zeiger, eds. "Anna Cook Beauchamp." In their *O Brave New World: American Literature from 1600 to 1840.* New York: Dell, 1968, pp. 636-39.

Jones, R., ed. "Wacousta or, the Curse." *Black Moss,* 2nd ser., No. 1 (Spring 1976), pp. 41-74.

Klinck, Carl F., introd. *Wacousta; or, The Prophecy.* By John Richardson. New Canadian Library, No. 58. Toronto: McClelland and Stewart, 1967.

Lecker, Robert. "Patterns of Deception in *Wacousta.*" *Journal of Canadian Fiction,* No. 19 (1977), pp. 77-85.

Mathews, Robin. "John Richardson: The Wacousta Factor." In his *Canadian Literature: Surrender or Revolution.* Ed. Gail Dexter. Toronto: Steel Rail, 1978, pp. 13-25.

Monkman, Leslie. "Richardson's Indians." *Canadian Literature,* No. 81 (Summer 1979), pp. 86-94.

Moss, John. *Patterns of Isolation in English Canadian Fiction.* Toronto: McClelland and Stewart, 1974.

————. *Sex and Violence in the Canadian Novel: The Ancestral Present.* Toronto: McClelland and Stewart, 1977.

Northey, Margot. *The Haunted Wilderness: The Gothic and Grotesque in Canadian Fiction.* Toronto: Univ. of Toronto Press, 1976.

Pacey, Desmond. "A Colonial Romantic, Major John Richardson, Soldier and Novelist; Part I: The Early Years." *Canadian Literature*, No. 2 (Autumn 1959), pp. 20-31. "Part II: Return to America." *Canadian Literature*, No. 3 (Winter 1960), pp. 47-56.

Reaney, James. *Wacousta: A Melodrama.* Erin, Ont.: Porcépic, 1979.

Riddell, William Renwick. *John Richardson.* Toronto: Ryerson, 1923.

Story, Norah. "Richardson, John." In *The Oxford Companion to Canadian History and Literature.* Toronto: Oxford Univ. Press, 1967.

Catharine Parr Traill (1802-1899)

CARL P. A. BALLSTADT

Biography

CATHARINE PARR STRICKLAND was a member of one of the remark-able literary families of nineteenth-century England. Her elder sister Agnes was famous for *Lives of the Queens of England* (1840-48), which she wrote jointly with another sister, Elizabeth. Immigration of three members of the family, Catharine, Susanna, and Samuel, to Canada extends the significance of the family to the development of Canadian literature, as well.

Catharine Parr was born 9 January 1802 in London, Kent, prob-ably in Rotherhithe parish, the fifth daughter of Thomas and Eliza-beth Strickland. Her father was manager of the Greenland Dock, and the family had resided on the south bank of the Thames for many years.[1] Shortly after Catharine's birth, Thomas Strickland retired, and the family moved to East Anglia, living first near Norwich and then at Stowe House on the Suffolk side of the River Waveney overlooking the river valley and the town of Bungay. Catharine's earliest memories were of Stowe House, but in 1808 her father bought Reydon Hall, a large red-brick mansion near the coastal village of Southwold, Suffolk. Although Reydon was the principal residence of the family, Thomas also acquired a house in Norwich at Saint Giles Gates, with a coach manufactory on the premises.[2] He lived there for portions of each year, usually the winter months, with some members of the family accompanying him and some remaining at Reydon.

All these early environs were important in the education and the formation of the tastes of the Strickland children. In her autobio-graphical writings, Catharine expresses vivid memories of the natural beauty of the Waveney valley, historical sites such as the ruins of Bungay castle, excursions in search of wild flowers, and details of life at Stowe House and the legends associated with it. Reydon, dating from Tudor times, and Southwold offered an even greater range of associations, historical, natural, and supernatural. The children heard stories of the Battle of Sole Bay during the reign of Charles II, of smugglers and adventures at sea, of Cardinal Wolsey and his bridge over Blythburgh Ford, of the ruined city of Dunwich, of ghosts and witches and other aspects of East Anglian folklore. Their rural location and proximity to the sea gave opportunities to keep pets, to collect and to grow flowers, to wander the seashore in search of shells and other marine life, and to encounter gipsies, while time spent in Norwich afforded experience of a busy industrial and commercial centre.

The more formal education of the Strickland girls was chiefly parental, although, eventually, the elder sisters tutored the younger. It included the usual feminine accomplishments of sewing, embroidery, and handicrafts, but it was exceptional in that they had a wide range of literary and linguistic experience, as well. The relative isolation of Reydon allowed plenty of time for study, and Thomas Strickland's well-stocked library offered reading in the classics, in history and natural history, in books of travel, and in English literature, both early and modern. There is evidence that they also studied French and Italian and had available translations of German literature.[3]

According to Catharine, the availability of books and the isolation of their lives sparked the impulse to write in herself and Susanna, "to break the tedium of the dull winter." Their writing, in turn, "influenced . . . [their] elder and more gifted sisters, to take up the pen of authorship."[4] Catharine was fifteen at the time, and by the date of her father's death in May 1818, she must have had a stock of manuscripts available. Within a few months, through the agency of one of the executors of her father's estate, Mr. Morgan, she was the first of the sisters to have a book published: *The Tell Tale: An Original Collection of Moral and Amusing Stories* (1818).[5] Following the publication of that book, five of the Strickland sisters found outlets for their work in the expanding literary markets of the pre-Victorian decades. They began shaping their knowledge of history, nature, Suffolk lore and legend, life in Norwich, and their own family life and travels into books of instruction and amusement for children, sketches and poems for the elegant annuals which flourished in England from 1823, and eventually their own collections of poetry and tales. Literary periodicals for women, especially *La Belle Assemblée* and *The Lady's*

Magazine, became very important to them, Agnes and Eliza having editorial connections with the latter publication during the 1830s.[6]

It was common practice in the early decades of the nineteenth century for the authorship of books and periodical pieces to be indicated only by reference to other items the writer had produced. Catharine, in fact, maintained this policy even when her career was well established, many of her works being identified as by the authoress of *The Backwoods of Canada* (1836), her best-known work. She seemed to prefer anonymity, with the results that the extent of her contributions to annuals and periodicals is not yet known, although she certainly did submit items to particular editors,[7] and some of her early books have been attributed by bibliographers to her sisters, Agnes and Susanna. Fortunately, Traill produced a list of her early books in her old age to enable correct identification of authorship, and internal evidence supports her claims in several cases.[8]

According to her list, between the ages of fifteen and thirty she had published more than nine books, including the following: *The Tell Tale: An Original Collection of Moral and Amusing Stories* (1818); *Nursery Fables* (n.d.); *Little Downy; or, The History of a Field Mouse: A Moral Tale* (1822); *Prejudice Reproved; or, The History of the Negro Toy-Seller* (1826); *The Young Emigrants; or, Pictures of Canada, Calculated to Amuse and Instruct the Minds of Youth* (1826); *The Keepsake Guineas; or, The Best Use of Money* (1828); *Sketches from Nature; or, Hints to Juvenile Naturalists* (1830); *Narratives of Nature, and History Book for Young Naturalists* (n.d.); and *The Step Brothers* (n.d.). To this list, we can add *Disobedience; or, Mind What Mama Says* (1819); *Reformation; or, The Cousins* (1819); *The Juvenile Forget-Me-Not; or, Cabinet of Entertainment and Instruction* (1827); *Amendment; or, Charles Grant and His Sister* (1828); *The Flower Basket; or, Botanical Blossoms* (n.d.); and some of the items in *Tales of the School-Room* (n.d.).

The list of works and Catharine's statement that she contributed many items to annuals and periodicals make it apparent that she was a very active writer in the dozen years preceding her immigration to Canada. Along with other members of the family, she also established friendships with other Suffolk literary figures, notably James Bird of Yoxford, and Thomas Harral and his family. Bird was a poet who wrote frequently on Suffolk historical subjects, and

Harral the editor of Suffolk newspapers and of *La Belle Assemblée* from 1821 to 1831. The Stricklands frequently visited the Birds and corresponded with them, and Catharine was affianced to Francis Harral, Thomas' son. She was much distressed when the engagement broke off in 1831. During that year, however, Catharine was also broadening her horizons. She followed Susanna to London and lived and travelled with her aunt, Mrs. Leverton of 13 Bedford Square, spending many months with her and visiting such places as Bath, Oxford, Cheltenham, and Waltham. The journey gave her opportunities to meet other relatives, visit historical sites and galleries, and to assist Mrs. Leverton in the conduct of a school for young girls.[9]

It was in London that she first met Thomas Traill, a friend of Dunbar Moodie and fellow officer in the Twenty-first Royal Scottish Fusiliers. She met him again at Susanna's house in Southwold the following year and married him on 13 May 1832. Two days later, the Traills left Southwold by steamer bound for Edinburgh, and after several weeks of visiting Thomas' friends and relatives in Edinburgh and the Orkneys, they sailed from Greenock bound for Upper Canada on 7 July 1832.

Catharine's life in Canada is much better known than her life in England, largely because much of it is reflected in her many Canadian books. She and Thomas settled first near her brother, Samuel, on the shores of Lake Katchawanook north of Peterborough, and they lived subsequently at various locations: Ashburnham (now part of Peterborough), the Wolf Tower, Mount Ararat, and Oaklands on the shores of Rice Lake. They were burned out at Oaklands on 26 August 1857 and lived in a house provided by their friend Frances Stewart until Thomas' death on 21 June 1859, following which Catharine built a house at Lakefield, where she lived the rest of her life.

From her early days in Canada, Traill maintained an active literary career, keeping daily journals for long periods of time and transmitting the raw data of those journals into stories, essays, novels, and botanical studies. Following the publication of *The Backwoods of Canada* (1836), stories and sketches by her appeared in numerous British, American, and Canadian periodicals. In the 1850s, she began to produce books again: *The Canadian Crusoes: A Tale of the Rice Lake Plains* (1852); *The Female Emigrant's Guide, and Hints on Canadian Housekeeping* (1854) (reissued the following year and in several subsequent editions as *The Canadian Settler's Guide*); and *Lady Mary and Her Nurse; or, A Peep into the Canadian Forest* (1856). These were followed by botanical studies and natural-history essays: *Canadian Wild Flowers* (1868); *Studies of Plant Life in Canada; or, Gleanings from Forest, Lake and Plain* (1885); *Pearls and Pebbles; or, Notes of an Old Naturalist* (1894); and another book for children, *Cot and Cradle Stories* (1895).

Late in her life, she received a good deal of public recognition for her contributions to Canadian literature and nature study. Through the efforts of Lady Charlotte Greville, she received £100 from Britain, and in Canada she was the recipient of a testimonial organized by Sir Sandford Fleming and contributed to by many notable Canadians.[10] She also carried on lengthy correspondence with Canadian botanists. She died in 1899 at the age of ninety-seven.

Tradition and Milieu

A full assessment of Catharine Parr Traill's literary career must acknowledge the richness and variety of the cultural contexts which she knew and within which she wrote. Those contexts include not only the wide reading of the Strickland sisters in history and literature, the development of literature for children and young ladies in the early nineteenth century, and the increasing importance of natural history throughout the century, but also the growing availability of literature on North America. Even before her own emigration, Traill was interested in American literature, and, following her emigration, her literary career was enlarged by the challenge of New World subjects and the search for forms appropriate to the development of literature in a new country.

In her autobiographical writing, Traill acknowledges that the Strickland sisters read Thomas Day's *Sandford and Merton* (1783-89), *Robinson Crusoe*, *Arabian Nights*, and many of the English mediaeval ballads.[11] Their own books suggest that they were familiar with other well-known children's literature, particularly Maria Edgeworth's *Moral Tales* (1801), Sarah Fielding's *The Governess* (1745), Charles Lamb's and Mary Lamb's *Mrs. Leicester's School* (1809), and Sarah Trimmer's *Fabulous Histories* (1786). Several of Traill's books, notably *Reformation, The Keep-*

sake Guineas, and *Charles Grant and His Sister*, reflect the example of Day's *Sandford and Merton* in that they contrast two boys in order to reveal the model of goodness, the generous and honest boy, and the reformation of his opposite, the imperious and brutal boy. More important to Traill, however, was the kind of book which combined natural history with the moral lesson. Here the model was Sarah Trimmer, and the principal device the wise parent or teacher who guides and informs the child. Trimmer, in turn, was influenced by Jean-Jacques Rousseau's *Emile* (1762). Such a device appears in Traill's first book, *The Tell Tale*, and in her most popular children's book, *Little Downy; or, The History of a Field Mouse*. In the 1820s, many other writers like the Stricklands were following the examples available to them and providing both moral tales and natural history in a prelude to the Victorian thirst for useful knowledge and good habits of industry, prudence, and honesty.

The growing interest in natural history was well suited to Traill's tastes and aptitudes. As noted above, the location of her Suffolk homes offered opportunities for nature study, and the practice was encouraged by her parents. Her father was an ardent fisherman, and she frequently accompanied him on his expeditions along the Waveney and the Blyth rivers. His favourite book, and hers, was Izaac Walton's *Compleat Angler*, but he was also profoundly interested in natural history and geology, as is indicated in a dialogue which Traill recalled in her old age. It serves as an indication of the milieu of curiosity and speculation in which she was nurtured, a milieu which is reflected in her own wide-ranging inquiry into the mysteries of the natural world:

I remember listening with interest to discussions that were carried on between a certain old Doctor Lewis and my father on the theory of the formation of the globe as it was and is, and often the old doctor got very warm on the subject. He was too conservative to be very liberal and my father was too imaginative and often there were quick passages at arms between them but it was only word warfare in which as listeners in duty bound, we took our father's arguments as truths not to be disputed. While the Doctor held firmly to the mosaic chronology of the days of Creation being days of twenty-four hours, my father regarded time as unmeasured periods, not marked or divided by our present mode of reckoning: the solar light not then having been appointed to chronicle time, dividing it into days and months and years. The old Doctor would growl at my father's idea that the globe we live on was formed from the disrupted materials of a yet older planet, destroyed by the decree of the Creator for some cause known only to the great Originator ... and that the gigantic fauna, and flora, that are entombed in the strata of the rocks, and in the coal measures, might be the remains of what had been living organisms in a former world of which we only see the fragments.[12]

Traill's view of the subject was that such problems would probably be forever beyond man's understanding, but she never ceased to probe the mysteries of the earth nor to wonder at the adaptation of species to environments.

Her interest was also sparked by her elder sister Elizabeth, the leader amongst the family in botanical study. It was Elizabeth to whom Traill wrote her first reports of botanical life in the New World and who set her the example for botanical essays. Starting in August 1830, almost two years before Catharine departed for Canada, Eliza wrote "Biographies of Flowers" and essays on the months of the year for *The Lady's Magazine*. Catharine's own writing at the time was oriented towards fauna and geologic phenomena rather than plants.

Obviously, then, Catharine's literary development was much influenced by the actions of other members of the family, and that influence continued into her Canadian years. It was through the agency of Agnes that her work appeared in British periodicals, Agnes' own fame as the author of *Lives of the Queens of England* and her association with publishers being a distinct advantage. Agnes also exercised some editorial capacity in the production of Catharine's books, although one suspects that it was mostly limited to the use of her name on title pages to help establish Catharine's identity and to encourage sales. In addition, the elder sisters kept her informed of literary activities in Britain and continued to provide intellectual nourishment by sending parcels of books and writing materials to Canada.[13]

Traill's books, both early and late, indicate that she read widely in natural history, as well. The early *Sketches from Nature* and

Narratives of Nature draw upon the *Encyclopaedia Britannica*, Buffon's *Natural History of Birds, Fish, Insects and Reptiles* (1793), and Hector St. John de Crèvecoeur's *Letters from an American Farmer* (1782). The latter work may fairly be seen as one of the models for her own *Backwoods of Canada: Being Letters from the Wife of an Emigrant Officer, Illustrative of the Domestic Economy of British America*. The letter form of *The Backwoods* also suggests some indebtedness to Gilbert White's *Natural History and Antiquities of Selborne* (1789), particularly the letters on birds and plants. Certainly Traill was familiar with White's work, and she acknowledges in *Studies of Plant Life in Canada* a wish to produce a book which would have the status in Canadian literature that White's does in English literature: that of providing engaging reflections of a life close to nature, of its spiritual and aesthetic effects.

Traill's only guide to natural history in America during her early years in the backwoods was Frederick Pursh's *Flora Americae Septentrionalis* (1814). Later she had recourse to such works as Thomas McIlwraith's *The Birds of Ontario* (1890), Alexander Wilson's *American Ornithology* (1808), and *Reports of the Ottawa Field Naturalist's Society*, but most of her work is based on her own careful observation and information gleaned from the Indians and old settlers.

Even before her emigration, Catharine was aware of other reports of New World life. Her early *Young Emigrants* is based upon knowledge acquired from the letters of a Suffolk family who settled in Canada in 1821, possibly from her brother, Samuel, who emigrated in 1825, and from John Howison's *Sketches of Upper Canada* (1821). By the time she wrote *The Backwoods*, she had also read William Cattermole's *Emigration* (1831) and Tiger Dunlop's *Statistical Sketches of Upper Canada* (1832). Since she refers in a general way to works on emigration, it is probable that she knew others, some of which were written in the form of letters.[14]

One other type of English work which bears a relationship to both *The Backwoods* and *The Female Emigrant's Guide* is the manual for the education of young ladies. The Stricklands themselves addressed the subject of female education in Agnes' *Tales of the School-Room*, and it is probable that one of them reviewed Mrs. John Sandford's *Woman in Her Social and Domestic Character* (1831) in *The Lady's Magazine*.[15] There were many of these books dealing with the duties, education, manners, and domestic habits of women, and Traill's own comments in the introductions to her books suggest that she had them in mind in producing her own guides to domestic economy in British America:

> Indeed, a woman's pen alone can describe half that is requisite to be told of the internal management of a domicile in the backwoods, in order to enable the outcoming female emigrant to form a proper judgment of the trials and arduous duties she has to encounter. . . . She likewise wishes to teach them to discard everything exclusively pertaining to the artificial refinement of fashionable life in England; and to point out that, by devoting the money consumed in these incumbrances to articles of real use, which cannot be readily obtained in Canada, they may enjoy the pleasures of superintending a pleasant, well-ordered home. (*The Backwoods*, pp. 1-2)

She frequently repeats in both *The Backwoods* and *The Female Emigrant's Guide* her own preference for simplicity in life-style over the artificiality of the drawing room.

Although Traill's personality and experience were suited to an exploration of the natural world, she also received encouragement in this direction from her close friend Frances Stewart, writer of the letters in *Our Forest Home* (1889), and possibly from other British settlers in the Peterborough area, as well. Her own impression is that American settlers were less interested in natural history, having a more pragmatic orientation to the environment. Of course, the history of American literature on the New World environment is extremely rich, and much of it predates Traill's work. She, however, has a prominent place in the development of Canadian literature devoted to the exploration of the peculiar characteristics of the New World. Many works on emigration included résumés of the natural features of the country or the opportunities for hunting and fishing which it offered, but Traill was one of the first to fulfil the directive of the early critics that the first step in the creation of a Canadian literature ought to be to take inventory of the distinctive features of the new country before more sophisticated forms of literature are pursued. To some extent, *The Backwoods* begins the process by providing catalogues of flora and fauna, a technique that is characteristic of the literature of discovery and exploration.[16]

From that beginning, Traill went on to become essayist, novelist, storyteller, and chronicler of pioneer days. In doing so, she assumed a prominent place in two major categories of our literature: the literature of arrival and adaptation, and the literature of nature and rural life. In the first category, Traill did in prose what many of our nineteenth-century poets, people such as Alexander McLachlan, Adam Burwell, and Oliver Goldsmith, did in their narrative and descriptive poems. Of course, there have been many Canadian novels devoted to the experiences of the immigrant and pioneer. In the second category, Traill's successors include such prominent figures as Grey Owl, Peter McArthur, Frederick Philip Grove, Roderick Haig-Brown, Ernest Seton, and Charles G. D. Roberts. Malcolm Lowry recognized Traill's importance and her essentially poetic role as a nature writer in his poem "The Dodder":

The early flowered everlasting,
The hooded violet, the branching white
Wood-violet, brooding in the May night
Send petals forth even in Spring's wasting,
— Sped by the monkish cellarage-tasting
Of cowled cuckoo-pint, jack-in-the-pulpit! —
All of these, where there was but one poet,
In Katchewanook, lacked no contrasting.[17]

Critical Overview and Context

Although critics have accorded Catharine Parr Traill and Susanna Moodie prominent places in our literary history, assessments of their works as literature have been neither acute nor thorough until recently. Nineteenth-century reviews, particularly of relatively minor literature, tended to rely heavily on plot summary and long excerpts from a work to give the reader a sense of a book's nature and quality. When Canadian critics did begin to celebrate the careers of Moodie and Traill, more attention was paid to biographical details, perhaps because of the autobiographical nature of many of their works, than to actual literary achievement. In addition, Traill became the victim of her longevity, being treated as the "grand old lady" of Canadian literature and botanical study. She has also been viewed frequently in the shadow of Moodie; that is,

Roughing It in the Bush has, generally, been given priority when their works have been examined together, or Traill has been simply associated with her sister and not considered as an individual.[18] More recent criticism has endeavoured to redress the earlier imbalanced treatment of books by the two sisters.

Amongst the early articles on Traill, Hampden Burnham's "Mrs. Traill" in *The Canadian Magazine* is one of the best.[19] Burnham writes of her character on the basis of his personal knowledge, suggesting that the "best of her is unwritten" and that she was remarkable for her gentleness and dignity. He does, however, write briefly of specific works and finds *Pearls and Pebbles* her most significant literary achievement. His view of other works is that they are more "useful" than "ornamental." For example, he sees *The Canadian Crusoes* as a work in which "the naturalist has overborne the romancist," the pleasure which the book yields deriving from its detailed descriptions rather than its dialogue or plot.

Other critics, notably Ray Palmer Baker and Alec Lucas, have acknowledged Traill as the forerunner of the animal story and nature essay in Canadian literature, but the treatment of the issue has not been very detailed.[20] The observation is made in passing as part of the literary-historical survey.

There have been two fairly recent biographical studies of Traill.[21] Audrey Morris' *Gentle Pioneers: Five Nineteenth-Century Canadians* (1968) traces the interwoven lives of the Traills, the Moodies, and Samuel Strickland's family. Her work is based on considerable archival searching and close attention to the autobiographical dimension of their works. It provides useful background and attention to their family and community lives but does not offer a literary assessment. Sara Eaton, in *Lady of the Backwoods: A Biography of Catharine Parr Traill* (1969), takes the facts from Traill's journals, letters, and books and uses them to create a biography in the manner of "a story." She, too, does not attempt a literary assessment.

Lloyd M. Scott's article "The English Gentlefolk in the Backwoods of Canada"[22] is one of those which examines Traill and Moodie together, giving Moodie more prominent treatment in a discussion of immigrant social values and attitudes. Scott discerns no difference between the two women, finding in them one voice expressing middle-class bigotry, hypocrisy, pride, and a patronizing attitude towards inferiors, all of which derive from entrenched

English characteristics such as reserve and class consciousness, a doctrine of work, and deification of nature. In other words, he sees Traill and Moodie as victims of their background. His use of Traill's work is slight, and the essay lacks cohesiveness.

Amongst recent critics of Traill and Moodie, Clara Thomas has been most prolific. She wrote the introductions to the New Canadian Library editions of *The Backwoods of Canada* and *The Canadian Settler's Guide*, contributed an article on "The Strickland Sisters" to *The Clear Spirit: Twenty Canadian Women and Their Times* (1966),[23] and published "Journeys to Freedom" in *Canadian Literature*[24] and "Traill's Canadian Settlers" in *Canadian Children's Literature*.[25] Her article "The Strickland Sisters" is a useful biographical piece, most attention being given to the contrasting personalities of Traill and Moodie. She observes Traill's "rational and empiric nature," her common sense and adaptability. Thomas also briefly reviews the principal publications, noting the primary qualities of each and emphasizing Traill's clarity of style and the keenness of her observation. "Journeys to Freedom" is similar in the points it makes concerning Traill's personality and literary strengths, as she is measured against her sister and Anna Jameson. In this assessment, Traill is affirmed as the writer who "came the closest ... to finding benign perfection in this land,"[26] the one of the three in whom one finds the most positive point of view. Traill's positive outlook is also emphasized in "Traill's Canadian Settlers," an examination of two of her works, *The Young Emigrants* (1826) and *The Canadian Crusoes* (1852). By comparing the early work with the later, Thomas is able to point out the consistency of Traill's optimism and Christian acceptance of necessity in human affairs, while also illustrating the modification in her social attitudes effected by her own emigration and Canadian experience, and the formation of a vision of Canada based on the cooperation of various races and the management of nature's gifts.

Thomas' introductions to *The Backwoods* and *The Canadian Settler's Guide* present basic biographical detail, some of it erroneous, review the contents of each book, and emphasize Traill's personal qualities and literary strengths: her "maturity and commonsense," "sense of wonder," and religious faith are noted, as well as the precision, elegance, and clarity of her style.

In the last decade, critics have begun to grapple more intensely with the qualities of *The Backwoods* and *Roughing It* as works of literature, using comparison as the basis for discussion. T. D. MacLulich, for example, examines them as versions of the "Crusoe" fable but finds that neither book emulates absolutely the shape and impact of Defoe's *Robinson Crusoe*.[27] Moodie receives far more attention than Traill in the article because MacLulich finds her work psychologically richer, with more dramatic tension. He suggests that, while Traill's book is a "journey to freedom," it lacks tension because of the author's willingness to accept her place of exile and make it a "habitable kingdom," to accept necessity and "be saved by works." Moodie, on the other hand, resists adaptation, creates projections for her discontent, and lives by faith in the richness of her former mode of existence.

William Gairdner, in his "Traill and Moodie: The Two Realities,"[28] does much more to correct the imbalance in the appraisals of the two writers; he begins his article by observing the subordinate ranking of Traill's *The Backwoods* and declaring his intention to deal with it as a work of art. Unfortunately, he bases his treatment on the New Canadian Library abridged editions of both *The Backwoods* and *Roughing It*. In terms of structure, he finds Traill's book framed by two religious views or visions; the one at the beginning, a description of a "misty curtain" (*The Backwoods*, p. 13) which is lifted by invisible hands, he interprets as a metaphor for the idea that nature's beauty is revealed to us by a transcendent God. The concluding vision is of "a splendid pillar of pale greenish light" (p. 313), which he interprets as a sign of Traill's realization that the Holy Land is attained and that God is immanent in nature. The form of *The Backwoods* is said to be that of a conversion experience, the text between the framing visions being characterized by biblical allusions to wandering in the wilderness of brute fact in quest of the promised land. In psychological terms, that wandering takes the form of ambiguity in Traill's attitude to her new home: she loves nature because it leads man to God, yet she derives pleasure in seeing it destroyed by fire and axe in the effort to bring European order to the New World. Gairdner sees Traill clinging to the concept of a rationally ordered world, sensing irrationality and disorder, but denying them. Although she adjusts her belief in the English class system and Puritan values to the Canadian realities of pragmatism and hard work, she does not abandon those values. In this context, the final vision of green light is seen as signalling the proud heart humbled, the arrival through

suffering at a "state of grace, that is, of acceptance."[29] His position
is somewhat undercut by his assertions that Traill remains "endur-
ingly rational" in contrast to her sister, who explores the irrational
in man and nature and is much less certain of an ordered existence
and a conventional spirituality.

David Jackel, too, disagrees with the emphasis which other critics
have given to *Roughing It in the Bush* in their efforts to define a
Canadian literary tradition. His endeavour in "Mrs. Moodie and
Mrs. Traill, and the Fabrication of a Canadian Tradition" is to
question the critical positions regarding *Roughing It* by pointing
out the weaknesses of the book. He then proceeds to defend Traill
against charges that she is the advocate of cool reason, a writer
without sympathy or sociability, producing a book of " 'monotone
blandness.' "[30] Jackel sees her qualities in a much more positive
way, emphasizing her openness to experience, her powers of observation, her good judgement, moral vision, and sensitivity. These
qualities are considered as marks of a tradition of serious thought,
emotional restraint, good taste, order, and a keen sense of reality: a
tradition reaching back to pre-Romantic England and finding
expression in Canada in the works of Thomas Haliburton, Stephen
Leacock, Sara Jeannette Duncan, and W. O. Mitchell. In marked
contrast to Gairdner, Jackel suggests that Traill evidences a willingness to see the forest as "other," rather than to resist it as alien and
threatening to her identity. He also finds in adaptability or growth a
principle of order on which her book is based.

Obviously, the debate on Moodie and Traill has been lively and
serious in recent years; the probing and analysis are likely to
continue as more materials on these writers become available.[31]
One limitation that will need to be overcome is that of confining
discussion to their two best-known books. Traill's *The Backwoods*
was written within her first three years in the country, but she went
on to produce much more and to devote herself to a considerable
range of subjects and forms.

Traill's Works

Since Catharine Parr Traill enjoyed a long and prolific career as a
writer, it is not feasible in an essay to consider in detail all of her
productions, English and Canadian. Nevertheless, as the overview

makes apparent, critical attention has been focused almost exclusively on *The Backwoods of Canada*, leaving the variety of other forms in which she addressed her basic subjects and themes to rest in relative obscurity. In this essay, therefore, her Canadian career will be surveyed, and her variety demonstrated by giving more particular attention to her most important works.

Her Canadian career may be said to begin with *The Young Emigrants; or, Pictures of Canada, Calculated to Amuse and Instruct the Minds of Youth* (1826) because it so obviously reveals the interest she had developed in Canada following the emigration of a Suffolk family of her acquaintance in 1821 and of her brother, Samuel, in 1825. Her book is based on letters received from these people and on her own reading of John Howison and Lieutenant Hall.[32] Descriptions of the country are often directly quoted from the latter sources, and, presumably, information on the emigration process and the settlement on a cleared farm come from letters received. Indeed, the principal technique of the book is a series of letters written by two members of the emigrant family to a sister who remains in England because of illness; the letters provide her with accounts of Canadian customs, crafts, and people, the natural features of the country, and the advantages of diligence, prudence, and humility in the management of affairs. The book is Traill's most original early work, anticipating Captain Frederick Marryat's *The Settlers in Canada* (1844) by almost twenty years and showing Catharine's awareness both of the exigencies of emigration and the suitability of letters as a device for settlement narrative, the device she was to use for her book of "entertaining knowledge," *The Backwoods of Canada: Being Letters from the Wife of an Emigrant Officer* (1836).

The review of criticism above reveals that *The Backwoods* has rarely been examined as a literary construction; rather, it has been seen largely as an historical text depicting life in a certain phase of Canadian development. And yet, that it has been so often referred to by historians, literary and social, indicates that it is a work of quality: it survives by its stylistic character and, perhaps by implication, its structural elements, as well.

With *The Backwoods of Canada*, Traill was addressing a fertile subject in Canadian literature; the subject of emigration had already been given form in statistical accounts, handbooks, journals, and letters and was to find expression in numerous poems and novels. Her choice of form is probably derived from her familiarity with Crèvecoeur's *Letters from an American Farmer*, her own experiment with *The Young Emigrants*, and possibly from a knowledge of other settlement accounts.

A volume of letters as a medium for reporting to the homeland what transpires and what is found in the New World has the advantage of combining a sense of immediacy with judicious observation and reflection on general issues. In Traill's *The Backwoods*, we find such a balancing of subjectivity and objectivity: that is, we discover what happens to the Traills on the journey and during settlement, personal illness, and unforeseen difficulties; but we also find the author distancing herself by choosing or creating other voices for the expression of opinions on the advantages of emigration, or desirable attitudes in the emigrant, or for reporting success stories and raising questions on emigration issues.

Balance is, in fact, the chief structural and thematic principle of *The Backwoods*, and it is explicitly stated by Traill in Letter xv, one of the letters addressed to the idea of Canada as a land of opportunity:

> Let the *pro* and *con* be fairly stated, and let the reader use his best judgment, unbiassed by prejudice or interest in a matter of such vital importance not only as regards himself, but the happiness and welfare of those over whose destinies Nature has made him the guardian. (p. 283)

Here Traill's intent and personality are succinctly reflected; she writes not to lure the prospective emigrant to a false paradise, as some emigrant writers had done, but to delineate advantages and disadvantages. To do this, she chooses a rhetoric of balance. One significant manifestation of balance is the emulation of biblical phraseology and the frequent use of biblical quotations to convey advice to the emigrant, as in the following example from Letter xi:

> Like that pattern of all good housewives described by the prudent mother of King Lemuel, it should be said of the emigrant's wife, "She layeth her hands to the spindle, and her hands hold the distaff." "She seeketh wool, and flax, and worketh willingly with her hands." "She looketh well to the

ways of her household, and eateth not the bread of idleness."
(pp. 181-82)

Such biblical parallelism provides a model for Traill's own prose,
which is characterized by compound and compound-complex
sentences with many parallel constructions, as in the following
typical passage:

> For my part, I see no reason or wisdom in carping at the good
> we do possess, because it lacks something of that which we
> formerly enjoyed. I am aware it is the fashion for travellers to
> assert that our feathered tribes are either mute or give utter-
> ance to discordant cries that pierce the ear, and disgust rather
> than please. It would be untrue were I to assert that our
> singing birds were as numerous or as melodious on the whole
> as those of Europe; but I must not suffer prejudice to rob my
> adopted country of her rights without one word being spoken
> in behalf of her feathered vocalists. Nay, I consider her very
> frogs have been belied: if it were not for the monotony of their
> notes, I really consider they are not quite unmusical. . . . Their
> note resembles that of a bird, and has nothing of the creek in
> it. (p. 173)

Since she is stating *pro* and *con*, the first half of *The Backwoods*,
especially, is marked by antithesis as the reader is given details
concerning Old World/New World, wilderness/cultivation, picturesque scenery/cholera-infested city, present evils/future good,
comfortable shanties/disgusting shanties, economic progress/de-
struction of natural scenery. A complete list of contrasting observations would be very long, indeed. Even in the detailing of the
antithetical elements, we are given parallelism: a bird's note is
"sweet and thrilling" (p. 173); flowers expand in "woods and clearings" (p. 173); Canada is a land of "vast lakes and mighty rivers"
(p. 112); the emigrant's wife is "pining . . . and lamenting" (p.
105); and the Yankees are "industrious and ingenious" (p. 292).
The book is replete with such balanced expression and antithesis as
Traill strives consciously to be honest and just in her assessment of
Canada.

In its overall structure, the book evidences this rhetorical balance, as well, having four basic parts, the first two predominantly negative and the last two positive: the journey, the settlement, the naming, and the expectation.

The first seven letters are devoted to the emigration journey from the Old World to the site of the new home, and although we find the characteristic balance of expression and fairness of attitude in these letters, their focus is on the difficulties of the journey, "the perils of the great deep and the horrors of the pestilence" (p. 92). The inland journey, particularly, is marked by a succession of *trials*: people with bad manners, a "surly Charon" (p. 76), night in a forest maze, a hazardous bridge, corduroy roads, untracked woods, evidences of bad taste, inferior trees, and a wearying "immensity" of landscape (p. 14). The following brief paragraph presents an image of the new immigrant's bewildered condition, a condition Traill alludes to and plays upon later in the book:

> Imagine our situation, at ten o'clock at night, without knowing a single step of our road, put on shore to find the way to the distant town as we best could, or pass the night in the dark forest. (p. 76)

Letters VIII to XII, the settlement, do contain Traill's wish to be a namer of new things, but the emphasis is upon present evils, the forces of expediency and necessity, the battle by fire and steel against the wilderness, trials by the elements of wind and fire, the afflictions of bad roads and insects, and the loss of Old World historic lore and mystery.

Letters XIII to XVII reveal the emergence of the author as namer and discoverer, for in this section, more than in any of the others, we find catalogues of the wonders of the new surroundings together with an accounting of Canadian advancement and success. At the beginning of Letter XIII, the author virtually rejects expressions of regret for her exile and proceeds to dwell on the splendours of the Canadian winter, a visit to the winter camp of the Indians, and the attractiveness of Canadian birds. Letter XIV is exclusively devoted to descriptions of the botanical life of Upper Canada, which Traill finds "flung carelessly from Nature's lavish hand among our woods and wilds" (p. 232). The most notable rhetorical feature of these sketches is the emphasis on the plentitude and superlative nature of the plant life. In observing that particular plants are "very handsome" (p. 240), "exceedingly large" (p. 245), "extensive" (p. 249), "beautiful" (p. 245), "very elegant and numerous" (p. 250), and even "strong scented" (p. 253), Traill is both showing the excitement of discovery and refuting the common charge of English immigrants that there are no beautiful birds or charming flowers in Canada.[33]

By this stage of the book, the author is sufficiently adapted to her surroundings that she can playfully threaten to lead her reader into "the pathless mazes of our wild woods, without a clue to guide you, or even a *blaze* to light you on your way" (p. 255), as she had been led and abandoned on the journey to Peterborough. What she does in Letter xv, however, is to celebrate the progress of settlement and testify to Canada as "the land of hope" (p. 258), newness, and excitement. She declares her own happiness with the simplicity of her life in an extended passage contrasting European etiquette and fashion with the Canadian primals of liberty, prudence, economy, and industry, and, to prove the effect of these virtues, she recounts a Canadian success story of movement from trials, such as her own early letters reflect, to the achievement of the blessings of flourishing settlement. The effect of the story on Traill herself is to give an "additional stock of contentment, and some useful and practical knowledge" (p. 281). Letters xvi and xvii continue the evidence of progress and add to the catalogue of wonders in Indian life and flora and fauna, even though the narrative aspect of the letters necessitates the account of the ague which afflicts the family in the autumn of 1834 and which she notes "few persons escape" (p. 299) in the second year.

The final letter, xviii, clearly embodies several features which make it an appropriate resolution to the whole work, first because it contains a restatement of the author's contentment:

> . . . yet I must say, for all its roughness, I love Canada, and am as happy in my humble log-house as if it were courtly hall or bower; habit reconciles us to many things that at first were distasteful. It has ever been my way to extract the sweet rather than the bitter in the cup of life, and surely it is best and wisest so to do. . . . My husband is becoming more reconciled to the country, and I daily feel my attachment to it strengthening. (pp. 310-11)

In part, this attachment stems from the achievement of a comfortable and friendly society. One of Traill's persistent themes is to transform the wild "by the hand of taste" (p. 310) and to create a human proportion in the bush setting; to this end, she repeatedly endeavours to cultivate the wild plants and make them part of her garden. In the final letter, she extends the accomplishment of this task by envisioning a future in which

> ... all will be different; our present rude dwellings will have given place to others of a more elegant style of architecture, and comfort and grace will rule the scene which is now a forest wild. (p. 311)

I think it is not extreme to interpret the aurora borealis and "a splendid pillar of pale greenish light in the west," which she describes on the last page of her text, as emblems of the promise she anticipates. Characteristically, she gives the pillar of light a scientific explanation as part of her balanced perception of things, but her treatment of it as "a vision" (p. 313) associated with "another and a better world" (p. 313), perhaps both temporal and spiritual, accords with her expectation of mature settlement.

As has been noted above, the structure of *The Backwoods of Canada* derives not only from chronological elements but from differences in tone, subject, and authorial attitude. In part, deviations from dominant aspects of each section are accounted for by the rhetoric of balance which issues from Traill's personality, but some deviations also result from the retrospective character of portions of the letters. For example, Letter IX, concerning the early trials in the construction of a log house during the winter, also contains a catalogue of wild fruits and their uses, but much of the information, including descriptions of blossoms and summer conditions for a walk along the lakeshore, could only have come from later observation by Traill. By April 1833, she had not spent a summer in the backwoods. Such additions to early letters of information and analysis, which Traill must have gained later and recorded in her journals, serve to maintain the balanced view of the whole pioneer process and to show the author as a person with curiosity, an open mind, and a determination to be a namer of New World phenomena, even in the midst of the hardships of first settlement.

By the time of the publication of *The Backwoods*, Traill was a devoted writer of daily journals, and she was to continue the practice, although not with absolute regularity, for most of her life in Canada. Early letters indicate that she was planning a sequel to *The Backwoods* based on her journals, but the sequel was not published as a book in the early years; rather, it took the forms of stories, essays, novels, and botanical studies, the journals forming the raw data for her writing, even for *Pearls and Pebbles* and *Cot and Cradle Stories*. The journals, therefore, deserve some attention in a consideration of her literary career.

Since they encompass so many years and are rich in detail concerning domestic life, nature, excursions, and the lives of other settlers, they cannot be fully dealt with in this essay, but a few observations are worth making. One is that they show Traill developing a more poetic style immediately subsequent to the publication of *The Backwoods*, the journals possessing a greater volume of imagery than the book. The image of the "splendid pillar of pale greenish light in the west" on the last page of *The Backwoods* is, indeed, a prelude to a frequently recurring motif in Traill's journals, a motif which helps to counter the usual conception of her as a cool rationalist interested only in the scientific description and utility of objects. In numerous passages, she reveals herself as one enchanted with the transforming power of mist, frost, and snow, three phenomena which she associates with the power of fancy because they have the capacity to "veil" or alter the otherwise harsh and displeasing aspects of bush scenery. The following passage from her journal entry for 11 December 1837 is typical in its poetic imagery and the expressed enthusiasm for the magic:

Nothing can surpass the loveliness of the woods after a still heavy snow shower has loaded every bough and spray with its feathery deposit. The face of the ground so rough and tangled choked with a strange mass of uptorn trees broken boughs and timbers in every stage of unsightly decay seems as by the touch of some powerful magician's wand to have changed its character; unrivaled purity softness and brilliancy has taken the place of confusion and vegetable corruption. It is one of the greatest treats this country affords me to journey through the thick forest after a heavy snow whether it be by the brilliant light of the noonday sun shining in cloudless azure and

giving a gemlike brightness to every particle that clothes the
surface of the ground — and in heavy masses on the evergreens converting their dark fan shaped boughs into foliage of
glittering whiteness and most fantastic form — or by the
softer light of the full moon and frosty stars looking down
through the snowy tops of the forest trees sometimes shining
through a veil of silvery haze which the frost converts into a
sparkling rime that encases every spray and twig with
crystal.[34]

It is primarily such transformations and the ensuing enchantment
that make winter Traill's favourite Canadian season, and she writes
at length upon it, both from the vigour and time which the season
gives her to expend upon her journal entries.

In entries for all seasons, however, she reveals her curiosity and
her openness to all aspects of her surroundings and restates her
favourite themes: that everything in nature, no matter how small, is
significant and wonderfully adapted; that God's goodness and
power are proclaimed in all things; and that she prefers "nature's
volume" to the crowded drawing room or ballroom. It is in the
journals, also, that she first gives form to the most significant theme
in her fiction, child lost — child found.

The theme first appears in an advertisement copied from *The
Cobourg Star* for 2 August 1837 which notes the loss of a child near
the Rice Lake plains and offers a reward for her discovery. Traill
gives further details in her entry and then adds to it the notice in the
same issue of *The Cobourg Star* that the child had been found near
Cold Springs, "having wandered in the woods five days and
nights." She proceeds to give accounts of other children lost and
found, both in her own district and in others, including one
concerning the loss of three children who entered the forest in
search of cows. The piece is fascinating because it reveals Traill
turning fact into fiction in one spontaneous, uninterrupted movement. The passage begins, "It must now be three or four years ago
since the sympathies of the inhabitants in the township of ———— in
one of the Western Districts of the Province were excited to a high
degree of most painful interest by the sudden disappearance of
three young persons, the eldest a girl about thirteen years of age
. . . ."[35] Before long, Traill gives names to the mothers of the children, gives an account of a consoling friendship which develops

between them during the months and years of the children's absence, creates conversations between them on earthly affliction and heavenly hope, and brings the story to a climax with the implied return of the children at a time when Thirza Hill, the mother whose cows were being sought, is near death by consumption. This is, of course, the prototype story for *The Canadian Crusoes*, Traill's most extended piece of fiction.

Before finding its form as a novel, however, the story of children lost in the woods underwent several changes and appearances. In 1843 Traill had a story published in *Chambers' Edinburgh Journal*, "A Canadian Scene," about the loss of, and search for, a neighbour's child.[36] Traill and her husband took part in the search, so that much of the story is about the techniques of searching and the progressive loss of energy for the search as hope wanes and the attention of the searchers is distracted by the profusion of berries and the pleasantness of the weather. The resolution, sudden and brief, is the discovery of the child near an abandoned house. The style here is very concrete and restrained, giving a vivid sense of the actions of the searchers and the irony of their exciting encounters with life in the forest. There is little sentiment here.

Another appearance of the motif, in "The Mill of the Rapids: A Canadian Sketch," is also restrained, the incident of children lost forming only a portion of the sketch, being an account by the daughter of the miller about an occasion when she and a brother were lost not more than a mile from their home. The chief interest of the sketch is that it contains the following statement by Traill:

> Now, I have almost as great a love for a story about being lost in the woods, as I had when a child on the knee for the pitiful story of the Babes in the Wood. I eagerly besought Miss Betty to favour me with the history of her own and her brother's wanderings.[37]

The comment helps to confirm what the frequency of Traill's attention suggests, that she was a fascinated collector of stories of children lost.

In 1849 "The Two Widows of Hunter's Creek" appeared in *The Home Circle*.[38] It is reportedly part of a letter addressed to Agnes Strickland, as are some of the other pieces which found publication in Britain; it is also a rewrite of the journal entry discussed above.

In the published story, however, the narrator is an old American major, although the setting is the Canadian woods near the Credit River. The two families are American settlers, the Hartley family being of New England Puritan stock, and the Bridges family staunch United Empire Loyalists. The names of the widows are the same as in the journal entry, Thirza and Mary, but the roles are reversed. Mary becomes the consumptive and dweller in hope, while Thirza is the nurse and comforter. The body of the story is about the mutual support of Mary and Thirza in their loss of Thirza's one child, Rachel, and Mary's two, Anne and Michael. On the day of Mary's death, five years after the disappearance of the children, she experiences a resurgence of hope, and the children return out of the bush in Indian dress, Rachel leading by the hand a child whom she had by her Indian husband. Missionaries near the Lake Huron shores have directed the children towards the homes they had never forgotten. The emphasis in this story is, of course, on the sufferings of the widowed mothers and the tension between Mary's earthly hope for her children and her longing for heavenly release; the dialogue, therefore, is sentimental, formal, and marked by biblical archaisms.

At the end of the story, the major rises saying, "I only am left of all whom they once knew as friends in this place," and he walks away, "his head bent down, and his thoughts evidently busy with scenes and friends of past days." The significance of this ending for us is that the words apply to Catharine Parr Traill, concerning both the treatment of the lost-child motif and the general character of her literary career. The Englishwoman who reports in *The Backwoods* that there is nothing of historic lore and supernatural mystery to stimulate the imagination becomes the voice of the Canadian pioneer, an apostle of his suffering, endurance, accomplishments, and the milieu in which he lived.

Certainly this is one of her major accomplishments in *The Canadian Crusoes: A Tale of the Rice Lake Plains*, the culmination of her lost-child entries and sketches. The story is set in the Rice Lake district immediately following the Seven Years' War, when the Indian in Upper Canada could still be thought of as enemy and the woods a few miles from major waterways were unknown or travelled only by the trapper. In choosing such a period and a setting, Traill intensifies the problems of pioneer life, creates her own story of the maze and enigma of the forest, and depicts the qualities of character necessary to confront it and survive in it.

As in its earlier versions, the story involves three children, Catharine and Hector Maxwell and their cousin Louis Perron, who enter the forest on a June day in search of the cows. They become lost, wander north to Rice Lake, and effect their own survival by their Crusoe-like resourcefulness over a two-year period. They also rescue an Indian girl from death by exposure; she becomes one of the party, and a mutual exchange of knowledge takes place. The climax of the story involves captivity by the Indians and a second rescue of Indiana; the resolution includes the return home of the young people by the guidance of the old trapper, Jacob Morelle, and the marriages of Hector and Indiana, Louis and Catharine.

The novel has two main levels of meaning: it is a fable about the creation of a civilized society, and it is a manual of elemental pioneering and survival. On both levels the story is interesting, and the considerable success which the book enjoyed may be attributed to both the timeless quality of this fable and the authoritative and detailed nature of its guidance. Its weaknesses are the rather stiff, formal dialogue and the excessiveness, for the modern reader, at least, of its religious sentiment and proselytizing.

As fable, *The Canadian Crusoes* has a wealth of association with all the lost-children stories of fairy tale, legend, and poetry. It also has specifically Canadian associations, for, as the evolution of Traill's book indicates, the incidence of children and hunters lost in the woods was, and still is, a common occurrence. Traill even extends its meaning by including in Appendix A a reference to the "Wild Man of the far West," indirectly connecting her tale with stories of the "Wild Man" and suggestions that he was a lost child.[39] In that it is a story of survival and self-realization celebrating the strengths of an earlier age, one may be tempted to see *The Canadian Crusoes* as related to Margaret Atwood's *Surfacing* with its four wanderers, even though the circumstances of challenge and survival are extremely different.

In any case, for its own time Traill's *Crusoes* expresses the myth of Canadian virtue deriving from contact with the immense wilderness. Her children are not brutalized by the experience, but made whole. Given the evidence of Traill's fascination with the lost child, her story may indeed be motivated by her own success in meeting the challenge of pioneer life, so different from what she had known in England.[40]

In its political rather than psychological character, *The Canadian Crusoes* offers a microcosm of the society Traill envisions. The cooperation of her characters with one another, Scots, French, and Indian, each contributing his or her strength to a common enterprise, suggests a model for Canada. Such an interpretation is warranted not only by the mutual instruction of the four young people but by the events, language, and vision of the concluding chapters.

The most significant event is that "Beam of the Morning," daughter of the Ojibwa chief and enemy to the Mohawk, Indiana, releases the latter from torture and execution, having been counselled to do so by Catharine. Thus, the violence of Indian law is replaced by Christian forgiveness and a "covenant of peace and good-will [is] entered upon by old Jacob and the chief" (p. 331). Following her release, Indiana decides to rejoin her white friends and accompanies Jacob and Catharine down the Otonabee River towards Rice Lake. In the account of their journey, the author gives a vision of a new order:

> The sun is now rising high above the pine trees, the morning mist is also rising and rolling off like a golden veil as it catches those glorious rays — the whole earth seems awakening into new life — the dew has brightened every leaf and washed each tiny flower-cup. . . . (p. 337)

The sense of newness in nature accords with the emotional state of the two girls, but the author takes the reader beyond this to a vision of the future: of Gore's Landing, the village church, the plank road, the tasteful garden, and the pretty farms. The Crusoes are the forerunners of this transformation, seeing in Mount Ararat and the Rice Lake shore a good place to settle. In the manner of romance, however, they return to their parents and follow their adventures with marriages and movement to a new settlement area.

In her preface to the book, Agnes Strickland dwells on its capacity as a manual to Canadian geography and natural history. The richness of its detail does, in fact, contribute a sense of authenticity to the book as well as help to display the practicality and resourcefulness of these Canadian children. In considerable degree, it is also a book of wisdom literature containing maxims on conduct and expressions of Christian faith. Many of the latter are directed to the savage, although physically superior, Indiana, as the white children, with a conviction of moral and intellectual superiority, seek to enlighten her. Their proselytizing zeal is an expression of Traill's own belief, but it is also an essential preparation for the Christian acts of the resolution: Indiana's willingness to give her life for Catharine's and Catharine's counselling of Beam of the Morning to forgive her enemy. Along with their missionary zeal, however, Traill's characters show their openness and tolerance, most fully expressed in the marriage of Hector to Indiana at the end.

In much of her fugitive prose, Traill continues to perform the role of chronicler of pioneer life. The writing falls into two divisions, the informal, discursive essay and the story, which she often characterizes as "Forest Gleanings" both in specific pieces of writing and in the title she gives to a major series published in *The Anglo-American Magazine*.[41] Most of the stories are less interesting to the modern reader than the essays. The former are not distinguished by any novelty of form or structure; their chief interest is thematic, and the theme is emigration and settlement. "The Blockhouse" is the tale which is least successful and which is also least devoted to the settlement process.[42] Although the setting is backwoods, the plot is a melodramatic unfolding of the secret of the English birth and history of the hero, Philip Harding, and his beloved neighbour, Alice. Not surprisingly, Philip returns to the Old World when he gains his inheritance. "The Lodge in the Wilderness" displays more irony and humour.[43] It is an incomplete fictionalized treatment of the arrival of an English gentleman and his lady at a prepared backwoods farm, the rude realities of the farm dispelling the dream in which they had journeyed. The Traills' own experience seems to be reflected in this tale.

The longest and most interesting treatment of the pioneer process is "The Settlers Settled; or, Pat Connor and His Two Masters."[44] It is a humorous story in four parts, "The Outset," "The Purchase," "The Progress," and "The Settlement," the humour being derived from ironic techniques and the lively dialect of the servant, Pat Connor. Arthur and Charles Windham, youngest sons in a disinherited family, adopt emigration as a means to maintain an appropriate station in life. With the blessing and financial support of their Uncle Philopson, they buy a cleared farm near Cobourg from a disillusioned Englishman, Tom Walker, who is very similar to Tom

Wilson of Susanna Moodie's *Roughing It in the Bush* and like him is returning to England with his pet bear. The story is advanced both by third-person narration and by the exchange of letters between Charles Windham and his uncle; it is by means of these two devices that the ironic treatment of the settlement process is rendered. While Uncle Philopson dispenses in his letters from afar impractical advice on farming, the engagement and management of servants, and the maintenance of social position, the narrative reveals Charles and Arthur facing the exigencies of settlement, including the problems created by a poor choice of land, the dishonesty of their hired domestic help, the borrowing propensities of their Yankee neighbours, and the harsh realities of Canadian agriculture. Contrary to their uncle's observations about Irish servants, Pat Connor turns out to be the boys' salvation, indeed, the true master. His industriousness and reliability, his homely and practical wisdom are balanced against the uncle's maxims based on English farming practice and aristocratic conduct. Under Pat's tutelage, Charles, whose tastes run to the simple and natural, acquires the humility, practicality, and habits of hard work necessary for success as a Canadian farmer, while Arthur, who is less suited to the hardness of pioneer life, finds a position in Toronto. The only exception to the following of Pat's advice is that Charles, instead of taking a Yankee girl as wife, chooses a neighbouring, recent English emigrant who is discovered to be a second cousin, a member of an estranged branch of his mother's family. The resolution of all is that the family is reunited; Uncle Philopson finds pleasure in Charles's progress and marriage, provides him with a more suitable farm, and even approves of Pat Connor.

The style of "The Settlers Settled" varies with the techniques employed, from the judicious, unpretentious observations of Charles on his affairs, to the more formal, imperative tone of Uncle Philopson and the lively, humorous brogue of Pat Connor, sprinkled as it is with Americanisms that remind one of Sam Slick's language in T. C. Haliburton's sketches. The following excerpt is a good example of the latter type:

> "If them praties arn't illigantly boiled, and dried too with the pickle (i.e. pinch) of salt just dusted over their jackets by way of sauce! There's a pretty go now — if the handle arn't

clean comed off the tea-pot! That tin-man's ware arn't worth the snuff of a rush candle."

"That was your setting the tea-pot on the hot coals," said Charles, somewhat tartly; "you know, Connor, I warned you of that a week ago, and told you, besides, I detested boiled tea. You Irish can never make tea without setting the tea-pot on the embers."

"Well, thin, if it isn't the raal Yankee fashion, your honour. Why bless you, their tea-pot stands it like anything."

The Windhams could hardly help laughing at the adroit way in which Pat turned the question from the tea to the tea-pot.

"But what is to be done? this is one of the miseries of this horrid place," broke forth Arthur, with a sigh, almost deep enough for a groan, "how is the tea to be poured out?"

"Why, Master Arter, the spout isn't gone yet, and worse things will happen in this country than the handle coming unsoldered of a tin tea-pot," said Pat, seizing the dilapidated vessel in his huge fist; and, pouring out the tea, set the cups reeking on the table, with an air of infinite satisfaction, remarking upon its superior strength and high colour from the mode of cooking it.[45]

In sketches and informal essays, such as "The Rice Lake Plains," "Female Trials in the Bush," "Society in the Bush," and "A Walk to Railway Point," Traill finds another medium for the celebration of the accomplishments of the pioneer.[46] Essentially she is showing that the promise of *The Backwoods of Canada* has been fulfilled, indeed, so successfully that by mid-century Canadians need to be reminded of the steps by which the "desert" has been transformed, with God's blessing, into a "fruitful garden."[47] She reminds her readers of the disillusionment and suffering of British gentlemen and gentlewomen, and of the endurance, industry, and self-sufficiency by which they survived and flourished. Together with the poor Irish and Scots immigrants, they are proclaimed as the heroes of Canadian development and mid-century prosperity.

Yet other essays are contradictory to her chronicles of the pioneer, revealing a degree of ambivalence about the impact of settlement and cultivation on the Canadian forest. In "A Glance within the Forest,"[48] "Voices from the Canadian Woods: The White Cedar,"[49] and "Love of Flowers,"[50] she is a natural-history essayist and ecologist developing her role as namer of Canadian life, showing the pleasure of examining and appreciating all natural phenomena, preserving a record of what was, and lamenting the disappearance of the flora and fauna that settlement destroys. The lament is implicit in, and one motivation for, her studies of plant life, but it is frequently stated explicitly in the resolutions of essays, as in the concluding paragraph of "A Glance within the Forest":

> To those who love the forest and its productions, the continual destruction of the native trees will ever be a source of regret, even while acknowledging its necessity, for with the removal of the sheltering woods must also disappear most of the rare plants, indigenous to the soil, that derive their nurture from them, some indeed so entirely dependent on the decaying vegetation of the trees beneath which they grow that they perish directly they are deprived of it. Exposed to the effects of drying winds and hot sunshine they wither away and are seen no more. Soon may we say, in the words of the old Scotch song —

> "The flowers of the forest are a'wede away."[51]

The reference to many of Traill's essays and stories as "Forest Gleanings" suggests that they were to form part of a book on life in the colony, and such an intention is confirmed by her unpublished manuscripts. She worked on several pieces of very large design. "The Pioneers" and "The United Empire Loyalists" are both drafts of novels meant to perform the same function as the essays, and "Under the Pines" was to be her autobiography and sequel to *The Backwoods*, including large-scale treatment of the Strickland family in England and the chronicle of her own trials as a backwoods settler who becomes a successful author devoted to the articulation of Canadian life.[52]

Of course, another of Traill's books on the accomplishments of the pioneer was published two years after *The Canadian Crusoes*. *The Female Emigrant's Guide, and Hints on Canadian Housekeeping* (1854), also known as *The Canadian Settler's Guide* (1855), was, to judge by the frequency of its publication, a very popular work.[53] As the original title indicates, this book is a further development of that facet of *The Backwoods of Canada* which is derived from the English manuals for women. In contrast to the English books, Traill's *Guide* is concerned with the useful arts rather than elegant manners, and doing for oneself rather than managing others.

Although *The Female Emigrant's Guide* has elements similar to *The Backwoods*, it exhibits differences in both content and tone. After more than twenty years as a resident of Upper Canada, Traill wished to remedy the earlier book's deficiencies in instruction by providing more essential information on horticultural and domestic resources and procedures, and less personal narrative, but a comparison of the two books shows a marked advance in the degree of Traill's Canadianization, as well. The promise of the earlier book has been realized and is conveyed in a very affirmative attitude towards the new country:

> Here all is new; time has not yet laid its mellowing touch upon the land. We are but in our infancy; but it is a vigorous and healthy one, full of promise for future greatness and strength. (p. 30)

> It is delightful this consciousness of perfect security: your hand is against no man, and no man's hand is against you. We dwell in peace among our own people. What a contrast to my home, in England, where by sunset every door was secured with locks and heavy bars and bolts; every window carefully barricaded, and every room and corner in and around the dwelling duly searched, before we ventured to lie down to rest, lest our sleep should be broken in upon by the midnight thief. (p. 58)

Throughout there is a sense of well-being and delight, dignity and independence to be found in the new land.

Another difference in the later book is that the emigrant is cautioned against having a too negative attitude to the forest. Its resources are celebrated, and this is nowhere more apparent than in the most "literary" section of the book, the series of appreciations of the months of the year and the extracts from "Letters from Canada" which form its conclusion. In these, as in all of her writing, Traill is affirmative: "there is good at all seasons, and in every-thing" (p. 213).

Throughout her long literary career, she sustained her positive attitude towards Canada, and towards life generally. In additional books for children, *Lady Mary and Her Nurse; or, A Peep into the Canadian Forest* (1856) and *Cot and Cradle Stories* (1895), she expresses her love of nature and her close observation, chiefly in stories of small animals. In the latter book, she draws heavily upon her own childhood years and some of her early literary work. *Lady Mary*, in contrast, depicts Canadian customs, Indians, and natural phenomena, mostly of the Rice Lake plains, and celebrates Canadian virtues of liberty and independence. The form is the dialogue between the wise teacher and the curious child, and the style successfully reflects the manners and enthusiasm of each. The distinctions are particularly apparent when the child tells a story; she is easily distracted from her main topic by associated ideas and by her own impetuosity. The nurse, as a persona for Traill, is rich with information, is aware of what appeals to children, and is constant in her praise of Canada.

Although Traill continued to write in many modes, including drafts of an autobiography following the publication of Jane Margaret Strickland's *Life of Agnes Strickland* (1887), her principal publications were on natural history. *Studies of Plant Life in Canada; or, Gleanings from Forest, Lake and Plain* was apparently prepared as early as the mid-1860s, but a publisher could not be found for the rather large work, and a selection was made to accompany lithographed illustrations of flowers by Agnes Fitzgibbon, Susanna Moodie's daughter, and issued as *Canadian Wild Flowers* (1868). The complete *Studies* was eventually published in 1885, with twenty plates of illustration by her niece.

In some degree, these are scientific works containing necessary technical, botanical information, but Traill conceived of them as literature, as "forest gleanings" which she hoped would be a Canadian version of Gilbert White's *Natural History and Antiquities of Selborne*. She was a self-taught botanist in whose philosophy the study of flowers is a civilizer and a medium for the development of love of country. It was the medium of her own attachment to Canada, and she seeks to promote it in others by the charming informality of botanical essays replete with anecdote, folklore, analogy, and historical, ethical, and religious observations. The lives of the old settlers and Indians are touched in her reminiscences, and poets, major and minor, are quoted to demonstrate the universality of the love of flowers. Often her own imagination is called into play to reflect the character of species, as in this description of the water lily with its imagery of courtship and its sense of the design in nature:

> On the approach of night our lovely water-nymph gradually closes her petals, and slowly retires to rest on her watery bed, to rise again the following day, to court the warmth and light so necessary for the perfection of the embryo seeds, and this continues till the fertilization of the germ has been completed, when the petals shrink and wither, and the seed-vessel sinks down to the bottom of the water, where the seeds ripen in its secret chambers. Thus silently and mysteriously does Nature perform her wonderful work, "sought out only by those who have pleasure therein."[54]

The shape of each piece is determined by the special character of the species and by the wide range of information which Traill has acquired, often from others, but mostly from her own observation. Thus it is that the essays contain many recollections of her first settlement and her life on the Rice Lake plains, and even a retelling of her favourite motif, the lost child, in her essay on the swamp blueberry.[55] Clearly, the botanical works are the culmination of the urge to explore and to name Canadian phenomena which Traill first declared in *The Backwoods of Canada*.

Pearls and Pebbles; or, Notes of an Old Naturalist (1894), Traill's last published work for adults, is an appropriate summation of her career, for it includes reflections of her life, both early and late, and a restatement of all her major themes: that all of nature is wonderfully ordered and adapted; that small things lead to great; that man will develop humility and awe, and find rules for his own conduct in the study of nature; that nothing is lost. Once again the reader is impressed with the balanced perception evidenced in style and structural elements, for these essays are organized about such concepts as yesterday and today, illusion and reality, great and small, life and death.

Even though the book is a collection of essays, like *The Backwoods of Canada* and *The Canadian Crusoes*, it has a discernible, artistic shape based upon the Bible. All three books begin with an exile or departure and end with the attainment of a new home. Such a pattern is obviously derived from Traill's religious convictions that man's earthly home, although fascinating, is not his true home. The first essay in *Pearls and Pebbles*, "Pleasant Days of My Childhood," is a reminiscence of May Day at the childhood home on the banks of the Waveney, "our Eden" where the children gathered flowers and "the garden was laid out right daintily."[56] But the reminiscence ends with a "Lament for the May Queen":

> The cowslip bends her golden head,
>   And daisies deck the lea;
> But ah! no more in grove or bower
>   The Queen of May we'll see.

(p. 42)

All that remains are memories which "come back to my wearied soul to cheer and soothe the exile in her far distant forest home" (p. 41).

The second essay, "Sunset and Sunrise on Lake Ontario: A Reminiscence," is similar in shape. It is about the beauty of the voyage up the Saint Lawrence, including "visions of pleasant rustic homes" (p. 44), "childish delight" (p. 44), the magic landscape of the Thousand Islands, and Lake Ontario, which "like a sea of gold" with "clouds of mist . . . broke into all sorts of fanciful forms" (p. 47). But "in a moment all was changed" (p. 48). The mist lifts and the fanciful illusion is gone leaving "but a dream of beauty on the gazer's mind — a memory to be recalled in after years when musing over past scenes of a life where lights and shadows form a mingled pattern of trials and blessings" (p. 48).

The essays which follow, for example, "The First Death in the Clearing" and "Alone in the Forest," give some sense of those trials and the unpleasantness of the pioneer landscape, but the emphasis is upon the blessings to be discovered in the place of exile. Even here there are ordered sequences. The essays on birds are followed by those on the forest in general and the people who dwell in it. The last segment of essays is on relatively obscure subjects, vegetable instinct, pollen, grasses, mosses, and lichens, as Traill endeavours to show that nothing is without significance.

Her investigation of the minute and the obscure prepares the reader for the insights and affirmations of her finest and concluding essay, "Something Gathers Up the Fragments." It is about natural processes and the interrelatedness of all things, themes which are rendered in lucid and concrete prose:

> As the lichens decay they give place to the mosses, and these, as they increase, send down their wedge-like roots between the fissures of the bark, penetrating into the tissue of the wood, already softened by the decomposition of the former occupants. The dew, the showers, the frosts and snows of winter, falling upon the sponge-like mosses, fill them with moisture, invigorate them and increase them till they form thick mats that hide the surface of the wood. . . .
> The very heart of the wood has yielded up its strength and hardness under the influences of the agencies brought to bear upon it. A few more years and that fallen tree will be no more seen. The once mighty tree, with the mosses and lichens alike, will have returned their substance to Mother Earth. "Ashes to ashes, dust to dust." (pp. 239-40)

The whole essay has a quality of consolation about it. Tragedy and death are not the end; nothing is lost. The fallen forest becomes "the rich black vegetable mould" in which "a stranger and an emigrant from a far-off land" may sow the grain "for the life-sustaining bread for himself and his children" in his new homeland (p. 241). In Traill's outlook, as in that of the early American Puritans, the white man's transformation of North America is part of God's design. Although, as we have seen, she laments the disappearance of specific forms, for her the ideal landscape is one reflecting human taste and order.

The structure of the book is reinforced by the longest essay in it, "In the Canadian Woods," a four-part piece on the seasons beginning with spring with its wild flowers, like the Indians "fast passing away" (p. 131), and ending with winter, which Traill makes the analogue of the change from wilderness to civilization:

> The Frost King is abroad, and as by the magic touch of an enchanter's wand has wrought a wondrous change within the forest as well as on lake and stream.
> What has become of the unsightly heaps of brushwood, the

débris of fallen rotting leaves, of stalks of withered flowers and rank herbage, the blackened stumps, the old prostrate wind-blown trees? Where are they now? Here is purity without a sign of decay. All that offended the sight in our forest walks has vanished. (p. 146)

As the snow transforms the stumps and fallen trees to "purity without a sign of decay," so "fair dwellings, tasteful gardens, fruitful orchards, . . . the steamboat, the railroad, the telegraph" replace "the primeval settlement house," "the disfiguring stump," and "the ugly snake-like rail fences" — "all are gone — things that *were*, not things that *are*" (p. 148).

Each of Traill's major works, therefore, *The Backwoods of Canada*, *The Canadian Crusoes*, *The Female Emigrant's Guide*, and *Pearls and Pebbles*, is ultimately ironic. While celebrating the achievement of a new home, each draws its energy from her own fascination with the primeval forest and its resources. She laments its passing and expresses her own ambivalence in a poem which concludes the essay "In the Canadian Woods":

Oh! wail for the forest! the green shady forest!
No longer its depths may the hunter explore;
.For the bright golden grain
Shall wave o'er the plain.
Oh, wail for the forest, its glories are o'er!

(p. 149)

Such fascination and ambivalence she shares with many other Canadian writers.

NOTES

[1] Mary Agnes Fitzgibbon, "Biographical Sketch," in *Pearls and Pebbles; or, Notes of an Old Naturalist*, by Catharine Parr Traill (Toronto: Briggs, 1894), p. iv. See also "Memorials of the Stricklands: A Family Chronicle," TS, in the Traill Family Papers (T.F.P.), VII, 10852; and "Family History," TS, T.F.P., V, 8262. These and all other unpublished papers cited in the Traill Family Papers are in the Public Archives of Canada, Ottawa.

[2] Thomas Strickland's Will, Somerset House, London, England.

[3] Catharine Parr Traill, *The Backwoods of Canada: Being Letters from the Wife of an Emigrant Officer, Illustrative of the Domestic Economy of British America* (London: Charles Knight, 1836), p. 15. All further references to this work appear in the text. See also T.F.P., VI, 8867. The Stricklands' cousin Thomas Cheesman, an artist, was a student of Italian and interested his cousins in the language.

[4] "Some Reminiscences of the Life of Mrs. C. P. Traill," TS, T.F.P., VI, 8864-65.

[5] Notebook, T.F.P., III, 4066. Mary Agnes Fitzgibbon calls this book *The Blind Highland Piper and Other Tales* (see Fitzgibbon, "Biographical Sketch," p. xiv), but I have found no evidence that the book was published with that title. "The Blind Highland Piper" is one of the stories in *The Tell Tale*.

[6] Susanna Moodie, "To the Editor of *The Literary Garland*," *The Literary Garland*, 4 (June 1842), 319. Internal evidence also suggests that Agnes and Eliza were heavily involved in *The Lady's Magazine*.

[7] Catharine Parr Strickland, Letters to Susanna and to James Bird [1831], Glyde Papers, Public Record Office, Ipswich, England.

[8] Notebook, T.F.P., III, 4066; see also the letter from Susanna to Mary Russell Mitford, in *The Friendships of Mary Russell Mitford as Recorded in Letters from Her Literary Correspondents*, ed. the Rev. A. G. L'Estrange (London: Hurst and Blackett, 1882), I, 212-13.

[9] Letter to James Bird, 17 July [1831], Public Record Office, Ipswich, England.

[10] "Auditor's Report" (Traill Testimonial), T.F.P., I, 1453. Some contributors were G. M. Grant, John G. Bourinot, James Macoun, James Fletcher, and Hugh Fleming.

[11] Catharine Parr Strickland, *Narratives of Nature, and History Book for Young Naturalists* (London: Edward Lacey, n.d.), p. 129; T.F.P., VI, 8861.

[12] "Fragments of Thoughts by an Aged Head," T.F.P., V, 7302-03.

[13] Correspondence, Catharine to Susanna and Agnes to Catharine, T.F.P., I.

[14] For example, the Rev. William Bell's *Hints to Emigrants in a Series of Letters from Upper Canada* (Edinburgh: Waugh and Innes, 1824) and Thomas Magrath's *Authentic Letters from Upper Canada*, ed. the Rev. T. Radcliff (Dublin: Curry, 1833). Over one hundred accounts of emigration were published in Britain during the 1820s and 1830s.

[15] Rev. of *Woman in Her Social and Domestic Character*, by Mrs. John Sandford, *The Lady's Magazine*, improved series, 5 (1832), 211-14.

[16] Wayne Franklin, *Discoverers, Explorers, Settlers: The Diligent Writers of Early America* (Chicago: Univ. of Chicago Press, 1979), pp. 23-24, 71.

[17] *Malcolm Lowry: The Man and His Work*, ed. George Woodcock (Vancouver: Univ. of British Columbia Press, 1971), p. 96.

[18] Ray Palmer Baker, "Memoirs," in *A History of English-Canadian Literature to the Confederation* (Cambridge: Harvard Univ. Press, 1920), pp. 117-24; V. B. Rhodenizer, *A Handbook of Canadian Literature* (Ottawa: Graphic, 1930), pp. 61-62; Lionel Stevenson, *Appraisals of Canadian Literature* (Toronto: Macmillan, 1926), pp. 201-02; Desmond Pacey, *Creative Writing in Canada* (Toronto: Ryerson, 1961), pp. 26-27.

[19] *The Canadian Magazine*, 4 (1895), 388-90.

[20] Baker, "Memoirs"; Alec Lucas, "Nature Writers and the Animal Story," in *Literary History of Canada: Canadian Literature in English*, gen. ed. and introd. Carl F. Klinck (Toronto: Univ. of Toronto Press, 1965), pp. 364-88.

[21] There is also one dissertation on Traill, J. J. McNeil's "Mrs. Traill in Canada," Queen's 1948, as well as the author's own dissertation on the Strickland family, "The Literary History of the Strickland Family," London 1965.

[22] *Dalhousie Review*, 39 (1959), 56-69.

[23] *The Clear Spirit: Twenty Canadian Women and Their Times*, ed. Mary Quayle Innis (Toronto: Univ. of Toronto Press, 1966), pp. 42-73.

[24] Clara Thomas, "Journeys to Freedom," *Canadian Literature*, No. 51 (Winter 1972), pp. 11-19.

[25] *Canadian Children's Literature*, Nos. 5-6 (1976), pp. 31-39.

[26] Thomas, "Journeys to Freedom," p. 19.

[27] T. D. MacLulich, "Crusoe in the Backwoods: A Canadian Fable?" *Mosaic*, 9, No. 2 (1976), 115-26.

[28] William Gairdner, "Traill and Moodie: The Two Realities," *Journal of Canadian Fiction*, 2, No. 3 (1973), 75-81.

[29] Gairdner, p. 78.

[30] *The Compass*, No. 6 (1979), p. 16.

[31] Professors E. Hopkins (Glendon College) and M. Peterman (Trent University), in conjunction with the present author (McMaster University), are currently working on a collection of letters by Catharine Parr Traill and Susanna Moodie.

[32] John Howison, *Sketches of Upper Canada* (Edinburgh: Oliver and Boyd, 1821); Francis Hall, *Travels in Canada and the United States in 1816 and 1817* (London: n.p., 1818).

33 Traill refers to such charges on pages 91 and 173. Susanna Moodie expressed similar disappointment in Canadian flora and fauna in correspondence as late as 1869.

34 TS, T.F.P., I, 3416.

35 TS, T.F.P., I, 3455.

36 *Chambers' Edinburgh Journal*, 12 (1843), 79.

37 *Chambers' Edinburgh Journal*, 7 (1838), 322-23.

38 *The Home Circle*, 21 July 1849, pp. 33-35.

39 Catharine Parr Traill, *The Canadian Crusoes: A Tale of the Rice Lake Plains*, ed. Agnes Strickland (London: Arthur, Hall, Virtue, 1852), pp. 353-68. All further references to this work appear in the text. Traill tells about the discovery of a type of "Sasquatch" monster — "his face and shoulders were enveloped with long streaming hair, his body was entirely hirsute, his progression was by great jumps of twelve or thirteen feet at a leap" (p. 357) — and proceeds to relate the discovery of the creature to the issue of the plausibility of her own tale:

All persons generally agreed that it was a child that had been lost in the woods, at the earthquake in 1811, now grown to meridian strength, in a solitary state. Thus the possibility of an European child living, even unassisted, in the wilderness, is familiar to the inhabitants of the vast American continent. Although we doubt that any human creature would progress by leaps, instead of the paces familiar to the human instinct. (p. 357)

40 In *Narratives of Nature* (London: Edward Lacey, n.d.), pp. 129-30, Catharine tells of the Strickland children's fascination with *Robinson Crusoe* and their attempts to build their own "Crusoe" home. Agnes Strickland wrote a version of the Crusoe fable, *The Rival Crusoes; or, The Shipwreck* (London: Harris, 1826), and Catharine's *The Young Emigrants* seems to emanate from the same fascination in that it dwells upon children using the resources at hand.

41 "Forest Gleanings" appeared in volumes I, II, and III of *The Anglo-American Magazine*, in 1852 and 1853.

42 *The Anglo-American Magazine*, 1 (1852), 513-18; 2 (1853), 33-39.

43 *The Anglo-American Magazine*, 3 (1853), 493-98.

44 Catharine Parr Traill, "The Settlers Settled; or, Pat Connor and His Two Masters," *Sharpe's London Journal*, 10 (1849), 107-10, 137-42, 274-77, 335-40.

45 Traill, "The Settlers Settled," p. 274.

⁴⁶ *The Anglo-American Magazine*, 1 (1852), 353-54; 2 (1853), 426-30, 603-10; 3 (1853), 401-04.

⁴⁷ Catharine Parr Traill, "The Rice Lake Plains," *The Anglo-American Magazine*, 1 (1852), 353-54.

⁴⁸ Catharine Parr Traill, "A Glance within the Forest," *The Canadian Monthly and National Review*, 6 (1874), 48-53.

⁴⁹ *The Canadian Monthly and National Review*, 9 (1876), 491-94.

⁵⁰ *The Literary Garland*, NS 1 (1843), 41-42.

⁵¹ Traill, "A Glance within the Forest," p. 53.

⁵² T.F.P., VI, 8946, and various manuscript drafts in T.F.P., III, IV.

⁵³ Catharine Parr Traill, *The Female Emigrant's Guide, and Hints on Canadian Housekeeping* (Toronto: Maclear, 1854). All further references to this work appear in the text. There were several editions of this book in one ten-year period. The Edward Stanford edition of 1860 claims to be the tenth.

⁵⁴ Catharine Parr Traill, *Studies of Plant Life in Canada; or, Gleanings from Forest, Lake and Plain* (Ottawa: A. S. Woodburn, 1885), p. 62.

⁵⁵ Traill, *Studies of Plant Life in Canada*, pp. 121-24.

⁵⁶ Catharine Parr Traill, *Pearls and Pebbles; or, Notes of an Old Naturalist* (Toronto: Briggs, 1894), p. 40. All further references to this work appear in the text.

SELECTED BIBLIOGRAPHY

Primary Sources

Books and Periodical Contributions

Strickland, Catharine Parr. *The Tell Tale: An Original Collection of Moral and Amusing Stories*. London: Harris, 1818.

———. *Nursery Fables*. London: Harris, [1821].

———. *Disobedience; or, Mind What Mama Says*. London: James Woodhouse, 1819.

———. *Reformation; or, The Cousins*. London: James Woodhouse, 1819.

———. *Little Downy; or, The History of a Field Mouse: A Moral Tale*. London: Dean and Munday, 1822.

———. *Prejudice Reproved; or, The History of the Negro Toy-seller*. London: Harvey and Darton, 1826.

———. *The Young Emigrants; or, Pictures of Life in Canada, Calculated to Amuse and Instruct the Minds of Youth*. London: Harvey and Darton, 1826.

———. *The Juvenile Forget-Me-Not; or, Cabinet of Entertainment and Instruction*. London: N. Hailes, 1827.

———. *The Keepsake Guineas; or, The Best Use of Money*. London: A. K. Newman, 1828.

———, and Susanna Strickland. *The Little Prisoner; or, Passion and Patience; and Amendment; or, Charles Grant and His Sister*. London: Dean and Munday, 1828.
Amendment is by Catharine Parr Strickland; *The Little Prisoner* by Susanna Strickland.

———. *Sketches from Nature; or, Hints to Juvenile Naturalists*. London: Harvey and Darton, 1830.

———. *Narratives of Nature, and History Book for Young Naturalists*. London: Edward Lacey, [1831].

———. *The Flower Basket; or, Poetical Blossoms: Original Nursery Rhymes and Tales*. London: A. K. Newman, n.d.

Traill, Catharine Parr. *The Backwoods of Canada: Being Letters from the Wife of an Emigrant Officer, Illustrative of the Domestic Economy of British America.* London: Charles Knight, 1836.

——. "The Mill of the Rapids: A Canadian Sketch." *Chambers' Edinburgh Journal*, 7 (1838), 322-23.

——. "Love of Flowers." *The Literary Garland*, NS 1 (1843), 41-42.

——. "The Two Widows of Hunter's Creek." *The Home Circle*, 21 July 1849, pp. 33-35. Rpt. in *The Maple Leaf*, 4 (1854), 86-94.

——. "The Settlers Settled; or, Pat Connor and His Two Masters." *Sharpe's London Journal*, 10 (1849), 107-10, 137-42, 274-77, 335-40.

——. *The Canadian Crusoes: A Tale of the Rice Lake Plains.* Ed. Agnes Strickland. London: Arthur, Hall, Virtue, 1852.

——. "Forest Gleanings No. 1." *The Anglo-American Magazine*, 1 (1852), 318-20.

——. "Forest Gleanings No. 2: The Rice Lake Plains." *The Anglo-American Magazine*, 1 (1852), 353-54.

——. "Forest Gleanings No. 3: Rice Lake Plains — The Wolf Tower." *The Anglo-American Magazine*, 1 (1852), 417-20.

——. "Forest Gleanings: The Block House." *The Anglo-American Magazine*, 1 (1852), 513-18; 2 (1853), 33-39.

——. "Forest Gleanings No. VI: Ramblings by the River." *The Anglo-American Magazine*, 2 (1853), 182-84.

——. "Forest Gleanings No. VII: Female Trials in the Bush." *The Anglo-American Magazine*, 2 (1853), 426-30.

——. "Forest Gleanings No. VIII: Society in the Bush." *The Anglo-American Magazine*, 2 (1853), 603-10.

——. "Forest Gleanings No. IX: Humours of Holy Eve." *The Anglo-American Magazine*, 3 (1853), 82-83.

——. "Forest Gleanings No. X: Female Servants in the Bush." *The Anglo-American Magazine*, 3 (1853), 83-85.

——. "Forest Gleanings No. XI: Bush Wedding and Wooing." *The Anglo-American Magazine*, 3 (1853), 276-78.

——. "Forest Gleanings No. XII: A Walk to Railway Point." *The Anglo-American Magazine*, 3 (1853), 401-04.

——. "Forest Gleanings No. XIII: The Lodge in the Wilderness." *The Anglo-American Magazine*, 3 (1853), 493-98.

——. *The Female Emigrant's Guide, and Hints on Canadian Housekeeping.* Toronto: Maclear, 1854.

——. *Lady Mary and Her Nurse; or, A Peep into the Canadian Forest.* London: Arthur, Hall, Virtue, 1856.

————. *Canadian Wild Flowers.* Montreal: John Lovell, 1868.

————. "A Glance within the Forest." *The Canadian Monthly and National Review*, 6 (1874), 48-53.

————. "Voices from the Canadian Woods: The White Cedar." *The Canadian Monthly and National Review*, 9 (1876), 491-94.

————. *Studies of Plant Life in Canada; or, Gleanings from Forest, Lake and Plain.* Ottawa: A. S. Woodburn, 1885.

————. *Pearls and Pebbles; or, Notes of an Old Naturalist.* Toronto: Briggs, 1894.

————. *Cot and Cradle Stories.* Ed. Mary Agnes Fitzgibbon. Toronto: Briggs, 1895.

Manuscripts and Typescripts

Traill, Catharine Parr. "Fragments of Thoughts by an Aged Head." Vol. 5. Traill Family Papers. Public Archives of Canada (P.A.C.).

————. "Historical and Genealogical Notes of the Strickland Family." Vol. 5. Traill Family Papers. P.A.C.

————. "Journal 1831-1895." Vol. 2. Traill Family Papers. P.A.C.

————. Letters to Susanna Moodie. Vol. 1. Traill Family Papers. P.A.C.

————. Letters to Susanna Moodie. Glyde Papers. Public Record Office, Ipswich, England.

————. "Memorials of the Stricklands: A Family Chronicle." TS. Vol. 7. Traill Family Papers. P.A.C.

————. "Notebook 1887-1894." Vol. 3. Traill Family Papers. P.A.C.

————. "Some Reminiscences of the Life of Mrs. C. P. Traill, Written by Herself." TS. Vol. 6. Traill Family Papers. P.A.C.

————. "Under the Pines." Vol. 6. Traill Family Papers. P.A.C.

Secondary Sources

Allibone, L. Austin. "Catharine Parr Traill." *Critical Dictionary of English Literature.* 3 vols. (1859-71).

"Auditor's Report." Vol. 1. Traill Family Papers. P.A.C.

Baker, Ray Palmer. *A History of English-Canadian Literature to the Confederation.* Cambridge: Harvard Univ. Press, 1920.

Ballstadt, Carl. "The Literary History of the Strickland Family." Diss. London 1965.

————, introd. *The Canadian Settler's Guide*. By Catharine Parr Traill. Vancouver: Alcuin Society, 1971.

Burnham, Hampden. "Mrs. Traill." *The Canadian Magazine*, 4 (Feb. 1895), 388-90.

Burpee, L. J. "Catharine Parr Traill (1802-1899)." In *A Little Book of Canadian Essays*. Toronto: Musson, 1909, pp. 56-64.

Eaton, Sara. *Lady of the Backwoods: A Biography of Catharine Parr Traill*. Toronto: McClelland and Stewart, 1969.

Fitzgibbon, Mary Agnes. "Biographical Sketch." In *Pearls and Pebbles; or, Notes of an Old Naturalist*. By Catharine Parr Traill. Toronto: Briggs, 1894.

Franklin, Wayne. *Discoverers, Explorers, Settlers: The Diligent Writers of Early America*. Chicago: Univ. of Chicago Press, 1979.

Gairdner, William. "Traill and Moodie: The Two Realities." *Journal of Canadian Fiction*, 2, No. 3 (1973), 75-81.

Guillet, E. C. *The Valley of the Trent*. Toronto: Champlain Society, 1957.

Hume, Blanche. *The Strickland Sisters*. Toronto: Ryerson, 1929.

Jackel, David. "Mrs. Moodie and Mrs. Traill, and the Fabrication of a Canadian Tradition." *The Compass*, No. 6 (1979), pp. 1-22.

Klinck, Carl F. "Literary Activity in the Canadas 1812-1841." In *Literary History of Canada: Canadian Literature in English*. Gen. ed. and introd. Carl F. Klinck. Toronto: Univ. of Toronto Press, 1965, pp. 125-44.

Logan, J. D., and Donald G. French. *Highways of Canadian Literature*. Toronto: McClelland and Stewart, 1924.

Lucas, Alec. "Nature Writers and the Animal Story." In *Literary History of Canada: Canadian Literature in English*. Gen. ed. and introd. Carl F. Klinck. Toronto: Univ. of Toronto Press, 1965, pp. 364-88.

————. *The Otonabee School*. Montreal: Mansfield Book Mart, 1977.

MacLulich, T. D. "Crusoe in the Backwoods: A Canadian Fable?" *Mosaic*, 9, No. 2 (1976), 115-26.

McNeil, J. J. "Mrs. Traill in Canada." Diss. Queen's 1948.

Mitford, Mary Russell. *The Friendships of Mary Russell Mitford as Recorded in Letters from Her Literary Correspondents*. Ed. A. G. L'Estrange. 2 vols. London: Hurst and Blackett, 1882.

Morris, Audrey. *Gentle Pioneers: Five Nineteenth-Century Canadians*. Toronto: Hodder and Stoughton, 1968.

Needler, G. H. *Otonabee Pioneers: The Story of the Stewarts, the Stricklands, the Traills and the Moodies*. Toronto: Burns and MacEachern, 1953.

Partridge, Florence. "The Stewarts and the Stricklands, the Moodies and the Traills." *Ontario Library Review*, 40 (Aug. 1956), 179-81.

Pope-Hennessy, Una. *Agnes Strickland: Biographer of the Queens of England 1796-1874*. London: Chatto and Windus, 1940.

Ritchie, James Ewing. *To Canada with Emigrants*. London: Fisher Unwin, 1885.

Scott, Lloyd M. "The English Gentlefolk in the Backwoods of Canada." *Dalhousie Review*, 39 (1959), 56-59.

Stevenson, Lionel. *Appraisals of Canadian Literature*. Toronto: Macmillan, 1926.

Strickland, Jane Margaret. *Life of Agnes Strickland*. Edinburgh: Blackwood, 1887.

Thomas, Clara, introd. *The Backwoods of Canada*. By Catharine Parr Traill. New Canadian Library, No. 51. Toronto: McClelland and Stewart, 1966.

———. "The Strickland Sisters." In *The Clear Spirit: Twenty Canadian Women and Their Times*. Ed. Mary Quayle Innis. Toronto: Univ. of Toronto Press, 1966, pp. 42-73.

———, introd. *The Canadian Settler's Guide*. By Catharine Parr Traill. New Canadian Library, No. 64. Toronto: McClelland and Stewart, 1969.

———. "Journeys to Freedom." *Canadian Literature*, No. 51 (Winter 1972), pp. 11-19.

———. "Traill's Canadian Settlers." *Canadian Children's Literature*, Nos. 5-6 (1976), pp. 31-39.

Weaver, Emily. "Mrs. Traill and Mrs. Moodie: Pioneers in Literature." *The Canadian Magazine*, 84 (March 1917), 473-76.

Three Writers of Victorian Canada

CAROLE GERSON

Rosanna Leprohon (1829-1879)

Biography

ROSANNA ELEANOR LEPROHON, née Mullins, was born in Montreal on 12 January 1829 and died in the same city on 20 September 1879. Her father, Francis Mullins, had emigrated from Ireland in 1819 and prospered in Canada as a ship chandler. He later expanded his business to include importing and real estate, eventually becoming a substantial Montreal landowner. Her mother, Rosanna Conelly, the daughter of a schoolmaster, presumably set a high value on education. Young Rosanna attended the Convent of the Congregation, at the time the best school for young ladies in the city. In November 1846, at the age of seventeen, she published her first poems in *The Literary Garland*. During the following four and a half years, she produced a steady stream of *Garland* contributions: fifteen poems, one story, and five serialized novels, all set in England. Rosanna's marriage to Dr. Jean-Lukin Leprohon in June 1851, coupled with the demise of *The Literary Garland* the following December, ended the first phase of her career.

Seven years his wife's senior, Dr. Leprohon was himself remarkably active in both professional and cultural circles. He founded *La Lancette Canadienne*, the country's first medical journal; was professor of hygiene at Bishop's College in Lennoxville; helped to establish the Women's Hospital in Montreal; served on the Catholic section of the provincial Council of Public Instruction and on the Montreal city council; helped to institute the National League; was vice-president of the College of Physicians and Surgeons; founded and belonged to various local and international medical societies; and from 1871 was Vice-Consul for Spain.[1]

After her marriage, Rosanna moved to Saint Charles on the Richelieu River, where her husband was then practising. For about eight years, her literary output declined to a trickle of poems published in Montreal newspapers, as she turned her attention to maternal and domestic concerns. Indeed, one wonders how she managed to write at all, considering that between 1852 and 1872 she bore thirteen children, five of whom (including her first) died in infancy. In 1855 the Leprohons returned to Montreal, which was to be Rosanna's home for the rest of her life. She resumed her production of fiction in 1859 with "Eveleen O'Donnell" (reputedly a prize-winning story),[2] published in *The Pilot* [Boston], and "The Manor House of de Villerai," serialized in the Montreal *Family Herald*. These were followed by her best-known work, *Antoinette de Mirecourt; or, Secret Marrying and Secret Sorrowing* (1864), her only novel in print today. Four years later, *Armand Durand; or, A Promise Fulfilled* was serialized in *The Daily News* [Montreal], then appeared in book form as her last separately published work. During the remainder of her life, her literary activity waned due to ill health and family cares, but she continued to write poems and produced five more tales: "Clive Weston's Wedding Anniversary" for *The Canadian Monthly and National Review* (1872), and four others for the *Canadian Illustrated News*: "Ada Dunmore; or, A Memorable Christmas Eve: An Autobiography" (1869-70); "My Visit to Fairview Villa" (1870); "Who Stole the Diamond?" (1875); and "A School-Girl Friendship" (1877). Her posthumously collected *Poetical Works* were published in 1881, with an introduction attributed to John Reade,[3] fellow poet and literary editor of *The Gazette* [Montreal].

Tradition and Milieu

Living and writing in Montreal from the 1840s to the 1870s, Rosanna Leprohon enjoyed a diversified literary and cultural milieu which touched on the English, French, and Irish-Catholic strands of Quebec society. Her English-speaking literary contemporaries included Isidore Ascher, Charles Heavysege, Thomas D'Arcy McGee, John Talon Lesperance, and John Reade. With Ascher and Heavysege there is no evidence of significant contact. Lesperance edited the *Canadian Illustrated News*, which published much of Leprohon's work during the 1870s; for several years, McGee lived close by;[4] and Reade is presumed to have edited her *Poetical*

Works. Although her language of composition was English, Leprohon was bilingual (in 1860 she translated Edouard Sempé's poem *Cantate en l'honneur de Son Altesse Royale Le Prince de Galles*), and her literary circle may have been predominantly French. According to her biographer, Henri Deneau, her three French-Canadian novels were inspired by the upsurge of literary activity in Quebec in the 1860s, which included the founding of the *Soirées Canadiennes* in 1861 and the historical fiction of Philippe Aubert de Gaspé, Antoine Gérin-Lajoie, Napoléon Bourassa, and Joseph Marmette.[5]

Interestingly, Leprohon's work appears to have reached a wider audience in French Canada than in English Canada. "Ida Beresford; or, The Child of Fashion," serialized in *The Literary Garland* in 1848, was translated into French and serialized in *L'Ordre* (1859-60); *Armand Durand*, never reprinted in English after its original publication in 1868, appeared in two French editions in 1869 and 1892 and was serialized in three Quebec newspapers; *Antoinette de Mirecourt* (1864), published only once in English until its 1973 reissue by both McClelland and Stewart and the University of Toronto Press, appeared four times in translation[6] and was dramatized in 1901. "The Manor House of de Villerai," which first ran in the Montreal *Family Herald* (1859-60) and is now almost inaccessible in English, proved an especial favourite in Quebec, its French version enjoying at least two serial runs in newspapers and five separate printings between 1861 and 1925.[7]

Given their sympathetic treatment of French-Canadian history and culture, it is hardly surprising that the three novels occasionally described as a trilogy ("The Manor House of de Villerai," *Antoinette de Mirecourt*, and *Armand Durand*) were warmly received in Quebec. Less obvious are the reasons for their lack of comparable popularity in English Canada. Unfortunately for her own reputation, Leprohon seems to have remained content with local publishers and presumably with local distribution. The only American periodical to publish her work appears to have been the Irish-Catholic Boston *Pilot*; most of the Canadian journals which printed her poems and stories originated in Montreal. Her French-Canadian novels were written at least a decade too early to benefit from the wave of English-Canadian interest in Quebec which was inspired by Parkman's histories and James Le Moine's series of *Maple Leaves* and which peaked after 1875 with John Talon

Lesperance's *The Bastonnais*, William Kirby's *The Golden Dog* (both published in 1877), and the rash of romances and local-colour stories written during the 1880s and 1890s by Gilbert Parker, Susan Frances Harrison, Blanche Macdonell, E. W. Thomson, D. C. Scott, and many others.

The literary tradition of Leprohon's early poetry and fiction is indicated by their publication in *The Literary Garland*, which put her in the company of fellow Montreal authors Mrs. E. L. Cushing and Mrs. H. V. Cheney, as well as Susanna Moodie and Catharine Parr Traill. Throughout her career, none of her work deviated from *The Literary Garland*'s standard of promoting gentility, good morals, and correct conduct, which tended to encourage fiction overlooking the lower orders of society. Her earliest work was warmly commended by Susanna Moodie, who described her in *The Victoria Magazine* as "one of the gifted, upon whom fancy smiled in her cradle, and genius marked her for his own."[8] Leprohon's place in the international tradition is less easy to discern. Carl F. Klinck sees similarities between *Antoinette de Mirecourt* and *Vanity Fair*,[9] while Mary Jane Edwards suggests that Balzac was an influence.[10] J. C. Stockdale finds resemblances to Emerson and Thomas Gray in her poetry,[11] and Henri Deneau frequently draws comparisons with Dickens.[12] As is the case with most minor writers, Leprohon echoes many of her more illustrious predecessors and contemporaries without being explicitly imitative. Other possible influences are earlier female writers like Jane Austen and Fanny Burney, with whom Leprohon shared a concern with social manners and the education of young ladies. A more accurate assessment of her early models would have to be based on detailed knowledge of the reading material available to, and approved for, a convent-bred girl growing up in Montreal in the 1840s. Presumably, she was familiar with the romance and melodrama of Scott, Dickens, Dumas, and Balzac, as her biographer suggests,[13] but her novels resemble theirs no more than does the mass of secondary nineteenth-century fiction. Within her stories, Leprohon frequently condemns the pernicious influence of sentimental novels (especially French ones), but she names few authors of acceptable fiction. Some of her comments suggest her approval of Scott,[14] while in "The Manor House of de Villerai" she denounces "the free bold immorality of the Sue and Balzac school" in favour of "such men as Fenelon [sic], Châteaubriand [sic] and Bourdaloue."[15] Since she does not appear to have written any reviews or literary criticism, she has left few other clues to the identity of her models and mentors.

James De Mille (1833-1880)

Biography

James Demill (he added the final "e" after 1865) was born in Saint John, New Brunswick, on 23 August 1833, the third child in a large family of Loyalist descent. At the time of his death in Halifax, on 28 January 1880, he was "the widest read and most productive of Canadian writers,"[16] although there is little in his early childhood to predict his later career. When James was nine, his father, Nathan Smith Demill, a prosperous merchant and shipowner, left the Church of England for the Baptists, his views on alcohol earning him the cognomen "Coldwater Demill." A colourful, rather eccentric figure, the elder Demill is reputed to have "burned a package of novels that had found their way into a cargo" and to have "rather disparaged book-learning." He put James and his elder brother, Elisha Budd, "at an early age into his counting-house" (MacMechan, p. 405), yet he was also a governor of Acadia College — founded as a Baptist school — to which he sent his sons. At the age of fifteen, James attended Horton Academy, the congenial Grand Pré School of his boys' adventure stories, then spent eighteen months at Acadia before moving on to Brown University (Providence, Rhode Island), which granted him his M.A. in 1854.

Before entering Brown, however, James and Budd set out on a year and a half of travels which deeply impressed the future novelist. In August 1850, the youths sailed from Quebec City for Liverpool. The two brothers toured Scotland and England, crossed the channel, then "followed the old diligence line, the route of the *Sentimental Journey*, through central France to Marseilles" (MacMechan, p. 406). Italy proved the most memorable country on their itinerary, providing James with scenes and incidents that were to enhance more than half his novels.

De Mille returned to North America to enter Brown in February 1852. His academic work was undistinguished — not from lack of ability, but from boredom, as Archibald MacMechan infers from the sketches and caricatures in the margins of De Mille's notebooks (MacMechan, p. 410). According to MacMechan, while at Brown De Mille began to toss off fiction for "story papers" like the *Waverly Magazine*, more for fun than for profit. Upon graduation, he spent a year and a half in Cincinnati helping friends investigate the affairs of a mining company in which Maritime Baptists (including Acadia College) had invested heavily. One of De Mille's biographers has suggested that his "lost" serial novel, "The Minne-haha Mines" (1870), may shed light on this period of its author's life.[17] The novel has since been found,[18] but in common with the rest of De Mille's light fiction, it simply transforms incidents drawn from his experiences into amusing fantasy. The Cincinnati episode ended tragically when one of De Mille's companions was murdered; the novel ends comically when the hero (with a good deal of aid from the heroine) trounces the villains, recovers the capital of the gullible investors (mostly clergymen), and turns the mine into a profitable enterprise.

For De Mille, however, success in business occurred more frequently in fiction than in fact. In 1855 he returned to Saint John to help with the family's failing lumber company. With a partner he opened a bookstore, but his partner proved "negligent, or dishon-est, or both" (MacMechan, p. 412) and De Mille was left with a burden of debt which he may not have paid off until shortly before his death. In 1859 he married Elizabeth Ann Pryor, daughter of Dr. John Pryor, first president of Acadia College. The following year he embarked on his academic career, first as professor of classics at Acadia, then as professor of history and rhetoric at Dalhousie College. During this time, he returned to the Church of England and published a pamphlet on its early history. In Halifax, De Mille was well known as an exciting teacher and a fine scholar, in 1878 producing *The Elements of Rhetoric*. According to one source, "Harvard had been for some years anxious to secure him for her services, and at the time of his death was making a special effort."[19] The immediate cause of De Mille's sudden early death, at the age of forty-six, was pneumonia; many felt overwork to be a contributing factor.

De Mille's frenzied literary career may have begun during his student days, but most of his more than twenty-five novels were published after 1868, at least three appearing posthumously. Most are utterly negligible adventure stories, dependent upon impossible coincidences and predictable characters and padded to suit serial publication. Even these, however, are often composed in a rather tongue-in-cheek manner; as MacMechan put it, they are "literary practical jokes on the public" (MacMechan, p. 414). De Mille's first commercial success was *The Dodge Club; or, Italy in MDCCCLIX* (1869), which pokes gentle fun at Americans abroad. He himself set great store by his major historical novel, *Helena's Household* (1867), a turgid reconstruction of first-century Roman life. More readable is his series of boys' novels, published between 1869 and 1873. To modern readers, however, he is known almost solely for *A Strange Manuscript Found in a Copper Cylinder*, not published until 1888 and possibly left unfinished.

Tradition and Milieu

De Mille's two identities — the respected university scholar and the hack producer of market fiction — seem curiously at odds with one another. Fluent in Latin, acquainted with nearly a dozen ancient and modern languages (including Persian and Icelandic), Professor De Mille hardly seems the man to specialize in spine-tingling cliff-hangers, fluffy travel comedies, or even boys' adventure stories. Financial need set the tenor of most of his fiction: "Like Scott he determined to pay ... off [his debts] and to do so by his pen" (Crockett, p. 124). Money was to be made in New York, where Harper, the publishing house, cultivated a group of native American writers for its magazines and "library of select novels." Here De Mille kept company with people like Elizabeth Stuart Phelps, Lew Wallace, and Thomas Bailey Aldrich — widely read during their time, but hardly household names today. Quite frequently, however, De Mille could not resist the temptation to indulge his erudition, creating delightful comic touches such as O'Halloran's translation of Homer into Irish dialect in *The Lady of the Ice* (1870).

De Mille achieved fame first as a humorist when *The Dodge Club* was serialized in *Harper's New Monthly Magazine* in 1867 and issued in book form two years later (with at least two reprintings, 1875 and 1897). Possibly written in 1860 (Crockett, p. 135) and based on De Mille's own youthful travels, the picaresque adventure takes its title from a group of American tourists determined to dodge the various swindlers who plague them. At times, their Pick-wickian naïveté recalls De Mille's affection for Dickens;[20] both the subject and the tone of De Mille's humour resemble those of Mark Twain in *The Innocents Abroad*, published the same year as the book version of *The Dodge Club*. So well did the latter sell that De Mille was inspired to tap the juvenile market with three frequently reprinted sequels about a group of travelling boys, subtitled "The Young Dodge Club."[21]

Although De Mille's "sensation novels" met with little critical approval at home, their many reprints indicate that they certainly found a market abroad. Contemporary critics likened *Cord and Creese* (1869) and *The Living Link* (1874) to the novels of Wilkie Collins, Jules Verne, Charles Reade, and Mary Braddon; of *The Living Link*, the *Canadian Illustrated News* complained that De Mille was trying to "out-Braddon" Miss Braddon by including in one short book "a surfeit of sensations that would suffice Miss Braddon for half a dozen novels."[22] More acceptable to Canadian critics was *Helena's Household: A Tale of Rome in the First Century* (1867), which De Mille dedicated to his father-in-law. Almost unreadable today, it appealed to those with a taste for fiction flavoured with a strong dose of piety. One of De Mille's admirers, however, suggests that it may have inspired later histor-ical novels about Rome, like Wallace's *Ben Hur* and Sienkiewicz's *Quo Vadis.*[23]

Ironically, the books by De Mille which failed to attract emula-tors are among his best — his six boys' adventure stories subtitled "The B.O.W.C." (The Brethren of the Order of the White Cross, a school-boy club). Refreshingly undidactic for Victorian children's literature, they acquaint their young readers with the history, geog-raphy, and natural history of the area around Wolfville and the Bay of Fundy as well as recount their heroes' exciting and humorous escapades. Issued only by American publishers, they were still in print in 1906 (MacMechan, p. 415), but they declined in popularity without ever mythologizing Grand Pré as L. M. Montgomery's "Anne" books later mythologized Prince Edward Island.

Archibald MacMechan believed that the essential De Mille was to be found in his long posthumous poem, *Behind the Veil* (which MacMechan edited for publication in 1893), which "shows the poet's deeply reverential nature and his unfaltering grasp of the things that are unseen and eternal. . . . In thought it owes something to Richter's version of immortality, in form to Poe's *Raven*" (Mac-Mechan, p. 415). Modern readers prefer to find the essential De Mille in *A Strange Manuscript Found in a Copper Cylinder.* Surprisingly, only two critics have placed De Mille within a tradition of Maritime satirists: George Stewart, whose comments linking De Mille with Haliburton appeared before *A Strange Manuscript* was in print and are based on similarities between De Mille's comic Yankees and Sam Slick;[24] and A. J. Crockett, who concurred with the view of "Dr. A. W. H. Eaton, the Historian of Kings County," that De Mille was "next to Judge Haliburton the most important writer of fiction that the Maritime Provinces have produced" (Crockett, p. 121). *A Strange Manuscript* is one of many books contributing to the late Victorian interest in socially critical utopian and antiutopian fiction; it was preceded by Lord Lytton's *The Coming Race* (1870) and Samuel Butler's *Erewhon* (1872), coincided in publication date with Edward Bellamy's *Looking Backward*, and was followed by William Morris' *News from Nowhere* (1890) and H. G. Wells's *A Modern Utopia* (1904).

Agnes Maule Machar (1837-1927)

Biography

Agnes Maule Machar was born on 23 January 1837 in Kingston, where she died ninety years and one day later on 24 January 1927. Her parents had immigrated to Canada in 1827; her mother, Margaret Machar (1798-1883), had been raised in a Scottish manse, and her father, Dr. John Machar (1796-1863), had studied theology in Edinburgh and was licensed to preach in the Church of Scotland. From 1827 until his death in 1863, John Machar served as minister of Saint Andrew's Church in Kingston and was principal of Queen's University from 1846 to 1854. Agnes and her younger brother, John (1841-99), grew up in an environment that was both religious and intellectual. With her father and private teachers, she "studied Greek and Latin before she was ten, and by the time she was fifteen she had made good progress in French, Italian, and German, besides mathematics, drawing and music."[25]

Machar's first poem, written at the tender age of seven, recounted "the painful deaths of two young emigrants"; shortly.

afterwards, "a few verses, descriptive of a mother preparing tea for her family, appeared in one of the Kingston papers."[26] One source claims that her first three books were "written before she was within sight of her twenties" (MacCallum, p. 355). However, two of these were not published until 1870 and 1871; more widely accepted is the story that her first novel, *Katie Johnstone's Cross: A Canadian Tale* (1870), was "written in six weeks" (Wetherald, p. 301) and garnered a prize offered by a Toronto publishing house, Messrs. Campbell and Son, "for the book best suited to the needs of the Sunday School library" (MacCallum, p. 355). Machar carried off Campbell's prize the following year, as well, with *Lucy Raymond; or, The Children's Watchword*. Three years later, she captured another literary honour when *For King and Country* won a competition sponsored by *The Canadian Monthly and National Review*, and in 1887 she won *The Week*'s prize for the best native poem on the Queen's Jubilee.

Despite these successes, Machar always avoided publicity, usually writing anonymously or under the pseudonyms "A. M. M.," "Canadensis," and possibly "A. M." and "F."[27] Her favourite and most familiar pen name was "Fidelis," because, as she is reported to have said, "Faithfulness is the quality I most value and care most to possess" (Wetherald, p. 300). Throughout her long and prolific career, she remained faithful to the social and religious principles inherited from her parents, who had cooperated with the Abolitionists in aiding escaped slaves. She advocated the application of Christian ideals to everyday life, her causes including better working conditions for labourers, charity towards the poor and unfortunate, improved education for women, love of country and Empire, and, of course, temperance. In 1926, near the end of her life, she appeared to be a relic from the past, "a true Victorian optimist" who viewed the world "from her parlour window [with] a naïve simplicity."[28]

Today, it is easy enough to dismiss Agnes Maule Machar as a second-rate, didactic writer whose imaginative work displays the inevitable shortcomings of morally earnest fiction and maple-leaf poetry. During the nineteenth century, however, she was at the centre of Canadian intellectual life, and sometimes considerably to the left of centre. She was a major contributor of poetry, fiction, book reviews, and articles to the country's most important periodicals, publishing over sixty-five items in *The Canadian Monthly and*

National Review (1872-78) and its successor, *Rose-Belford's Canadian Monthly and National Review* (1878-82);[29] more than one hundred pieces in *The Week*;[30] countless items in unindexed Canadian periodicals like *The Canadian Magazine* and the *Canada Presbyterian*; and various pieces in important British and American periodicals for both adults and children, including *Scribner's, The Century, The Westminster Review, St. Nicholas Magazine,* and *Wide Awake*.

Only a small proportion of Machar's total output appeared in book form, all of it now out of print. In addition to her prize-winning Sunday-school novels, she appealed to young readers with *Marjorie's Canadian Winter: A Story of the Northern Lights* (1892), in which she intertwined stories about old Quebec with discussions of proper Christian behaviour. She sought to reach an adult audience with *Roland Graeme, Knight: A Novel of Our Time* (1892), which proposes Christian brotherhood and understanding as a solution to labour problems. Her other novels include *Down the River to the Sea* (1894), essentially a travelogue extolling the beauties of the Saint Lawrence Valley, and *The Heir of Fairmount Grange* (1895), a romance which ends with the heroine choosing a life of service over the comforts of an English estate. As well, she published several chapbooks of poetry and one major collection, *Lays of the "True North" and Other Canadian Poems* (1899), which was popular enough to require an enlarged edition in 1902. In addition, she wrote a number of biographies, including one of her father, and translated several others from French. She also produced, or contributed to, eight volumes of historical writing, three of them about Kingston, and three others for young readers. Unfortunately, all her writings on social issues remain buried in the periodicals where they first appeared. She was a competent artist, as well, but never exhibited her sketches and watercolours.

Machar never married, and her personal life seems to have been uneventful and healthy. (In 1888 she claimed to have "never spent a sick day in bed in her life" [Wetherald, p. 300].) Her life in Kingston was punctuated by several trips abroad, but she usually spent her winters at her house in town and her summers at Ferncliffe, her cottage near the Thousand Islands, which figure so prominently in her poetry. Although almost unknown today, she was an acknowledged figure during her lifetime: her poetry was anthologized in Canadian school texts and read at the Royal Society of Canada's

1895 "Evening with Canadian Poets," and in 1903 she was elected vice-president of the Canadian Society of Authors.

Tradition and Milieu

Machar's cultural milieu was provided by mid-nineteenth-century Kingston society, enhanced by the intellectual stimulation of close ties with Queen's University. Among her acquaintances were:

> the Rev. Dr. James Williamson (1806-1895), one time vice-principal and professor of astronomy, brother-in-law to Sir John A. Macdonald; the Rev. George Romanes, professor of classics during her father's principalship and father of George Romanes, eminent biologist concerned with the theories of Darwin and Wallace; the Rev. Professor J. H. Mackerras, professor of classics in the 1860's; and George Monro Grant, principal from 1877 until his death in 1902. (Chenier, p. 11)

She was attracted to current issues as much from personal associations as from the social orientation of her upbringing: her father's church "was also the church of Hugh Macdonald, father of John A. Macdonald, and of John Mowat, father of Oliver Mowat, future premier of Ontario" (Chenier, pp. 3-4). Machar also knew Ontario politicians Richard Cartwright and Alexander Campbell.[31] Her Kingston literary contemporaries included Charles Sangster, Grant Allen (whose sister married Agnes' brother), and Evan McColl; in addition, she corresponded with Lady Aberdeen and Sir Wilfrid Laurier.

Her close involvement with nineteenth-century Canadian history and society notwithstanding, the literary tradition to which Machar belongs is international as well as Canadian. Under the leadership of George Monro Grant, Queen's became the centre of the social gospel movement in Canada during the last decades of the nineteenth century. Machar shared Grant's "gospel of active social service . . . directed towards a spiritual end"[32] as well as the concerns and proposals of Victorian liberals in England and America. In her fiction, she identifies some of her influences as the economic theories of Henry George, the Christian poetry of John Keble, and the novels of Charles Kingsley.

Although committed to moderate social reform, her fiction lacks the passion and imaginative power found in the work of her British mentors. A comparison of her handling of labour relations in *Roland Graeme* with Dickens' treatment of the same topic in *Hard Times* reveals her evasion of any implicit or explicit analysis of class and industrial structures which could jeopardize the security of her middle-class liberalism. Dickens compensates for his misrepresentation of the labour movement and the Preston strike through his magnificently sombre imagery which bares the black heart of Victorian capitalism; Machar, in contrast, presents only a lukewarm optimistic vision of the best men and women of the middle class leading the workers and the factory owners towards a spirit of Christian cooperation. Her pious solutions to problems of social and domestic conduct were typical of the strain of Sunday-school writing which dominated so much of the women's and children's literature of her age; in Canada, her notion of the moral purpose of fiction was shared by most of her fellow writers. As a preacher of the "social gospel" as an antidote to doubt and scepticism, Machar was an important precursor of two of the most popular writers Canada has produced: Charles W. Gordon ("Ralph Connor") and Nellie McClung.

In his chapter on "Literature of Protest" in *Literary History of Canada: Canadian Literature in English*, Frank Watt places Machar closer to the fringes than to the centre of Victorian Canada's rather pallid radical tradition.[33] She shared with Goldwin Smith, a fellow contributor to *The Canadian Monthly and National Review*, an interest in many aspects of "social revolution" and with Sara Jeannette Duncan, a fellow contributor to *The Week*, a commitment to improving the lot of women. These two periodicals, which published so much of her work, themselves define her tradition and milieu in Canada by placing her in the company of men and women who shaped the country's intellectual and literary environment: inquiring and occasionally esoteric, but always genteel and, ultimately, safe.

Critical Overview and Context

The fates of Leprohon, De Mille, and Machar at the hands of their critics have been roughly parallel. Each enjoyed substantial recognition at home and/or abroad while alive but slipped into disregard shortly after death. The New Canadian Library reissues of *A Strange Manuscript Found in a Copper Cylinder* in 1969 and *Antoinette de Mirecourt* in 1973 sparked some renewal of interest in De Mille and Leprohon; Machar, however, has enjoyed no such attention. In the case of each writer, the modern scholar is indebted to enterprising graduate students for valuable primary research: to Henri Deneau for "The Life and Works of Mrs. Leprohon" (M.A. Thesis Montréal 1948); to Douglas MacLeod for "A Critical Biography of James De Mille" (M.A. Thesis Dalhousie 1968); and to Nancy Miller Chenier for "Agnes Maule Machar: Her Life, Her Social Concerns, and a Preliminary Bibliography of Her Writing" (M.A. Thesis Carleton 1977). Bibliographical information is available on two of these writers: Chenier lists all of Machar's books, monographs, and contributions to Canadian periodicals; and in 1974 Tom Flemming, a Dalhousie Library School student, prepared a helpful but not exhaustive bibliography of De Mille. An adequate bibliographical study of Leprohon has yet to appear.

James De Mille

During De Mille's lifetime, his work received little attention from the press of central Canada. In the 1870s none of his books reached the reviewers of the most important periodical of the decade, *The Canadian Monthly* [Toronto], or its successor, *Rose-Belford's Canadian Monthly*. The *Canadian Illustrated News* [Montreal] evinced some familiarity with De Mille's work when it said of *The Living Link* (1874), "It would be better for the author's fame if it had never been written. . . . It has neither the fascination of 'Cord and Creese' nor the sparkling *verve* and crispness of 'The Dodge Club.' "[34] Maritimers, not surprisingly, looked upon their native son with greater favour. Sir William Young, chairman of the Dalhousie Board of Governors when *Helena's Household* appeared in 1867, regretted that De Mille's name had not appeared on the title page: "It would have enhanced your own reputation and reflected credit on Dalhousie."[35] George Stewart, editor of *Stewart's Quarterly* [Saint John] and later a prominent newspaperman in Quebec, was one of De Mille's earliest champions. In 1870 he declared *Helena's Household* "a brilliant work . . . to be expected from a University Professor," described *The Dodge Club* as "rollicking merry sketches," but found *Cord and Creese* "much too sensational for our taste."[36]

South of the border, *Harper's Magazine* reviewed De Mille's novels enthusiastically, which is hardly unexpected considering that Harper happened to be De Mille's main publisher. However, *The Atlantic Monthly* also approved of his work, attempting in one review to "claim him for our nationality" (Crockett, p. 136). De Mille's American popularity endured into the early years of the twentieth century, as evidenced by readers' letters to *The Nation* after Harper reprinted *Cord and Creese* in 1906 (Crockett, p. 137).

The anonymous publication of *A Strange Manuscript Found in a Copper Cylinder* in 1888 did little to enhance De Mille's Canadian reputation. *The Week*, ignorant of the author's identity, published a review consisting almost entirely of plot summary, its only criticism being that "the story seems to be a sensational satire." The review noted further, "It has some of the characteristics of the *Arabian Nights*, and the works of Jules Verne and Rider Haggard."[37]

From 1880 to the present, the purpose of nearly all commentary on De Mille has been to call attention to an unduly neglected author. When *Behind the Veil* appeared in 1894, Charles G. D. Roberts declared in *The Week*:

> The name of de Mille [sic] is all too little known among Canadians. The recent growth of interest in Canadian literature has called forth many articles on our native writers, but in these articles de Mille's name seldom appears. Yet both the quality and the bulk of James de Mille's work entitle him, I think, to be ranked as one of the most distinguished of Canadian writers.[38]

Archibald MacMechan's important article of 1906, "De Mille, the Man and the Writer," provided biographical information which formed the basis of all subsequent criticism until Douglas MacLeod's M.A. thesis of 1968. MacMechan offers many cogent and witty comments about De Mille's work (including his view that *The Dodge Club* has been highly overrated), but his article scarcely has the space necessary for substantial criticism. During the 1920s, interest in De Mille revived briefly with articles in *The Vancouver*

Daily Province and *The Canadian Bookman* by appreciative readers, including Lawrence J. Burpee (a nephew of De Mille), who drew heavily on MacMechan's essay. In the outlines and handbooks of Canadian literature published during this decade, De Mille is identified as "the father of the Leacockian type of humour"[39] and a specialist in "exaggerated nonsense or nonsense said with a face of seriousness."[40]

Until the late 1960s, which saw both the completion of MacLeod's thesis and the New Canadian Library reissue of *A Strange Manuscript*, there appeared only two serious studies of De Mille, again with a biographical emphasis. Both these have been quoted from earlier: Judge A. J. Crockett's collaboration with De Mille's former student, George G. Patterson, on "Concerning James De Mille" (1941); and A. R. Bevan's detailed description in 1955 of MacMechan's planned, but never completed, biography of De Mille.

The 1969 reprinting of *A Strange Manuscript* prompted the only intensive literary analysis De Mille's work has yet received. Most critics agree on the nature and general intention of De Mille's satire, but they differ concerning his specific targets and his sources. In his introduction to the New Canadian Library edition, R. E. Watters argues for De Mille's originality, defending him against unjust accusations of indebtedness to utopian and/or adventure stories which appeared during the long interval between the writing and the publication of *A Strange Manuscript*.[41] He reads the book as an exposure of the hypocrisy and materialism underlying "current Western and Christian values"[42] and describes it as a utopian fiction. George Woodcock, in a 1973 article which grew out of an earlier editorial in *Canadian Literature*, takes issue with Watters' use of the term "utopian." De Mille, Woodcock argues, is not working in a utopian or antiutopian mode because he does not construct a futuristic vision of human development or present a complete society which shows "the positive and the negative results of carrying out certain theories of social reconstruction to their practical and logical conclusions."[43] Rather, he creates the polar world of the Kosekin to criticize existing social conditions in the manner of Swift. His models were Mallock, Butler, and Lytton, and his book drew heavily on popular nonfiction of the 1870s. Woodcock narrows De Mille's target to Victorian society, seeing the dark-loving, apparently selfless Kosekin as an embodiment of the death wish implicit in Victorian society and its conventions. Crawford Kilian, however, places the book in a specifically Canadian context, describing it as an example of Frye's Menippean satire.[44] He looks to De Mille's own life to account for the disillusionment expressed in *A Strange Manuscript* and finds in the book specific critiques of Canada and of godlessness, a trait Adam More shares with the Kosekin. Kilian contends that the novel was written in the 1860s, a point supported by M. G. Parks in "Strange to Strangers Only."[45] Hence, Parks argues, De Mille did not imitate the writers of the 1870s cited by Woodcock. Parks analyses *A Strange Manuscript* as an attack on religious extremism, which plays off the "extreme self-denial and consequent life-denial" of the Kosekin against the "extreme self-indulgence and consequent denial of transcendence" of modern Western society.[46] De Mille, he suggests, was satirizing the evangelical fundamentalism and religious cant he found among the Baptists and supported a temperate philosophy — the *via media* of the Anglican church to which he returned after his father's death.

A different approach to De Mille's antecedents comes from Wayne R. Kime, who has traced *A Strange Manuscript*'s indebtedness to Poe, Melville, and William H. Prescott, proposing that De Mille's main influences were not English and European, but American. Kime submits that De Mille's "radical eclecticism" and "great resourcefulness as an adapter of used literary material" contribute to the novel's strength, inviting the educated reader to trace its sources and to scrutinize both the manuscript and the book as a whole, as do the characters aboard Featherstone's yacht.[47] Kenneth J. Hughes's recent, rather tenuous attempt to reverse previous readings of *A Strange Manuscript*, by arguing that the book "is a positive Utopia,"[48] requires him to describe Adam More as a Promethean figure bringing a Western European renaissance to the benighted Kosekin. He thus ignores More's obvious impercipience, which is pointed out by Kilian and Parks, and discounts their reliable evidence concerning De Mille's own difficulties with the novel's end.

Few other works by De Mille have been noticed by modern critics. *The Dodge Club* was reprinted in 1981 with an informative introduction by Gwendolyn Davies,[49] and his juvenile fiction received attention from Sheila Egoff in her chapter on "Early Canadian Children's Books" in *The Republic of Childhood*. Egoff finds the B.O.W.C. books "startlingly original"[50] for their time and place, preferring them to the "Young Dodge Club" series because of the authenticity of their Canadian setting.

Rosanna Leprohon

Unlike De Mille, Rosanna Leprohon has enjoyed no discernible upsurge of serious critical attention following the recent reprinting of one of her major novels. Indeed, J. C. Stockdale's entry on Leprohon in the *Dictionary of Canadian Biography*, published the year before the reissue of *Antoinette de Mirecourt; or, Secret Marrying and Secret Sorrowing*, describes the latter as "a romantic, stilted novel, the worst of the later group."[51]

Romantic and stilted as Leprohon's work may appear to modern readers, it met the wholehearted approval of her contemporaries. Susanna Moodie quickly identified Leprohon as a kindred elevating writer in 1848 when "Ida Beresford; or, The Child of Fashion," Leprohon's second serialized novel, was in the midst of its run in *The Literary Garland*. In her short-lived *Victoria Magazine*, Moodie declared: "Let her keep truth and nature ever in view, and scorn not the slightest teaching of the 'Divine Mother,' and she may become the pride and ornament of a great and rising country."[52] According to Henry Morgan, Leprohon was well on her way to fulfilling this promise by 1862, when he commended her *Garland* stories as "tales of fiction and pathos of so high a character, that they may, without exaggeration, be ranked among those of the same class, by the best English or American contributors to the periodical press" and lauded "The Manor House of de Villerai" as "the very best [work] written on Canada."[53]

Antoinette de Mirecourt (1864) was warmly welcomed in both national languages, but not without reservations. *The Saturday Reader* called it "our best Canadian novel, *en attendant mieux*," noting some inconsistency in Leprohon's moral stance: "The lesson of Miss de Mirecourt's misery and sufferings, brought on by foolish and imprudent conduct, will be totally lost on the romantic young reader, when she learns that the said Miss de Mirecourt's misfortunes ultimately resolve themselves in a happy union with the man she loves and by whom she is beloved."[54] The French press did not begrudge Antoinette her wedding bells but took issue instead with

Leprohon's treatment of relations between the two cultures. Mary Jane Edwards has described *Antoinette* as "probably the best novel about English-French relations in Canada published in the nineteenth century," seeing Antoinette's eventual marriage to Colonel Evelyn as a symbolic "union of the old and the new orders in Canada and the emergence of a new society."[55] Herself partner to a bicultural marriage, Leprohon would probably have agreed with this view of her novel. However, reviewers for both *L'Ordre* and *La Revue Canadienne* disliked the "anglomanie" implicit in Mrs. D'Aulnay's eagerness to greet "avec tant d'empressement les militaires étrangers, et ouvrir ses salons à ceux-là même qui auraient dû être les derniers admis,"[56] and in Antoinette's final choice of husband: "Il est vrai que le Col. Evelyn, le second mari d'Antoinette, était catholique; c'est quelque chose, mais ce n'est pas tout ce que je désire voir dans l'époux d'une de mes jeunes compatriotes: il n'était pas Canadien."[57]

After 1865, criticism of Leprohon's work declined to bland appreciation. In an 1877 article on "The Literary Standing of the New Dominion," John Talon Lesperance placed Leprohon "at the head of Canadian novelists"[58] for "The Manor House of de Villerai," *Antoinette*, and "Ada Dunmore." Obituary notices praised her "élévation de pensées et . . . noblesse de sentiments"[59] as well as her charity, purity, delicacy, and devotion, naming her "the Canadian Mrs. Sadlier."[60] When her *Poetical Works* appeared in 1881, *Rose-Belford's* chose to treat the book respectfully, lauding its "national themes" and downplaying the fact that "there is not a little in the volume which, from a literary point of view, had better have been left out."[61] The book's introduction, understandably, expresses no such reservations, but concentrates on presenting Leprohon as a literary pioneer whose poetry "contains the emotional record of a blameless and beautiful life."[62] This reverential tone, suitable for obituaries and memorial editions, was appropriated by Henri Deneau, whose 1948 thesis on "The Life and Works of Mrs. Leprohon" consists of substantial biographical research mixed with vague adulatory comments which pass for criticism. His most significant discovery was that Leprohon was born in 1829, not 1832, refuting the myth that she published her first poems at the age of fourteen. Fortunately, Carl Klinck's succinct, lucid introduction to the New Canadian Library reprint of *Antoinette* condenses most of Deneau's salient information, supplementing it with a judicious assessment of Leprohon's shortcomings and achievements.

Few other modern critics have paid attention to Leprohon. Linda Shohet appreciatively reviewed the 1973 reissue of *Antoinette*,[63] and Mary Jane Edwards devoted several pages to the same work in her 1972 article "Essentially Canadian" (cited above) on English-French relations in early Canadian writing. A look at the sexual and religious politics of *Antoinette* appears in Elizabeth Brady's article "Towards a Happier History: Women and Domination," which draws parallels between British imperialism and Leprohon's depiction of the patriarchal structure of family, church, and society.[64] Editors of recent anthologies have been constrained by Leprohon's preference for lengthy narratives. Mary Jane Edwards reprinted "Clive Weston's Wedding Anniversary" in *The Evolution of Canadian Literature in English: Beginnings to 1867*, and David Arnason selected "Alice Sydenham's First Ball" for his *Nineteenth-Century Canadian Stories*, both stories being typical expositions of Leprohon's fictional world.

Agnes Maule Machar

During the second half of the nineteenth century, Agnes Maule Machar reached a wider audience in Canada than did De Mille or Leprohon, yet since her death in 1927 she has been almost universally dismissed as a quaint literary lady of a bygone era. The prizes she won attest to her literary stature during her lifetime, as do contemporary comments on her work. According to *The Canadian Monthly*, the serialized version of *For King and Country* (1874) "was received by our readers with unqualified approval";[65] to W. D. Lighthall she was "one of those who well disputes the palm for the leadership among Canadian poetesses";[66] while *The Week* described her as "our most gifted authoress."[67] Machar's novels were applauded by critics who liked their fiction to contain "a healthy tone of morality and a warm, though not obtrusive vein of practical piety,"[68] as well as "a true picture of life . . . , the spirit of enlightened patriotism and . . . noble precepts and sterling examples."[69]

More sophisticated readers cited Machar's obtrusive didacticism as her greatest fault. In 1888 Ethelwyn Wetherald delicately observed that "some of her poetry is produced by a collaboration of the artist and moralist within her, and . . . we are not so grateful for the moral as we are for the picture" (Wetherald, pp. 300-01). Machar's most ambitious novel, *Roland Graeme, Knight: A Novel of Our Time* (1892), received more intensive criticism than her other books, which were usually greeted with bland, generous praise. *The Week*'s review of *Roland Graeme* found fault with several minor characters but sympathized with Machar's attitudes towards literature and social problems. "Miss Machar is not a realist," it noted approvingly, for "she does not dwell on the haunts of sin and poverty." Rather, she "passes through them," showing that "there is a nobility of soul in the poorest classes of society that cannot be surpassed by any deeds of those in a higher station." Hence, while not a realist in the Zolaist sense, she succeeds "in painting life as it is."[70] Machar's subordination of artistry to moral purposes was approved by *The Week*, but not by William Wilfred Campbell, who stated that "with all its strong points as an earnest attempt to portray the influence of religion as a social lever, [*Roland Graeme*] falls below the ideal as a literary achievement, and there is not a spark of genius from cover to cover." Nonetheless, Campbell commended Machar's "strong and abiding interest in the social and religious problems of our present humanity" and described her as "a woman who will always be more human and more interesting than any book she will ever write."[71]

Machar as an interesting woman, rather than as a significant writer, is the subject of several articles written after the turn of the century, many of them by R. W. Cumberland, a graduate student and English instructor at Queen's University during the 1920s. Based on personal interviews and memories, they provide warm portraits of a "tiny, old lady" of "indomitable spirit" (MacCallum, p. 354), "a cultured Victorian echoing the notes characteristic of her age."[72] Of these, only Cumberland's article published in *Queen's Quarterly* just after Machar's death contains any literary criticism. His perspective shaped by the anti-Victorian modernism of the 1920s, Cumberland describes Machar as "an historic figure in Canadian literature," "a minor poet" whose "literary reputation will not increase."[73] Although he frequently calls attention to her limitations, he also pleads that she be sympathetically appreciated as a product of her age.

Cumberland's 1927 prophecy that Machar's reputation would

decline has proven true. She is barely mentioned in modern historical surveys of Canadian literature, and in *Literary History of Canada: Canadian Literature in English* she receives more than passing attention only in Frank Watt's comments on *Roland Graeme*, which he describes as "essentially a romantic story of high society," which "preaches not social or political revolution but *noblesse oblige.*"[74] However, the recent appearance of two serious considerations of her work may herald a revival of interest in Machar.

In 1975, Mary Vipond, a cultural historian, published a study of "the labour question in Canadian social gospel fiction."[75] Grouping *Roland Graeme* with Albert R. Carman's *The Preparation of Ryerson Embury* (1900) and Ralph Connor's *To Him That Hath* (1921), she evaluates the three novels' treatment of contemporary social issues in relation to similar fiction from Britain and the United States. Despite their artistic failings, she concludes that these three books "did at least attempt to grapple with contemporary problems," "did discuss some of the imperfections of prevailing conditions and attitudes," and "did speak sympathetically of certain reform ideas."[76] The most recent and comprehensive study of Machar is Nancy Miller Chenier's well-researched M.A. thesis, "Agnes Maule Machar: Her Life, Her Social Concerns, and a Preliminary Bibliography of Her Writing." Chenier argues that "for her time and her place, Agnes Maule Machar stands out as an aware and versatile person" (Chenier, p. vi), substantiating her position with detailed references to Machar's periodical writings and brief comments on her fiction.

Works

Rosanna Leprohon, James De Mille, and Agnes Maule Machar were born in separate colonies of British North America between 1829 and 1837 and established their careers in the 1860s and 1870s in the country which by then was known as Canada. Despite their common nationality, they appear to have operated in completely separate spheres, although they could scarcely have remained oblivious to one another.[77] They each received appreciative local criticism, yet due to a variety of personal and cultural circumstances they chose to subordinate the writing of fiction to other concerns: Leprohon to domestic life, De Mille to paying off his debts and pursuing an academic career, Machar to journalism and social causes. Hence none was tempted to leave his or her native environment for London or New York, or even Toronto, which became the centre of English-language Canadian publishing during the second half of the nineteenth century. As a result, they remained physically and culturally isolated from Canadian writers outside their local communities, although Machar did maintain an active international correspondence and De Mille successfully exploited the New York popular market.

In common with most other Canadian writers of the period, De Mille, Leprohon, and Machar had little sense of belonging to a national literary movement. Until Roberts, Carman, Lampman, Scott, and Campbell formed a loose circle in the 1890s (the last three having as their focus their "At the Mermaid Inn" column in *The Globe*), nearly all Canadian poets and novelists — not just tragic figures like Isabella Valancy Crawford or vociferous protesters like John Richardson and Sara Jeannette Duncan — suffered the absence of a stimulating, self-critical artistic community transcending civic and provincial boundaries. One can only speculate wishfully on the benefits that a richer cultural milieu might have brought to post-Confederation writing. In the case of Leprohon, De Mille, and Machar, a combination of choice and chance shaped their literary fortunes, destining them to support their country's conservative cultural values and to refrain from challenging the limits of their own talents.

As minor writers, they usually favoured conformity over innovation, employing traditional plot structures, conventional narrative methods, and stereotyped characters. At the same time, however, they occasionally incorporated into their works comments on the art of writing and bits of literary criticism, thereby presenting their views on the proper nature and function of fiction. The women's approach was almost uniformly serious, De Mille's frequently comic. Together they shared a sense of self-consciousness about their role as writer in relation to both the words on the page and the community at large. Their purpose was more often pragmatic than artistic, for they usually treated literature as a didactic medium providing historical and geographical facts or promoting social, moral, or literary reform. In all but his most frivolous stories, even De Mille frequently donned the hat of teacher, imparting information under the guise of entertainment: *Cord and Creese*, one of his most popular adventure stories, includes Greek quotations from Aeschylus and the *Odyssey* as well as information on Sable Island and Byzantine hymns.

While the best-known works of Machar, Leprohon, and De Mille vary considerably in style and content, all three writers were strongly influenced by the religious environments in which they were raised. Machar's first published book was *Faithful unto Death: A Memorial of John Anderson, Late Janitor of Queen's College* (1859), an account of an exemplary Presbyterian life, in the tradition of religious biography and autobiography which traces its roots back to seventeenth-century evangelical works like John Bunyan's *Grace Abounding to the Chief of Sinners*. When she turned to fiction, Machar structured her novels — some of which were intended for Sunday-school readers — as religious romances: most of her plots centre on an innocent, well-intentioned young man or woman who needs, and often seeks, further instruction in the Christian life. A suitable mentor, frequently a member of a clerical family, takes the young person in hand, safely guiding him or her past the pitfalls of materialism and self-indulgence. The narratives owe their blandness to their emphasis on instruction; few of Machar's heroes or heroines suffer much inner struggle, and except for young Katie Johnstone of *Katie Johnstone's Cross: A Canadian Tale*, who enjoys a model Christian death, they all find happiness and fulfilment in Christian service.

Although De Mille owed his commercial success to his comic and sensational potboilers, he likewise began his career with religious fiction influenced by his evangelical upbringing. In 1860 and 1861 he published stories in a Baptist paper, *The Christian Watchman* [Saint John], edited by his brother, Elisha Budd De Mill, who later rose to prominence as a Baptist minister. His first separately published book, *The Martyr of the Catacombs: A Tale of Ancient Rome* (1865), like Machar's first books, is an instructive religious tale for the young. De Mille went in for greater historical and dramatic colour than did Machar. Both *The Martyr of the Catacombs* and *Helena's Household* (1867) describe the persecution of the Christians in first-century Rome, allowing their author to display his scholarly knowledge of the period and to illustrate the superiority of the Christian doctrine of love over previous religions and philosophies with numerous conversions and scenes of martyrdom. Throughout her long career, Machar never significantly modified her religious views. In the late nineteenth-century debate between doubt and belief, she stood out as "one of the most articulate and intelligent Canadian lay defenders of Christian orthodoxy during one of the most difficult periods in the history of the Christian religion,"[78] her fiction frequently depicting the conversion of a sceptic or an atheist. De Mille, however, left his father's Baptist faith for the Anglicanism of his grandparents and reputedly later "took delight in ridiculing everything like cant,"[79] poking fun at matters he had treated more seriously in his early fiction. The Christians hiding in the catacombs and longing for martyrs' deaths in his first two novels may have inspired his satiric portrayal of the death-loving, cave-dwelling Kosekin in A Strange Manuscript, while in Cord and Creese the Reverend Courtenay Despard abhors "pietistic books," despising "the emotional, the rhapsodical, the meditative style of book in which one garrulously addresses one's soul from beginning to end."[80] One of De Mille's funniest victims of misguided religious zeal is feather-brained Mrs. Lovell, the much pursued merry widow of A Comedy of Terrors (1872), who acquired her dislike of men from her governess:

"... I assure, I have always had a very, very low opinion of men! When I was a little girl, my governess gave me a proof-book. Each page was headed with a statement about the nature of man. The first page was headed, 'Man is corrupt'; the second, 'Man is sinful'; the third, 'Man is a child of wrath'; the fourth, 'Man is weak'; the fifth, 'Man is desperately wicked'; and many more. Now ... I had to find texts from the Bible to prove all these; and I found no end of them, and I filled the book, and really, when I had finished, the impression that was left on my mind about man ... was that he was very, very shocking, and that it was a great pity that he was ever created. And I don't want ever, ever to be married again."[81]

While De Mille revelled in parodying religiosity and favoured a nondenominational state-supported system of higher education,[82] his poem Behind the Veil indicates that he entertained no doubts regarding the basic tenets of Christianity. Found among his papers after his death, already "prepared for the press with the greatest care,"[83] the poem is quite likely a late work. It recounts a vain quest into the world of spirits, after which the speaker returns to earth satisfied with his place in the divine scheme. The existence of this declaration of faith suggests that, like Machar and Leprohon, De Mille may have been concerned about contemporary attacks on the bastion of Christianity, even though his later fiction does not depict the conversion of disbelievers.

Rosanna Leprohon, educated in a convent, presumably received as thorough a grounding in her faith as the two Protestant writers did in theirs. However, the pattern of her treatment of religion differs from those of the other two writers and appears to have been tailored, in part, by her fictional models and her awareness of her audience. In her first stories, published in *The Literary Garland* between 1847 and 1851 and all set in England, she preaches morality while carefully avoiding specific references to church or religion, advocating general Christian principles which would meet the approval of Catholic and Protestant alike. That she could produce sectarian fiction is evidenced by "Eveleen O'Donnell" (1859), an evangelical Catholic romance written for *The Pilot* [Boston], an Irish-Catholic paper, in which a pious young orphan converts several Protestants and marries the most eligible. After this story, Leprohon's religious bias became less obtrusive. In her three Quebec novels, clerical characters scarcely appear and there is little appended religious moralizing; the religious dimension of *Antoinette de Mirecourt* emerges naturally from Antoinette's situation as a young woman in conflict with a church-dominated patriarchal society, the book's only evangelical detail being the return of Colonel Evelyn, the reputed infidel, to the Catholic fold. Because none of the characters in "The Manor House of de Villerai" or *Armand Durand* is tempted to marry outside the faith, religion is even less an issue in these novels. Indeed, the Catholic church is a more dominant presence in fiction written about Quebec by Protestant outsiders like William Kirby, Gilbert Parker, and Susan Frances Harrison than in Leprohon's work, although in private life she was devoutly religious. In her final stories in *The Canadian Monthly* and the *Canadian Illustrated News*, intended for a broad readership, she reverted to the manner of her *Garland* fiction, again avoiding references to specific denominations.

As strong as these writers' faith in Christianity was their dependence on romance. Love, adventure, and happy endings provide the structural framework of nearly all their fiction, whatever its content. Like many of their more illustrious contemporaries and predecessors, they laid a claim to realism by parodying or denigrating romance, yet they could not escape the plot conventions imposed by the forms of their stories.[84] Of the three, De Mille was most conscious of the irony of the novelist's dilemma: of his dependence upon inherently ridiculous situations to further his intrigues and structure his narratives. In many of his potboilers, he maintained a tongue-in-cheek approach, deliberately distancing himself from his material in order to parody the conventions he was compelled to use. Simple humorous padding by frequently repeating the obvious, a device probably arising from serial publication, is one of his less subtle indulgences; more witty are his games with coincidence, disguise and mistaken identity, sensational situations, and timely rescues. His serious adventure stories, such as *Cord and Creese*, *The Cryptogram*, and *The Living Link*, are elaborate brain-teasers, continually challenging the reader to decipher the next twist of the plot. In *An Open Question*, he calls attention to the puzzles he enjoys posing to both his characters and his readers by frequently arresting the narrative to present a point-by-point summary of the facts so far, as they appear to a specific character. The reader, who is allowed more information than the characters, knows each of these summaries to be faulty but lacks the details to piece together the entire picture. De Mille relinquishes his game of one-upmanship only at the very end, when he finally sorts out the identities of all the characters but one, whose fate, in the last words of the book, remains "an open question."[85]

Many of the most hallowed and hackneyed conventions of romance are amusingly caricatured in De Mille's lighter fiction. The duel — employed seriously by Leprohon to dispose of both Antoinette's nasty husband and the suitor preferred by her father — is pilloried in *The Lady of the Ice*, when the hero, having fallen in love with his friend's wife under the illusion that she was his daughter, is persuaded that since the two are gentlemen the affair must be resolved with a duel. The conflict between the code of duelling and the combatants' truly gentlemanly desire to reconcile their differences amicably is resolved by the Canadian winter, which provides such treacherous footing that the parties have to fight from sleighs and conveniently manage to miss one another. Another staple of romance used seriously by both Leprohon and Machar — the rescue of the heroine by a gentleman who courts her — provides the comic centre of De Mille's *The American Baron*, which stars foolish Minnie Willoughby as a helpless maiden whose primary concern is to escape the attention of suitors who have saved her life. While awaiting rescue from imprisonment by one of her more persistent admirers, Minnie complains, "I've *longed* so to be saved by a priest. These horrid men, you know, all go and propose the moment they save one's life; but a priest *can't*, you know — no, not even if he saved one a thousand times over."[86] In *The Babes in the Wood, a Tragic Comedy: A Story of the Italian Revolution of 1848*, De Mille opens by mocking the convention of the solitary horseman "slowly wending his way"[87] and continues to toy with this genre by calling attention to its staginess. Several climactic scenes close with the author calling "Tableau!" and some of the characters liken their plight of being tourists caught up in the Italian revolution of 1848 to "a bit from Verdi."[88] Stereotypical melodramatic villains also tickled De Mille's fancy, resulting in caricatures such as Count Girasole of *The American Baron*: "He was a crafty, wily, subtle, scheming Italian, whose fertile brain was full of ploys to achieve his desires, and who preferred to accomplish his aims by a torturous path, rather than by a straight one."[89]

When Machar and Leprohon criticized the conventions of romance, they usually did so with less deftness and more high seriousness than De Mille. Both writers use characters' literary tastes to signal their moral worth, often setting up a contrast between a virtuous heroine who shuns frivolous romances and an egotistical young lady with no higher purpose in life than reading novels. Machar's Katie Johnstone, whose taste has been "purified by drinking the living water" of the Bible, turns away "instinctively" from the novels preferred by her opposite, Clara Winstanley.[90] Marjorie Fleming learns to ration her reading of storybooks (although Walter Scott is permitted),[91] and Lottie Ward of "Lost and Won: A Canadian Romance" has been so corrupted by her penchant for "morbid sensational romances" such as *The Woman in White*, which are "not only vapid and unprofitable, but positively pernicious, from their highly coloured and false view of life,"[92] that she nearly ruins her lover's life by expecting him to behave like a romantic hero.

Despite her insistence that both her characters' reading and her own fiction relate directly to the improvement of life in the real world, Machar herself frequently slipped into romantic conventions. "Lost and Won" contains a Cinderella motif when an old Indian woman gives the hero a pair of beaded moccasins which are too small for his first choice, the undeserving Lottie, but fit perfectly the saintly Lenore. *Lucy Raymond: or, The Children's Watchword* concludes with the unexpected reunion of a long-lost brother and sister. Part of the plot of *Roland Graeme, Knight: A Novel of Our Time*, Machar's most serious attempt at social realism, turns, not on events in the union movement, but on a picture in a locket revealing the true identity of one character and the villainy of another, while the novel itself concludes with the four most admirable characters suitably paired off and an unexpected inheritance for the hero.

Ironically, of the three writers under discussion, it was Rosanna Leprohon who viewed most seriously the deleterious consequences of unsuitable literature, and yet she was the most dependent upon romantic conventions to structure her own novels. In the following description of an acceptable library, she rejects both high romance and "immoral" realism:

> No sentimental Miss fond of pathetic love verses would there have found much amusement — no young gentleman, admirer of the free bold immorality of the Sue and Balzac school could have gleaned even a pamphlet to his taste, but the works of such men as Fenelon [sic], Châteaubriand [sic] and Bourdaloue who had turned their brilliant genius to the improvement of their kind and the glory of Him who gave it to them, were there in profusion, attesting well the judgment of the careful mind and heart that had presided over their selection.[93]

A later story, however, concedes some educative value to contemporary fiction when Ada Dunmore, raised in great seclusion by an embittered father, complains that she and her brother "were as innocent as two children, destitute of the worldly knowledge which the perusal of even a few novels of the day would have imparted."[94] In Leprohon's *Garland* fiction, as in *Antoinette*, a character addicted to "silly French novels"[95] is immediately identifiable as misguided, albeit seldom actually wicked. Ida Beresford's troubles stem partly from her exposure to a collection of "silly novels and insipid poems," including "not one historical work . . . , not one volume containing the slightest matter, either useful or improving";[96] Antoinette owes her brush with tragedy to the meddling of Mrs. D'Aulnay, whose mind has been shaped by "novels, love-tales of the most reprehensible folly."[97] In addition, Sternfield teaches Antoinette English using as his text "some impassioned poem, — some graceful tale of fiction" (*AM*, p. 55), with the result that she too gives up "useful" reading in favour of "silly novels and exaggerated love-poems" (*AM*, p. 61). Despite Leprohon's denunciation of romantic literature, in *Antoinette* she creates an almost archetypal tale of love and adventure in which the heroine appears hopelessly trapped between an overbearing father on the one side and a secret marriage on the other, only to enjoy a timely delivery from her dilemma and eventual marriage to her most attractive suitor. Few readers can help concurring with Mrs. D'Aulnay's verdict that Antoinette's story ends "like a romance, a fairy tale" (*AM*, p. 366); in her concluding remarks, Leprohon herself evades this contradiction by focusing instead on her book's moral purpose, the inculcation of "a prudent horror of secret marriages" (*AM*, p. 369).

The happy ending of romance and fairy tale dominates the work of all three writers; indeed, William Kirby proved a notable exception to the Canadian romantic tradition when he terminated *The Golden Dog* "in all sadness" because in "most tales of this world" there is "neither poetic nor human justice."[98] Machar, Leprohon, and De Mille were essentially optimists, most of whose fiction demonstrates that in literature, even if not in life, justice can prevail. This attitude was shared by the community for whom they wrote: *The Canadian Monthly* commended Machar's handling of an attempted seduction in *For King and Country* because her version "fortunately ends, as such an episode does not always end, in the discomfiture of vice."[99]

In the work of Leprohon and Machar, the romantic structure clearly fortifies a moral structure. Until she turned to writing adventure stories rather like De Mille's for the *Canadian Illustrated News*, Leprohon employed quite consistently the same basic narrative pattern (whose prototype can be found in Jane Austen). The central character is a young woman who is entangled in the complexities of adult social and sexual relationships and who is without appropriate guidance, because she is either an orphan, the child of delinquent parents placed under an inadequate guardian, or simply because she is too strong-minded for her own good. Emotionally and morally threatened, she is eventually rescued. When her mentor is an older woman or a priest, the heroine ends up wedded to Mr. Right; when her deliverer is an eligible suitor, he marries her himself. In *Armand Durand; or, A Promise Fulfilled*, the sexual roles are reversed, Armand being saved by his "good angel," who becomes his second wife. Leprohon's last story of this nature, "Clive Weston's Wedding Anniversary," contains an important variation, for Virginia must act alone, without the comfort of a guide or confidante, to reclaim the love of the husband she has alienated.

Leprohon's stories frequently include the familiar romantic device of pairing characters who act as foils for one another: in *Antoinette*, the initially attractive Sternfield turns villainous, while the aloof Colonel Evelyn becomes an appealing Byronic hero; Blanche de Villerai,[100] despite her apparent coolness, is far more virtuous than the flighty socialite, Pauline de Nevers; Florence Huntingdon,[101] an Emma figure with more wit than wisdom, is given two contrasts, one almost unbearably virtuous, the other a novel-reading schemer. This doubling appears even more consistently in Machar's fiction, where the moral structure frequently overrides the romantic structure, resulting in novels with greater social relevance, but less unity of plot and overall appeal. Machar's basic narrative design is similar to Leprohon's: her main character is young (male or female), innocent, and well intentioned, but is in need of moral guidance. Two alternatives usually appear: worldly, self-interested characters who range from simply thoughtless to almost evil, and models of Christian virtue. The latter guide the main characters, imparting lessons in charity and goodness which contrast vividly with the self-indulgence of those dedicated only to pleasure. In the books where the principal character is old enough to marry, she or he is appropriately matched with the guide (if available) or with an equally public-spirited spouse.

While Leprohon may have owed her basic plot structure to Jane Austen, Machar seems to have been inspired in at least one of her stories by George Eliot. "Lost and Won" appears to be a Canadian version of *Adam Bede*: it is set in an idyllic agricultural community where Alan Campbell, like Adam, is attracted to a pretty but self-centred young woman. Lottie Ward toys with Alan's affections only to betray him — not as tragically as poor Hetty Sorrel, but by marrying a business schemer named Sharpley. Alan's subsequent depression is relieved by two characters who together add up to Eliot's Dinah Morris: Ralph Myles, a backwoods evangelist who ministers to logging camps (a forerunner of Ralph Connor's sky pilots); and saintly Lenore Arnold, who had converted Alan's brother on his deathbed and finds her "highest happiness in serving."[102] Alan eventually marries Lenore and enjoys a romantic benefit not given to Adam Bede when an apparently useless piece of inherited property turns out to contain valuable minerals. Machar's adaptation of Eliot is indicative of the precarious position of the nineteenth-century Canadian novelist who wanted to write about real life but could not escape conservative social values and romantic literary conventions. Nothing as devastating as the death of Hetty Sorrel's illegitimate child appears in any Canadian book of the period, nor is it likely that Canadians, who adored *Adam Bede*, would have tolerated at home as iconoclastic a figure as Dinah Morris. Hence Machar's versions of both Hetty and Dinah are significantly modified, while her hero is given extra virtues by performing such deeds as rescuing his father-in-law's mill from a forest fire. At the same time, however, Machar took pains to inject some details of Canadian life into her narrative, describing the unsuccessful attempt of Alan's friend, Philip Dunbar, to run for parliament against a ministerial incumbent and Alan's loss of his job for refusing to work against Dunbar.

Despite their dependence upon romantic conventions, Machar, Leprohon, and De Mille frequently wished to write concretely about the real world. Their solutions to the problem of marrying realism with romance ranged from clumsy authorial intrusion to clever manipulation of narrative form. All resorted at times to simply inserting wholesale into their fiction chunks of historical or geographical information, sometimes disguised as the utterances of knowledgeable characters, at others (for example, chapter five of *Antoinette*, which presents the historical setting) coming directly from the author. Throughout her career, Machar proved the least able of the three to gracefully incorporate factual information into her plots; her best effort occurs in *For King and Country*. Her plots tend to be diffuse and rambling, more often contrived to carry moral and educative messages than to develop characters and tell a story. Also the author of a number of books presenting British and

Canadian historical heroes to the young, and of travel sketches in periodicals, Machar frequently mixed the genres of historical and travel narrative into her fiction, especially her juvenile novels. Sections of three of her last books, *Marjorie's Canadian Winter* (1892), *Down the River to the Sea* (1894), and *The Heir of Fairmount Grange* (1895), turn into tourist guides, their didacticism overpowering their entertainment.

During the course of her literary career, Leprohon learned to resolve the problem with considerably more finesse than Machar. Her earliest fiction was high-life romance, utterly removed from real Canadian life in both content and diction and fablelike in its moral structure. Its flavour can be illustrated by the words of the heroine of "The Stepmother" (1847), whose widowed father brings home a young, pretty second wife. Looking at a portrait of her beloved mother, Amy tells her father, "Your second bride's fair semblance will better replace the plain, unpretending lineaments of her who will so soon be forgotten by all save her child. But fear not; the cherished image will not remain to wound the delicacy of your bride, or perchance to be exposed to her sneering remarks."[103]

When she turned closer to home with "The Manor House of de Villerai" (1859), Leprohon continued to write primarily about upper-class characters in suitably elevated language, but she also blended her romantic plot with Canadian history (taken from Garneau) by enlisting her hero in the Royal Rousillon Regiment, which conquered Fort William Henry in the summer of 1757 and attacked Ticonderoga in 1758. In this story, her characters participate more actively in actual historical incidents than in *Antoinette de Mirecourt* (1864), which is set against, rather than within, the events of the Conquest. In both works, Leprohon occasionally resorts to detailing historical matters in separate chapters and to footnoting comments on historical Montreal buildings, after the manner of Sir Walter Scott, the mentor of all Canadian historical novelists. Leprohon adds many of these details because they are essential to the reader's understanding of her characters' circumstances, not, as does Machar, solely to instruct both her readers and her characters.

Leprohon's last works demonstrate increasing control over her fictional material. *Armand Durand* (1868) is her most realistic novel, presenting a spectrum of Quebec life including the farm, the professions, and the aristocracy. While her earlier novels culminated in fairy-tale marriages, this book provides an extended analysis of marital failure (from which the hero is eventually released, to live happily ever after with his "good angel"). Leprohon's greatest technical advance in this book is her authorial restraint. She avoids the blatant pronouncements which mar *Antoinette*, allowing moral statements to develop through her characters instead of being imposed upon them. Judgements abound nonetheless: Captain de Chevandier is immediately identifiable as a scoundrel when we are told that "no religious principle guided him";[104] Armand Durand survives his unhappy first marriage and overcomes his drinking to become a brilliant political figure known for his "unwavering integrity" (*AD*, p. 77); while Gertrude, his second wife, fulfils the stereotype of the perfect wife, "the noble and superior woman who was the sharer of his thoughts, his hopes, his plans as she was of his life's destiny" (*AD*, p. 77). In *Armand Durand* the application of the fiction to real life is made abundantly clear, but the author wields a gavel instead of a sledgehammer.

It is unfortunate that due to illness and family cares Leprohon's literary activity declined during the last decade of her life. Her stories in the *Canadian Illustrated News* and *The Canadian Monthly* show the stylistic spareness she developed in *Armand Durand* but otherwise fail to develop the promise of the latter. In most she returns to the high-life world of her *Garland* fiction, the Canadian setting of these stories having little bearing on their content. She verges on social realism with "Clive Weston's Wedding Anniversary," which begins, rather than ends, with a marriage and describes a breakdown in communication between husband and wife. Perhaps the best-written tale of this last group is "Ada Dunmore," a cleanly narrated adventure story set in Upper Canada, in which the sensational plot, more typical of De Mille than of Leprohon, is toned down by the heroine's final conclusion that "the discipline of sorrow was of benefit to [us]. . . . It taught us to live, or try to live, for better and holier things than we had yet done — to turn our thoughts and aspirations to that life beyond the grave to which our paths on earth eventually lead. . . ."[105]

For De Mille, realism was scarcely an issue in most of his fiction; indeed, he frequently revelled in spinning tales distinguished by a total lack of relevance to the real world. In his series of juvenile stories set in Nova Scotia, however, reality predominates, despite the attempts of his schoolboy heroes to heighten their activities with exotic colour. Their efforts to transfer storybook romance from the realm of the imagination to everyday life meet with humorous deflation, but at the same time De Mille indicates that growing up in Grand Pré is itself an adventure; the land and its history provide ample excitement without the artificial enhancement of imaginary fortresses, robbers, pirates, and buried treasure. In the first book, *The B.O.W.C.* (The Brethren of the Order of the White Cross, a secret club founded by five boys), his youthful heroes embark on a voyage to gather geological specimens, during the course of which they acquire much practical information about survival in Minas Basin, but no rocks. De Mille sends them off on a mock-heroic note: "Now as Homer, at the outset of his poem, enumerates the ships and chieftains, so will I complete the enumeration of the voyageurs in this adventurous expedition."[106] Their games become serious when at various times they are lost in the fog, stranded on an apparently uninhabited island, cast adrift, or attacked by a shark. None of their misadventures proves fatal, for the boys continue to romp through five more books. Their activities are lightened by the comically inept Captain Corbett, a character almost out of Haliburton, Solomon, a stereotypical Negro servant, and Pat, an equally stereotypical Irish lad. Like Machar and Leprohon, De Mille incorporates factual information into his characters' adventures, inviting the reader to share the boys' discoveries and their teachers' knowledge of botany, zoology, and local history. The benignity of their physical environment is reflected in the way the B.O.W.C. black pirate flag, originally emblazoned with a skull, soon fades to look "more than ever like the face of some mild, venerable, and paternal monitor."[107] When the boys dig for treasure, they discover instead Acadian artefacts and the history of the expulsion; they try to find Captain Kidd's money hole on Oak Island, only to learn that legends are best left as legends; their frightening but ultimately innocuous experience with a minor forest fire leads to information about the great Miramichi fire of 1825; they know of Indians only as the perpetrators of "Indian warfare and Indian vengeance" from their "reading in Cooper's Leatherstocking series, and kindred works"[108] until they see Milicete Indians doing ordinary work in a sawmill.

In *A Strange Manuscript Found in a Copper Cylinder*, De Mille closed the gap between romance and realism in a particularly ingenious manner, his double narrative structure allowing him to have his cake and eat it too. Adam More's manuscript is more farfetched than any of De Mille's sensation novels, and as repetitious and carelessly assembled as some of De Mille's serial tales. But De Mille cleverly forestalls adverse external criticism by providing the commentary of the characters aboard Featherstone's yacht, who disagree whether they are reading an authentic account of a sailor's adventures, a sensation novel, or a "satirical romance."[109] At the same time, he indulges his gift for parody, mimicking literary critics and reviewers in the speeches of Otto Melick, a fatuous "*littérateur* from London ... with the restless manner of one who lives in a perpetual fidget" (*SM*, pp. 65-66). Melick initially comes up with the preposterous notion that the manuscript has been set afloat by "some fellow who wanted to get up a sensation novel and introduce it to the world with a great flourish of trumpets" (*SM*, p. 66). He later decides to analyse More's work as a satire "on things in general" which "mocks us by exhibiting a new race of men, animated by passions and impulses which are directly the opposite of ours, and yet no nearer happiness than we are," extracting the platitudinous message that "the happiness of man consists not in external surroundings, but in the internal feelings" (*SM*, p. 245). Melick, ironically, shares More's evaluation of the superiority of Western civilization in that he too fails to see that far from being "opposite" to us, the Kosekin manifest many of the life-denying elements of the current era and partake in the same hypocrisies, intrigues, injustices, and power struggles which darken the "enlightened" world. Whatever De Mille's personal interpretation of his fantasy novel, he quickly disposes of Melick, who meets Oxenden's challenge that he is reading too deeply into a simple travel document by retreating into the pat phraseology of the book reviewer. Denouncing More in favour of Defoe and Swift, Melick echoes the reviewers of De Mille's own potboilers, describing the author as "tawdry" and "a gross plagiarist," having "the worst vices of the sensational school ... [such as] marks of haste, gross carelessness, and universal feebleness," and violating "in the most glaring manner all the ordinary proprieties of style" (*SM*, p. 247).

Literary critics and reviewers are not the only butts of De Mille's wit. The book's symposium structure allows De Mille long passages of factual exposition: Dr. Congreve's detailed disquisitions on Ross's expedition to the Antarctic, extinct animals, and coral islands; Oxenden's lectures on Hebrew, Grimm's law, and comparative religion. These realistic sections balance the fantasy, giving the illusion that De Mille is himself submitting More's adventures to the objective scrutiny of science. Yet, within the book as we have it, science illuminates only the backdrop to the real drama, which is philosophical, and fails to provide a significant analysis of the meaning of More's encounter with the Kosekin, which is left to the reader to resolve for himself. Even the authenticity of the manuscript remains a question of faith: Oxenden believes it to be genuine, Melick denounces it as a fake, Congreve avoids the matter altogether, and Featherstone cares only about dinner.

The social criticism contained in the satire of *A Strange Manuscript* has attracted the attention of a number of excellent critics, who see in the Kosekin De Mille's criticism of some of the basic ills of his age — materialism, moral and religious hyprocrisy, and Victorian "anti-vitalism."[110] In form, the book appears to be unique in Victorian Canada; in content, it is not untypical of its time and place in that it offers and invites moral commentary while it provides entertainment.

Social criticism in nineteenth-century Canadian fiction was much milder than in England, for most Canadian writers evaded controversial topics such as the economic and political effects of the Industrial Revolution, labour unrest, and sexual morality. This evasion can itself be seen as a form of social commentary, however, as in Henry Morgan's entry on Leprohon in his *Bibliotheca Canadensis* (1867), which commends Leprohon's novels of the era of the Conquest: ". . . by her often graphic descriptions of the refinement and chivalry of that period, [she] has sought to exert a salutary influence over the present matter of fact and 'hard money' world in which we live."[111] When nineteenth-century Canadian writers did look at contemporary troubles, they preferred safe subjects, one of the safest being temperance. De Mille restricted his comments on alcohol to his juvenile fiction. In *Fire in the Woods* (1871), the boys hear of the comic drunkenness of Solomon's wife and are terrified by the less comic drunkenness of their Indian guide. In *The Seven Hills* (1873), the second book in his "Young Dodge Club" series, De Mille partially retracted the racist slant of his earlier novel when he declared, "It is unfortunate that the Anglo-Saxon, or English-speaking race, if it be the greatest on earth, is also the most prone to drunkenness."[112]

Alcoholism is not an identified vice in the elegant upper-class world of Leprohon's early romances and appears only in *Armand Durand*, her most realistic novel. Trapped by an unhappy marriage to a "shallow, violent tempered, though beautiful woman," Durand escapes into drink and is rescued when Gertrude, the "dignified, refined girl" (*AD*, p. 68) he should have married, makes him take the pledge. His fortitude, to the extent of not touching a drop of wine at a friend's wedding, is one of the tests which eventually earn him Gertrude's hand after his first wife conveniently dies.

Machar's fiction indicates that like Leprohon she saw intemperance as a problem primarily of the middle and lower classes. Upper-class characters, like Jack Howard of *The Heir of Fairmount Grange*, may drink themselves to death with impunity, but to families who are not independently wealthy alcoholism spells disaster. Machar debated the issue of prohibition in a series of articles in *The Canadian Monthly* (Chenier, pp. 39-48, 77), arguing in favour of restrictive legislation to protect the poor, particularly women and children, from the economic hardships and physical and emotional abuse resulting from alcoholism. Her novels reinforce her position that the restriction of alcohol must be a central plank in any platform of social reform. In her first, *Katie Johnstone's Cross*, Machar depicts the effects of intemperance on two families: the Egans, where the children are neglected because both parents drink, and Katie's, whose father dies penniless as a result of his indulgence. In "Lost and Won," Machar attacks the social practice of "treating," asking:

> . . . to what remote region does not the tavern-keeper penetrate, with his "bitters" and whiskey bottles; and where is the innocent Arcadian district which does not abound with temptations to that insidious poison which, like a canker worm, destroys both the flower and the fruit of many an otherwise happy and useful life? *Not* in Canada, at all events![113]

Her broadest analysis of the problem occurs in *Roland Graeme, Knight: A Novel of Our Time*, her most serious exposition of the ills of the day. Due to her dual allegiance to realism and romance, Machar's treatment of alcoholism in this book contains interesting inconsistencies. On the realistic level, she shows how the frustrated, underpaid proletariat (represented by Jim Mason) frequently seeks solace in drink. When alternative forms of entertainment are available, in this case the "Helping Hands Society," which offers books, lectures, and lemonade, many workers embrace temperance (although Jim himself proves rather recalcitrant). Members of the upper classes, represented by Harold Pomeroy, idle son of the factory owner, are prone to "a life of unrestrained self-indulgence,"[114] presumably including alcohol, because they know no higher purpose. In contrast to these two believable, if rather simplified, situations, is that of Mrs. Travers, the character at the centre of the book's romantic subplot. Initially a mysterious figure, ill and impoverished, she is distinguished from her working-class neighbours by her "soft musical English voice, decidedly the voice of a lady" (*RG*, p. 38). The cause of her illness turns out to be alcoholism, but she is absolved of any responsibility because she is "the poor victim of a hereditary craving" (*RG*, p. 226) for which her husband had abandoned her and which Dr. Blanchard, the novel's medical authority, fears may be passed on to her daughter. Machar thus suggests that there are two kinds of alcoholism: one for which society is responsible, and one which is the result of genetic inheritance. The former receives greater consideration in most of her writing, but in *Roland Graeme* her commitment to a romantic plot requires her to pay considerable attention to hereditary dipsomania, since Mrs. Travers' derelict husband turns out to be the Reverend Cecil Chillingworth, a fashionable preacher seeking the hand of Nora Blanchard. Both Machar's didactic purpose and her plot demand that Chillingworth (who had believed his wife to be dead) be unmasked as a hypocrite so that Nora can marry Roland and Machar's idealized minister, the Reverend John Alden, can be suitably esteemed.

Roland Graeme is one of the few Canadian novels of the nineteenth century to acknowledge the existence and debilitating effects of industrialization. The hero of the book is Canadian, but Machar could not bring herself to set the mill town where the action occurs in Canada, which appears in most of her fiction as a rather Arcadian agricultural nation. In "Lost and Won" (1875), Machar mentioned but avoided discussing "the relative duties of wealth to poverty, of capital to labour," describing this issue as one "far more interesting to [her character, Philip Dunbar] than it would be in these pages."[115] By 1892, however, she found the problem serious enough to make it the theme of her most important novel.

Roland Graeme, son of a Scottish-Canadian clergyman, first

comes to Minton, U.S.A., as a reporter. Reputedly an agnostic, he is moved by the evils of industrialization to embark on a secular mission, joining the Knights of Labour and founding his own newspaper, *The Brotherhood*, to promote the workers' interests. Not overly modest, he sees himself as a latter-day Red Cross Knight, whose ideal is "to ride abroad redressing human wrongs" (*RG*, p. 124), a quotation which also serves as the book's epigraph. The workers are represented by the Mason family, whose idealized daughter, Lizzie, has chosen factory work over domestic service in order to stay at home to help her family and who is "as truly chained by invisible fetters to her daily toil among those relentless wheels and pulleys, as if she were a galley slave" (*RG*, p. 67).

Within the novel, Machar offers several solutions to the conflict of labour and capital. A visitor from England describes her father's successful experiment in setting up a profit-sharing cooperative and mentions also the enterprises of "Monsieur Godin, a disciple of Fourier's, who had consecrated his life to elevate the condition of workingmen" (*RG*, p. 102). So radical a reorganization of labour relations would be too much for Minton, however, where Pomeroy, owner of the textile mill, is trying to cut wages and lengthen hours. When a strike threatens, Roland supports it, at the same time pleading to the workers to "act, not in a factious, selfish spirit, but in that of brotherly fairness and generous trust" and to "think not only of rights but of *duty*, of helping others as well as themselves" (*RG*, p. 168). Pomeroy eventually does increase wages and give a Saturday half-holiday — not because he has seen the light, but to reward the men for putting out a fire in his mill and to buy their cooperation in filling a large order.

Roland, meanwhile, loses some of his love for the lower classes, finding in them the same "spirit of selfishness" (*RG*, p. 212) as in their employers. Disillusioned by the town's hostile reception of his good intentions and chastened by dramatic events in the romantic side of the plot (the death of a beautiful sixteen-year-old girl he had admired and the attempted suicide of a friend), Roland rides off to start a cooperative factory elsewhere, hand-in-hand with Nora Blanchard, whose charitable work among the poor had earlier identified her as Roland's true mate. By the end of the story, Roland has been converted from religious doubt to belief, has received an unexpected legacy, and has modified his aims from initiating a Golden

Age of fraternal cooperation to working on behalf of the Eight Hours Movement.

In *Roland Graeme*, Machar's solution to labour unrest is, as Frank Watt puts it, *"noblesse oblige."*[116] Roland cannot conceive of the workers gaining ground without the help of their social betters, "a whole army of intelligent, energetic, educated young men to take up their cross and help them win the day" (*RG*, p. 125). Machar approaches the problem in the same manner as *The Brotherhood*, Roland's paper, which is characterized by "the temperate and moderate tone in which it set forth existing wrongs and grievances, and appealed to the sense of justice and humanity of those with whom it lay to remedy them" (*RG*, p. 12). She appears to believe that once the upper classes are properly informed of the hardships of the workers, their innate sense of justice will impel them to act, just as Pomeroy's daughter helps administer a club for working-class girls and tries to persuade her father to enact certain reforms. Underlying Machar's moderate stance may be a fear of violence and class warfare. At one point Roland asks, "If we can't wake up the rich, why mayn't we wake up the poor?" To which the Reverend John Alden, Machar's spokesman throughout the novel, replies, "Let the horrors of the French Revolution answer that question, once for all! . . . There is enough to wake up the poor to, in regard to their shortcomings. Let us try to wake each class up as to what lies in its own power to reform" (*RG*, p. 148). Above all, Machar preaches that the solution to social ills is to be found through a spirit of active Christianity. Alden tells Roland that his work will be valuable only if he "can, at the same time, raise this great mass of toiling humanity in the moral and spiritual scale, as well as in the material and intellectual one" (*RG*, p. 125); Nora Blanchard performs her little acts of charity under the principle that (quoting Goethe) "Man is not born to solve the problem of the universe, but to find out what he has to do, and then do that" (*RG*, p. 68). Machar's analysis of the problem and her proposed solutions are, at best, simplistic and naïve in the manner of turn-of-the-century social gospel fiction. Nonetheless, *Roland Graeme* addresses the issues far more directly than do Archibald Lampman's dream-vision (and nightmare) poems, which are frequently hailed as literary manifestations of late nineteenth-century Canadian socialist thought.

One particular area of social concern in which De Mille and Leprohon shared an interest with Machar was the education and entertainment of children and adolescents. None wrote a word which could bring a blush to the cheek of the young person, and all three acknowledged a need for literature especially intended for youthful readers. They all stressed that happy, well-guided children grow into moral, responsible adults. This interest in the imaginative development of the young was shared by several of their contemporaries: Mrs. Cushing and Mrs. Cheney, who founded *The Snow Drop* (1847-53); Susanna Moodie and Catharine Parr Traill, who wrote juvenile fiction in England and in Canada; Isabella Valancy Crawford, who wrote fairy tales and an adventure book for boys; and James Macdonald Oxley, who published more than two dozen juvenile adventure stories between 1885 and 1905.

Among these nineteenth-century Canadian writers, Rosanna Leprohon, taking as her province the preparation of young women for marriage, held a decidedly conservative position. Unlike Machar and De Mille, she wrote for a family rather than a specifically juvenile audience, directing much of her fiction towards adolescent girls. It is possible that, like Jane Austen, she was influenced by eighteenth-century courtesy books;[117] most of her novels are, on one level, fictionalized conduct manuals, illustrating the obligations of parents to bring up their daughters properly and of daughters to obey their parents, marry wisely, and, above all, become good, supportive wives. Beginning with her first *Garland* tale, published in 1847 just after she turned eighteen, Leprohon preached that a happy marriage must grow from "felicity based not on an affection the result of a passing fancy, but on the innate conviction of each other's long tried and well proven worth."[118] In *Antoinette*, written to dissuade impetuous teenagers from the temptations of secret marriages, her authorial voice intrudes to comment that "mutual love and community of soul and feeling" are not enough; these must be supplemented by "mutual esteem, moral worth, and prudence in point of suitable choice" (*AM*, p. 24).

Once married, a young woman undertakes the serious obligations of wifehood. The duty of a husband is to "shield" his wife from "life's trials and cares" (*AM*, p. 226), but if he proves reprobate, the duty of his wife is still to submit. Antoinette, in the depths of her misery, prays that "God would give her strength and grace to preserve unsullied till death, even by one rebellious thought, the fidelity she had vowed to Audley" and asks for "a wifely spirit of submission which would enable her to patiently bear all the bitter trials Sternfield's unkindness might yet inflict upon her" (*AM*, p. 240). So much is submission a woman's lot that, at the end of "The Manor House of de Villerai," Blanche explains her desire to remain in Quebec after the Conquest, with no conscious irony, as follows: "I will remain in Canada, my home, my birth-place, and even though I will henceforth be under a foreign rule, I am a woman and can easily bow my neck to it."[119] However, not all Leprohon's female characters are submissive: Ada Dunmore receives the same education as her brother, without appearing to suffer or benefit particularly; Eveleen O'Donnell converts several Protestants; Eva Huntingdon reforms her brother; and Gertrude de Beauvoir reforms her future husband. But, in Leprohon's eyes, the purpose of female education is to prepare girls for "the high and important offices of wives and mothers,"[120] and in many of her stories delinquent wives are the cause of marital discord. Rose Lauzon's shrewish stepmother makes life miserable for her husband and family; selfish Delima, Armand Durand's first wife, fails to provide a cheerful home; beautiful Virginia Weston fritters her time and energy on social activities; Mrs. D'Aulnay, whose own marriage is scarcely exemplary, presumes to select a mate for her younger cousin.

For Agnes Maule Machar, female education was a much broader issue, although she too subscribed to the Victorian convention that women, by virtue of their greater moral sensibility, could and should reclaim their prodigal brothers and reform their social and moral inferiors. In two juvenile novels, *Katie Johnstone's Cross* and *Marjorie's Canadian Winter*, she presents her young heroines as models of charitable Christian conduct. Following the example of a minister's daughter, fourteen-year-old Katie helps to regenerate the deprived, impoverished Egan family by sewing for them and teaching the children to read; Marjorie, spending a winter in Montreal with the idealized Ramsay family, learns to do good works such as visiting a boy injured in a factory which exploits child labour. In this book, Machar (like Leprohon) chides women who fail to approach life seriously. She recommends that girls learn to talk less, avoid desultory work habits, and keep up with current events. Above all, she advocates that girls be allowed to choose the education that suits their temperaments, abilities, and future goals.

The author of many articles advocating improved higher education for women and university coeducation, she shows Dr. Ramsay sending Marion, his "not particularly intellectual" daughter,[121] to a girls' finishing school, while Millie, who wishes to become a doctor, attends grammar school with her brother. However, she cautions girls against seeking scholastic excellence simply out of prideful ambition; Lucy Raymond learns to study "with very little reference to prizes, or even the approbation of masters, but from a deep interest in the studies themselves, and a feeling of their beneficent effect in leading her to higher ranges of thought."[122]

De Mille likewise expressed liberal views on feminism and education, although he had far more to say about the latter than on the former. In some of his potboilers, such as "The Minnehaha Mines," he presents vigorous women with greater intellectual powers than the hero, while in *A Strange Manuscript* More's discomfort when Layelah "take[s] the initiative" (*SM*, p. 193) in courting him reveals an additional chink in the armour of this stalwart representative of middlebrow British values. Seth Grimes, one of De Mille's comic travelling Americans, puts the case for female equality quite succinctly: "Women . . . have certain inalienable rights, among which may be mentioned as self-evident truths their natural right to life, liberty, the pursuit of happiness, and the privilege of travelling wherever they darn please, so long as they're able to pay their way."[123]

The education of boys, however, concerned him more than that of girls. Female characters appear only on the periphery of his schoolboy stories, and in his published inaugural addresses, delivered at Dalhousie in 1873 and 1878, he assumes that higher education is only for men. In these two speeches, De Mille champions liberal education. While not denying that there is a need for both denominational and utilitarian training, he argues that the state should support a nondenominational system of higher education to give young men mental discipline and broader culture. A classical liberal education may have little practical value (as evidenced by Bob Laidlaw of "The Minnehaha Mines"), but it trains the mind:

> ... the average college graguate exhibits a lamentable ignorance of his Latin, his Greek, his Mathematics, and, it may be sorrowfully added, sometimes even of his English. What then? The effect of his education remains, and will remain, if he can

think with accuracy; if he show a strengthened understanding, a chastened imagination; if he can study methodically, and reason correctly.[124]

In addition, the student of Greek will acquire "Culture" — an appreciation of "true refinement . . . , simple elegance . . . , purest grace."[125] In the 1878 address, De Mille acknowledges the claims of the rising physical sciences and resolves the conflict between what he calls the "old" and the "new" learning by advocating that students be allowed to select their preferred course of study, although he does not disguise his partiality for the old.

The heroes of his B.O.W.C. stories, who attend grammar school, not college, receive both the old and the new learning under the guidance of teachers who "stimulate the mind and develop its powers."[126] At Grand Pré School, the students learn lessons in prudence and responsibility by encountering situations in which they must exercise their own judgement, while their teachers take advantage of the school's location by incorporating classroom learning with field trips and on-the-spot lessons in geology, biology, and local history. Education is presented as part of, not an appendage to, the experience of growing up, and the opening of the school term is continually deferred by the boys' adventures. The boys also receive a solid grounding in the classics: when they plan to dig for treasure at midnight and concoct a mysterious ceremony for the occasion, each recites the most solemn thing he can think of: passages from English history, Euclid, and "Arnold's Latin Exercises"; Latin grammar rules; and the opening of Caesar's *Conquest of Gaul*.[127] Masters in their own spheres, the teachers are warm, fallible individuals, who frequently prove less able than their students at handling practical matters. The comedy and misadventures in these books are usually constructive, underscoring lessons in survival and judgement without heavy-handed moralism.

As well as illustrating their views on education, Machar, De Mille, and Leprohon used their fiction to teach young Canadians about Canada. Aside from his B.O.W.C. books, De Mille paid little attention to his native land. He set two novels in Canada, *The Lady of the Ice* in Quebec and *The Lily and the Cross* in Acadia, and he slipped Canadian references into several others — more, one senses, to expand the territory of his fiction market (and perhaps to tease his American readers) than to contribute seriously to the development of a native literature. The B.O.W.C. novels, in contrast, despite their publication in the United States, depict their region with great fidelity, occasionally including paeans to its natural beauty.

In De Mille's Canadian fiction, local pride does not lead to political nationalism; for Machar, however, the inculcation of patriotic fervour was one of the duties of the Canadian writer. Leprohon included passages of historical information in "The Manor House of de Villerai" and *Antoinette de Mirecourt* to enrich their backgrounds; while she creates sympathy for the victims of history, she does not exalt historical figures and makes no appeals to her readers' sense of patriotism. Her purpose was to avoid chauvinism and to heal the breach between French and English without rekindling potentially dangerous feelings, while at the same time reminding both groups of the many connections between past and present. Machar, on the other hand, often wrote to inspire patriotic emotions. *For King and Country* (1874), an early venture into the field of nationalistic fiction, canonizes Isaac Brock as "as brave and heroic a leader as ever bled for Britain on any world-renowned battlefield"[128] and is dedicated "To All Young Canadians" as follows: "In the hope that the memories which it records may stimulate them to endeavour, in the strength of that righteousness which alone exalteth a nation, to make the future of CANADA abundantly worthy of its past."

In 1894, in tune with the nationalist and imperialist fervour of the time, she declared in *The Week*:

> Above all, we want Canadian writers inspired with the true sentiment of patriotism. . . . With our racial differences and warring factions we can never be fused into *one people* without the *love of country* which it is one of the highest offices of poetry to foster.[129]

This patriotic spirit underlies her history books for children — *Stories of New France* (1890), *Heroes of Canada* (1893), *Stories of the British Empire for Young Folks and Busy Folks* (1913) — and inspires much of the didactic content of *Marjorie's Canadian Winter* (1893). In this novel, Machar waves her flag on three fronts: she advocates greater rapprochement between Canadians and Americans; she arouses imperialist sentiments by having her characters eagerly follow General Gordon's plight at Khartoum through the winter of 1884-85; and she tries to reconcile English and French by giving her young readers many lessons in the romantic history of Quebec. Curiously, although the book is set in Montreal, there is little sense that French Canadians exist in the present. The Ramsay children know Latin and Greek better than French, and only one French-Canadian character enters the contemporary narrative. Hence for Machar, as for Leprohon and for De Mille in *The Lily and the Cross*, French Canada was of literary value primarily for its picturesque past. The history of English Canada needed to be enlivened with an infusion of Quebec and Acadian romance, yet contemporary French Canada remained almost a foreign country.

Juxtaposing and comparing the work and careers of Rosanna Leprohon, Agnes Maule Machar, and James De Mille reveals both the range and the limitations of fiction in Victorian Canada. Their books included didactic thesis novels and escapist romances; their concerns varied from simply making money, to serious social matters, to the art of fiction. The book market, Canadian conservatism, and their own limited talents dictated the restrictions within which they worked as they wrestled with the conventions of romance. None can claim to be the great undiscovered Canadian genius, but all three were recognized as important writers in their day. As literary pioneers, they deserve our consideration and understanding, for they too ". . . had their being once / and left a place to stand on."[130]

NOTES

[1] Henry Morgan, *Canadian Men and Women of the Time* (Toronto: Briggs, 1898), II, 577-78.

[2] Henry Morgan, "Leprohon, Mrs.," in *The Dominion Annual Register and Review for 1879* (Ottawa: MacLean, Roger, 1880), p. 409.

[3] Archibald MacMurchy, *Handbook of Canadian Literature* (Toronto: Briggs, 1906), p. 89.

[4] For several years, until 1862, the Leprohons lived at 6 Rue St. Antoine and McGee at 220 Rue St. Antoine.

[5] Henri Deneau, "The Life and Works of Mrs. Leprohon," M.A. Thesis Montréal 1948, pp. 64-66.

[6] *Antoinette de Mirecourt* appeared in book form in French in 1865 and 1881 and was serialized in *Le Pionnier de Sherbrooke* in 1866-67 and *Les*

Nouvelles Soirées Canadiennes in 1886-87. Information on the French publication of Leprohon's work is to be found in the Dictionnaire des Oeuvres Littéraires du Québec, I (1978).

[7] 1861, 1884, 1892, 1901, 1925. Deneau, p. 93.

[8] Susanna Moodie, "Editor's Table," The Victoria Magazine, I (June 1848), 240.

[9] Carl F. Klinck, Introd., Antoinette de Mirecourt; or, Secret Marrying and Secret Sorrowing, by Rosanna Leprohon, New Canadian Library, No. 89 (Toronto: McClelland and Stewart, 1973), p. 10.

[10] Mary Jane Edwards, "Essentially Canadian," Canadian Literature, No. 52 (Spring 1972), p. 9.

[11] J. C. Stockdale, "Mullins, Rosanna (Leprohon)," Dictionary of Canadian Biography, X (1972).

[12] Deneau, passim.

[13] Deneau, p. 56.

[14] Rosanna Leprohon, "Florence; or, Wit and Wisdom," The Literary Garland, NS 7 (1849), 247-48.

[15] Rosanna Leprohon, "The Manor House of de Villerai," Family Herald [Montreal], 4 Jan. 1860, p. 61.

[16] Archibald MacMechan, "De Mille, the Man and the Writer," The Canadian Magazine, 27 (1906), 404. All further references to this work (MacMechan) appear in the text.

[17] Douglas MacLeod, "A Critical Biography of James De Mille," M.A. Thesis Dalhousie 1968, p. 70.

[18] James De Mille, "The Minnehaha Mines," The New Dominion and True Humorist, 4 (8 Jan.-25 June 1870). A complete run of The New Dominion and True Humorist for 1870 is held by the University of British Columbia library.

[19] A. J. Crockett and George Geddie Patterson, "Concerning James De Mille," in More Studies in Nova Scotian History, by George Geddie Patterson (Halifax: Imperial, 1941), p. 146. All further references to this work (Crockett) appear in the text.

[20] MacLeod, p. 52.

[21] Among the Brigands (1871), The Seven Hills (1873), and The Winged Lion; or, Stories of Venice (1876).

[22] Rev. of The Living Link, Canadian Illustrated News, 22 Aug. 1874, p. 118.

[23] Lawrence J. Burpee, "Who's Who in Canadian Literature: James De Mille," The Canadian Bookman, 8 (1926), 204.

[24] George Stewart, "Canadian Literature," *Stewart's Quarterly Magazine*, 3 (Jan. 1870), 404; "Professeur James De Mille," in *"Scrap-Book" Contenant Divers Souvenirs Personnels du Canada et des "21," Quelques Poésies, etc.*, by Comte de Premio-Real (Québec: C. Darveau, 1880), p. 183.

[25] Ethelwyn Wetherald, "Some Canadian Literary Women — II. 'Fidelis,' " *The Week*, 5 April 1888, p. 300. All further references to this work (Wetherald) appear in the text.

[26] F. L. MacCallum, "Agnes Maule Machar," *The Canadian Magazine*, 62 (1924), 354. All further references to this work (MacCallum) appear in the text.

[27] Nancy Miller Chenier, "Agnes Maule Machar: Her Life, Her Social Concerns, and a Preliminary Bibliography of Her Writing," M.A. Thesis Carleton 1977, p. 2. All further references to this work (Chenier) appear in the text.

[28] R. W. Cumberland, "Agnes Maule Machar," *Queen's Quarterly*, 34 (Jan. 1927), 331, 335.

[29] Marilyn Flitton, *An Index to* The Canadian Monthly and National Review *and* Rose-Belford's Canadian Monthly (Toronto: Bibliographical Society of Canada, 1976), pp. 87-88.

[30] D. M. R. Bentley and Mary Lynn Wickens, *A Checklist of Literary Materials in* The Week (Ottawa: Golden Dog, 1978), pp. 14-16, 55, 81, 114, 150.

[31] R. W. Cumberland, "Agnes Maule Machar," *Willison's Monthly*, 3 (June 1927), 34.

[32] A. B. McKillop, *A Disciplined Intelligence: Critical Enquiry and Canadian Thought in the Victorian Era* (Montreal: McGill-Queen's Univ. Press, 1979), pp. 217-18.

[33] Frank Watt, "Literature of Protest," in *Literary History of Canada: Canadian Literature in English*, gen. ed. and introd. Carl F. Klinck (Toronto: Univ. of Toronto Press, 1967), p. 461.

[34] Rev. of *The Living Link*, *Canadian Illustrated News*, 22 Aug. 1874, p. 118.

[35] A. R. Bevan, "James De Mille and Archibald MacMechan," *Dalhousie Review*, 35 (Autumn 1955), 211.

[36] Stewart, "Canadian Literature," pp. 403-04.

[37] Rev. of *A Strange Manuscript Found in a Copper Cylinder*, *The Week*, 26 July 1888, p. 561.

[38] Charles G. D. Roberts, "De Mille's 'Behind the Veil,' " *The Week*, 23

Feb. 1894, p. 301.

[39] Lorne Pierce, *An Outline of Canadian Literature* (Toronto: Ryerson, 1927), p. 164.

[40] J. D. Logan, *The Highway of Canadian Literature* (Toronto: McClelland and Stewart, 1924), p. 323.

[41] R. E. Watters, Introd., *A Strange Manuscript Found in a Copper Cylinder*, by James De Mille, New Canadian Library, No. 68 (Toronto: McClelland and Stewart, 1969), p. viii.

[42] Watters, p. ix.

[43] George Woodcock, "De Mille and the Utopian Vision," *Journal of Canadian Fiction*, 2, No. 3 (1973), 177.

[44] Crawford Kilian, "The Cheerful Inferno of James De Mille," *Journal of Canadian Fiction*, 1, No. 3 (1972), 61-67.

[45] M. G. Parks, "Strange to Strangers Only," *Canadian Literature*, No. 70 (Autumn 1976), pp. 61-78.

[46] Parks, p. 74.

[47] Wayne R. Kime, "The American Antecedents of James De Mille's *A Strange Manuscript Found in a Copper Cylinder*," *The Dalhousie Review*, 55 (Summer 1975), 285-86, 300.

[48] Kenneth J. Hughes, "*A Strange Manuscript*: Sources, Satire, a Positive Utopia," in *The Canadian Novel: Beginnings*, ed. John Moss (Toronto: NC, 1980), p. 123.

[49] James De Mille, *The Dodge Club; or, Italy in MDCCCLIX*, introd. Gwendolyn Davies (1869; rpt. Sackville, N.B.: Ralph Pickard Bell Library, 1981).

[50] Sheila Egoff, *The Republic of Childhood* (Toronto: Oxford Univ. Press, 1975), p. 299.

[51] Stockdale, p. 537.

[52] Moodie, p. 240.

[53] Henry Morgan, *Sketches of Celebrated Canadians* (Quebec: Hunter, Rose, 1862), p. 747.

[54] "The Old Thing," rev. of *Antoinette de Mirecourt*, *The Saturday Reader*, 9 Sept. 1865, p. 4.

[55] Edwards, pp. 9, 20.

[56] "Antoinette de Mirecourt," *L'Ordre*, 12 déc. 1864, p. 2.

[57] E. Lef. de Bellefeuille, "*Antoinette de Mirecourt*," *La Revue Canadienne*, 1 (juil. 1864), 444.

[58] John Talon Lesperance, "The Literary Standing of the New Dominion," *Canadian Illustrated News*, 24 Feb. 1877, p. 118.

[59] J. D., "Madame Leprohon," *L'Opinion Publique*, 2 oct. 1879, pp. 469-70.

[60] "The Late Mrs. Leprohon," *Canadian Illustrated News*, 4 Oct. 1879, p. 211.

[61] "The Poetical Works of Mrs. Leprohon," *Rose-Belford's Canadian Monthly*, 8 (1882), 325.

[62] Rosanna Leprohon, *The Poetical Works of Mrs. Leprohon* (Montreal: Lovell, 1881), p. 4.

[63] Linda Shohet, "Love and Marriage — Canada 1760," *Journal of Canadian Fiction*, 2, No. 3 (1973), 101-03.

[64] Elizabeth Brady, "Towards a Happier History: Women and Domination," in *Domination*, ed. Alkis Kontos (Toronto: Univ. of Toronto Press, 1975), pp. 17-31.

[65] Rev. of *For King and Country*, *The Canadian Monthly and National Review*, 6 (Dec. 1874), 571.

[66] W. D. Lighthall, *Songs of the Great Dominion* (London: Walter Scott, 1889), p. 458.

[67] "Roland Graeme: Knight," *The Week*, 25 Nov. 1892, p. 826.

[68] Rev. of *For King and Country*, *The Canadian Monthly and National Review*, 6 (Dec. 1874), 572.

[69] Rev. of *Marjorie's Canadian Winter*, *The Week*, 14 Oct. 1892, p. 731.

[70] "Roland Graeme: Knight," *The Week*, 25 Nov. 1892, pp. 826-27.

[71] W. W. Campbell, "At the Mermaid Inn," *The Globe* [Toronto], 26 Nov. 1892; rpt. in *At the Mermaid Inn: Wilfred Campbell, Archibald Lampman, Duncan Campbell Scott in* The Globe *1892-3,* introd. Barrie Davies (Toronto: Univ. of Toronto Press, 1979), pp. 195-96.

[72] Cumberland, *Queen's Quarterly*, p. 333.

[73] Cumberland, *Queen's Quarterly*, pp. 332-33.

[74] Watt, p. 461.

[75] Mary Vipond, "Blessed Are the Peacemakers: The Labour Question in Canadian Social Gospel Fiction," *Journal of Canadian Studies*, 10, No. 3 (1975), 32-43.

[76] Vipond, p. 42.

[77] In 1872, for example, Leprohon published "Clive Weston's Wedding Anniversary" in *The Canadian Monthly and National Review*, to which Machar was a major contributor.

[78] McKillop, p. 137.

[79] Bevan, p. 205.

[80] James De Mille, *Cord and Creese* (New York: Harper, 1869), p. 59.

[81] James De Mille, *A Comedy of Terrors* (Boston: Osgood, 1872), pp. 42-43.

[82] "Professor D'Mill's [sic] Inaugural Address," *Dalhousie Gazette*, 15 Nov. 1873, pp. 1-6.

[83] Archibald MacMechan, "Editor's Note," in *Behind the Veil*, by James De Mille (Halifax: T. C. Allen, 1893), n. pag.

[84] Northrop Frye, *The Secular Scripture: A Study of the Structure of Romance* (Cambridge: Harvard Univ. Press, 1976), pp. 39-40.

[85] James De Mille, *An Open Question: A Novel* (New York: Appleton, 1873), p. 233.

[86] James De Mille, *The American Baron* (New York: Harper, 1871), p. 67.

[87] James De Mille, *The Babes in the Wood, a Tragic Comedy: A Story of the Italian Revolution of 1848* (Boston: Gill, 1875), p. 9.

[88] De Mille, *The Babes in the Wood*, p. 110.

[89] De Mille, *The American Baron*, p. 67.

[90] Agnes Maule Machar, *Katie Johnstone's Cross: A Canadian Tale* (Toronto: Campbell, 1870), p. 145.

[91] Agnes Maule Machar, *Marjorie's Canadian Winter: A Story of the Northern Lights* (Boston: Lothrop, 1893), p. 243.

[92] Agnes Maule Machar, "Lost and Won: A Canadian Romance," *The Canadian Monthly and National Review*, 7 (1875), 211, 481.

[93] Leprohon, "The Manor House of de Villerai," *Family Herald* [Montreal], 4 Jan. 1860, p. 61.

[94] Rosanna Leprohon, "Ada Dunmore; or, A Memorable Christmas Eve: An Autobiography," *Canadian Illustrated News*, 1 (1870), 123.

[95] Rosanna Leprohon, "The Stepmother," *The Literary Garland*, NS 5 (1847), 166.

[96] Rosanna Leprohon, "Ida Beresford; or, The Child of Fashion," *The Literary Garland*, NS 6 (1848), 114.

[97] Rosanna Leprohon, *Antoinette de Mirecourt; or, Secret Marrying and Secret Sorrowing* (Montreal: Lovell, 1864), p. 221. All further references to this work (*AM*) appear in the text.

[98] William Kirby, *The Chien d'Or; The Golden Dog: A Legend of Quebec* (Montreal: Lovell, Adam, 1877), p. 678.

[99] Rev. of *For King and Country*, *The Canadian Monthly and National Review*, 6 (Dec. 1874), 571.

[100] Heroine of "The Manor House of de Villerai."

[101] Heroine of "Florence; or, Wit and Wisdom."

[102] Machar, "Lost and Won," *The Canadian Monthly and National*

Review, 8 (1875), 105.

[103] Leprohon, "The Stepmother," *The Literary Garland*, NS 5 (1847), 78.

[104] Rosanna Leprohon, *Armand Durand; or, A Promise Fulfilled* (Montreal: Lovell, 1868), p. 12. All further references to this work (*AD*) appear in the text.

[105] Leprohon, "Ada Dunmore," *Canadian Illustrated News*, 12 Feb. 1870, p. 235.

[106] James De Mille, *The "B.O.W.C."* (Boston: Lee and Shepard, 1869), p. 42.

[107] James De Mille, *Lost in the Fog* (Boston: Lee and Shepard, 1870), p. 20.

[108] James De Mille, *Fire in the Woods* (Boston: Lee and Shepard, 1871), p. 113.

[109] James De Mille, *A Strange Manuscript Found in a Copper Cylinder* (New York: Harper, 1888), p. 245. All further references to this work (*SM*) appear in the text.

[110] Woodcock, p. 178. See also the criticism of Crawford Kilian, M. G. Parks, and R. E. Watters.

[111] Henry Morgan, *Bibliotheca Canadensis* (Ottawa: Desbarats, 1867), p. 224.

[112] James De Mille, *The Seven Hills* (Boston: Lee and Shepard, 1873), p. 237.

[113] Machar, "Lost and Won," *The Canadian Monthly and National Review*, 7 (1875), 28.

[114] Agnes Maule Machar, *Roland Graeme, Knight: A Novel of Our Time* (Montreal: Drysdale, 1892), p. 203. All further references to this work (*RG*) appear in the text.

[115] Machar, "Lost and Won," *The Canadian Monthly and National Review*, 7 (1875), 485.

[116] Watt, p. 461.

[117] See Marian Fowler, " 'Substance and Shadow': Conventions of the Marriage Market in *Northanger Abbey*," *English Studies in Canada*, 6 (Fall 1980), 277-91.

[118] Leprohon, "The Stepmother," *The Literary Garland*, NS 5 (1847), 261.

[119] Leprohon, "The Manor House of de Villerai," *Family Herald* [Montreal], 1 Feb. 1860, p. 93.

[120] Rosanna Leprohon, "A School-Girl Friendship," *Canadian Illustrated News*, 16 (1877), 134.

[121] Machar, *Marjorie's Canadian Winter*, p. 83.

[122] Agnes Maule Machar, *Lucy Raymond; or, The Children's Watchword* (Toronto: Campbell, n.d.), p. 166.

[123] De Mille, *A Comedy of Terrors*, p. 46.

[124] "Professor DeMill's [sic] Address," *Dalhousie Gazette*, NS 4 (1878), 5.

[125] "Professor DeMill's Address," p. 6.

[126] "Professor DeMill's Address," p. 16.

[127] James De Mille, *The Boys of Grand Pré School* (Boston: Lee and Shepard, 1870), pp. 176-86.

[128] Agnes Maule Machar, *For King and Country* (Toronto: Adam, Stevenson, 1874), p. 245.

[129] Agnes Maule Machar, "Views of Canadian Literature," *The Week*, 23 March 1894, pp. 391-92.

[130] Al Purdy, "Roblin's Mills (2)," in *Selected Poems* (Toronto: McClelland and Stewart, 1972), p. 117.

SELECTED BIBLIOGRAPHY

Rosanna Eleanor Mullins Leprohon: *Primary Sources*

Mullins, Rosanna Eleanor. "The Stepmother." *The Literary Garland*, NS 5 (Feb.-June 1847).

—. "Ida Beresford; or, The Child of Fashion." *The Literary Garland*, NS 6 (Jan.-Sept. 1848).

—. "Alice Sydenham's First Ball." *The Literary Garland*, NS 7 (Jan. 1849), 1-14. Rpt. in *Nineteenth-Century Canadian Stories*. Ed. David Arnason. Toronto: Macmillan, 1976, pp. 96-127.

—. "Florence; or, Wit and Wisdom." *The Literary Garland*, NS 7 (Feb.-Dec. 1849).

—. "Eva Huntingdon." *The Literary Garland*, NS 8 (Jan.-Dec. 1850).

—. "Clarence Fitz-Clarence." *The Literary Garland*, NS 9 (Jan.-May 1851).

Leprohon, Rosanna Eleanor. "Eveleen O'Donnell." *The Pilot* [Boston], 24 Jan.-26 Feb. 1859.

—. "The Manor House of de Villerai." *Family Herald* [Montreal], 16 Nov. 1859-8 Feb. 1860.

—, trans. *Cantate en l'honneur de Son Altesse Royale Le Prince de Galles*. By Edouard Sempé. Montréal: Louis Perrault, 1860.

—. *Antoinette de Mirecourt; or, Secret Marrying and Secret Sorrowing*. Montreal: Lovell, 1864. Rpt. Toronto: Univ. of Toronto Press, 1973. Rpt. New Canadian Library, No. 89. Toronto: McClelland and Stewart, 1973.

—. *Armand Durand; or, A Promise Fulfilled*. Montreal: Lovell, 1868.

—. "Ada Dunmore; or, A Memorable Christmas Eve: An Autobiography." *Canadian Illustrated News*, 1 (25 Dec. 1869-12 Feb. 1870).

—. "My Visit to Fairview Villa." *Canadian Illustrated News*, 14 May-28 May 1870.

—. "Clive Weston's Wedding Anniversary." *The Canadian Monthly and National Review*, 2 (July-Aug. 1872). Rpt. in *The Evolution of Canadian Literature in English: Beginnings to 1867*. Ed. Mary Jane Edwards.

Toronto: Holt, Rinehart and Winston, 1973, pp. 266-301.
————. "Who Stole the Diamonds?" *Canadian Illustrated News*, 2 Jan.-9 Jan. 1875.
————. "A School-Girl Friendship." *Canadian Illustrated News*, 25 Aug.-15 Sept. 1877.
————. *The Poetical Works of Mrs. Leprohon*. Montreal: Lovell, 1881. Rpt. Toronto: Univ. of Toronto Press, 1973.

James De Mille: *Primary Sources*

De Mille, James. *The Martyr of the Catacombs: A Tale of Ancient Rome.* 1865; rpt. New York: Hunt and Eaton, n.d.
————. *Helena's Household: A Tale of Rome in the First Century.* 1867; rpt. London: Nelson, 1883.
————. *The "B.O.W.C."* [Brethren of the Order of the White Cross]. Boston: Lee and Shepard, 1869.
————. *Cord and Creese*. New York: Harper, 1869.
————. *The Dodge Club; or, Italy in MDCCCLIX.* New York: Harper, 1869. Rpt. Sackville, N.B.: Ralph Pickard Bell Library, 1981.
————. *The Boys of Grand Pré School*. B.O.W.C. Series. Boston: Lee and Shepard, 1870.
————. *The Cryptogram*. New York: Harper, 1870.
————. *The Lady of the Ice: A Novel.* New York: Appleton, 1870.
————. *Lost in the Fog.* B.O.W.C. Series. Boston: Lee and Shepard, 1870.
————. "The Minnehaha Mines." *The New Dominion and True Humorist*, 8 Jan.-25 June 1870.
————. *The American Baron*. New York: Harper, 1871.
————. *Among the Brigands.* Young Dodge Club Series. Boston: Lee and Shepard, 1871.
————. *Fire in the Woods.* B.O.W.C. Series. Boston: Lee and Shepard, 1871.
————. *A Comedy of Terrors*. Boston: Osgood, 1872.
————. *Picked Up Adrift.* B.O.W.C. Series. Boston: Lee and Shepard, 1872.
————. *An Open Question: A Novel.* New York: Appleton, 1873.
————. *The Seven Hills.* Young Dodge Club Series. Boston: Lee and Shepard, 1873.
————. "Professor D'Mill's Inaugural Address." *Dalhousie Gazette*, 15 Nov. 1873, pp. 1-6.

———. *The Treasure of the Seas*. B.O.W.C. Series. Boston: Lee and Shepard, 1873.

———. *The Lily and the Cross: A Tale of Acadia*. Boston: Lee and Shepard, 1874.

———. *The Living Link: A Novel*. New York: Harper, 1874.

———. *The Babes in the Wood, a Tragic Comedy: A Story of the Italian Revolution of 1848*. Boston: Gill, 1875.

———. *The Winged Lion; or, Stories of Venice*. Young Dodge Club Series. 1877; rpt. New York: Dillingham, 1899.

———. "Professor DeMill's Address." *Dalhousie Gazette*, NS 4 (1878), 1-7, 13-17.

———. *A Castle in Spain: A Novel*. New York: Harper, 1883.

———. *Old Garth: A Story of Sicily*. New York: Munro, 1883.

———. *A Strange Manuscript Found in a Copper Cylinder*. New York: Harper, 1888. Rpt. New Canadian Library, No. 68. Toronto: McClelland and Stewart, 1969.

———. *Behind the Veil*. Halifax: T. C. Allen, 1893.

Agnes Maule Machar: *Primary Sources*

Machar, Agnes Maule. *Faithful unto Death: A Memorial of John Anderson, Late Janitor of Queen's College*. Kingston: Creighton, 1859.

———. *Katie Johnstone's Cross: A Canadian Tale*. Toronto: Campbell, 1870.

———. *Lucy Raymond; or, The Children's Watchword*. Toronto: Campbell, n.d.

———. *For King and Country*. Toronto: Adam, Stevenson, 1874.

———. "Lost and Won: A Canadian Romance." *The Canadian Monthly and National Review*, 7 (Jan. 1875)-8 (Dec. 1875).

———. *Stories of New France, Being Tales of Adventure and Heroism from the Early History of Canada*. Boston: Lothrop, 1890.

———. "Parted Ways." *The Week*, 19 June 1891, pp. 461-63.

———. *Roland Graeme, Knight: A Novel of Our Time*. Montreal: Drysdale, 1892.

———, and T. G. Marquis. *Heroes of Canada*. Toronto: Copp Clark, 1893.

———. *Marjorie's Canadian Winter: A Story of the Northern Lights*. Boston: Lothrop, 1893.

———. *Down the River to the Sea*. New York: Home Book, 1894.

————. "Views of Canadian Literature." *The Week*, 23 March 1894, pp. 391-92.

————. *The Heir of Fairmount Grange*. London: Digby Long; Toronto: Copp Clark, 1895.

————. *Lays of the "True North" and Other Canadian Poems*. Toronto: Copp Clark, 1899.

————. *Stories of the British Empire for Young Folks and Busy Folks*. Toronto: Briggs, 1913.

Rosanna Eleanor Mullins Leprohon: *Secondary Sources*

"Antoinette de Mirecourt." *L'Ordre*, 12 déc. 1864, p. 2.

Brady, Elizabeth. "Towards a Happier History: Women and Domination." In *Domination*. Ed. Alkis Kontos. Toronto: Univ. of Toronto Press, 1975, pp. 17-31.

Champagne, Guy. "Cantate en l'honneur de Son Altesse Royale Le Prince de Galles, par Edouard Sempé." *Dictionnaire des Oeuvres Littéraires du Québec*, I (1978).

D., J. "Madame Leprohon." *L'Opinion Publique*, 2 oct. 1879, pp. 469-70.

de Bellefeuille, E. Lef. "*Antoinette de Mirecourt*." *La Revue Canadienne*, 1 (juil. 1864), 442-44.

Deneau, Henri. "The Life and Works of Mrs. Leprohon." M.A. Thesis Montréal 1948.

Edwards, Mary Jane. "Essentially Canadian." *Canadian Literature*, No. 52 (Spring 1972), pp. 8-23.

Klinck, Carl F., introd. *Antoinette de Mirecourt; or, Secret Marrying and Secret Sorrowing*. By Rosanna Leprohon. New Canadian Library, No. 89. Toronto: McClelland and Stewart, 1973.

Lesperance, John Talon. "The Literary Standing of the New Dominion." *Canadian Illustrated News*, 24 Feb. 1877, p. 118.

Moodie, Susanna. "Editor's Table." *The Victoria Magazine*, 1 (June 1848), 240.

Morgan, Henry J. "Leprohon, Mrs." In *The Dominion Annual Register and Review for 1879*. Ottawa: MacLean, Roger, 1880, p. 409.

Shohet, Linda. "Love and Marriage — Canada 1760." *Journal of Canadian Fiction*, 2, No. 3 (Summer 1973), 101-03.

Stockdale, John C. "Mullins, Rosanna (Leprohon)." *Dictionary of Canadian Biography*, X (1972).

———. "Ada Dunmore," "Antoinette de Mirecourt," "Armand Durand," "Ida Beresford," and "Le Manoir de Villerai." *Dictionnaire des Oeuvres Littéraires du Québec*, I (1978).

"The Late Mrs. Leprohon." *Canadian Illustrated News*, 4 Oct. 1879, p. 211.

"The Old Thing." Rev. of *Antoinette de Mirecourt*. *The Saturday Reader*, 9 Sept. 1865, p. 4.

"The Poetical Works of Mrs. Leprohon." *Rose-Belford's Canadian Monthly*, 8 (1882), 325.

James De Mille: *Secondary Sources*

Bevan, A. R. "James De Mille and Archibald MacMechan." *Dalhousie Review*, 35 (Autumn 1955), 201-15.

Burpee, Lawrence J. "Who's Who in Canadian Literature: James De Mille." *The Canadian Bookman*, 8 (1926), 203-06.

Crockett, A. J., and George Geddie Patterson. "Concerning James De Mille." In *More Studies in Nova Scotian History*. By George Geddie Patterson. Halifax: Imperial, 1941, pp. 120-48.

Douglas, R. W. "Concerning James De Mille." *The Canadian Bookman*, 4 (1922), 39-44.

Flemming, Tom. "James De Mille: A Bibliography." Unpublished MS. Dalhousie School of Library Service, 1974.

Hughes, Kenneth J. "*A Strange Manuscript*: Sources, Satire, a Positive Utopia." In *The Canadian Novel: Beginnings*. Ed. John Moss. Toronto: NC, 1980, pp. 111-25.

Kilian, Crawford. "The Cheerful Inferno of James De Mille." *Journal of Canadian Fiction*, 1, No. 3 (1972), 61-67.

Kime, Wayne R. "The American Antecedents of James De Mille's *A Strange Manuscript Found in a Copper Cylinder*." *The Dalhousie Review*, 55 (Summer 1975), 280-306.

Koopman, Harry Lyman. "Literary Men of Brown, III: James De Mille." *Brown Alumni Monthly*, 8 (1907), 27-30.

MacLeod, Douglas. "A Critical Biography of James De Mille." M.A. Thesis Dalhousie 1968.

MacMechan, Archibald. "An Important Canadian Poem." *The Week*, 9 Dec. 1892, pp. 36-37.

———. "De Mille, the Man and the Writer." *The Canadian Magazine*, 27 (1906), 404-16.

————. "Concerning James De Mille." *The Canadian Bookman*, 4 (1922), 125-26.

Parks, M. G. "Strange to Strangers Only." *Canadian Literature*, No. 70 (Autumn 1976), pp. 61-78.

Rev. of *A Strange Manuscript Found in a Copper Cylinder*. *The Week*, 26 July 1888, p. 561.

Rev. of *The Living Link*. *Canadian Illustrated News*, 22 Aug. 1874, p. 118.

Roberts, Charles G. D. "De Mille's 'Behind the Veil.'" *The Week*, 23 Feb. 1894, p. 301.

Stewart, George. "Canadian Literature." *Stewart's Quarterly Magazine*, 3 (Jan. 1870), 403-04.

————. "Professeur James De Mille." In *"Scrap-Book" Contenant Divers Souvenirs Personnels du Canada et des "21," Quelques Poésies, etc*. By Comte de Premio-Real. Quebec: C. Darveau, 1880, pp. 175-92.

Tracy, Minerva. "De Mille, James." *Dictionary of Canadian Biography*, x (1972).

Watters, R. E., introd. *A Strange Manuscript Found in a Copper Cylinder*. By James De Mille. New Canadian Library, No. 68. Toronto: McClelland and Stewart, 1969.

Woodcock, George. "Absence of Utopias." *Canadian Literature*, No. 42 (Autumn 1969), pp. 3-5.

————. "De Mille and the Utopian Vision." *Journal of Canadian Fiction*, 2, No. 3 (1973), 174-79.

Agnes Maule Machar: *Secondary Sources*

Campbell, William Wilfred. "At the Mermaid Inn." *The Globe* [Toronto], 26 Nov. 1892. Rpt. in *At the Mermaid Inn: Wilfred Campbell, Archibald Lampman, Duncan Campbell Scott in* The Globe *1892-3*. Introd. Barrie Davies. Toronto: Univ. of Toronto Press, 1979, pp. 195-96.

Chenier, Nancy Miller. "Agnes Maule Machar: Her Life, Her Social Concerns, and a Preliminary Bibliography of Her Writing." M.A. Thesis Carleton 1977.

Cumberland, R. W. "Agnes Maule Machar." *Queen's Quarterly*, 34 (Jan. 1927), 331-39.

————. "Agnes Maule Machar." *Willison's Monthly*, 3 (June 1927), 34-37.

———. "Remembering Agnes Maule Machar." *Historic Kingston*, No. 21 (April 1972), pp. 22-27.

Guild, Leman A: "Canadian Celebrities: No. 73 — Agnes Maule Machar." *The Canadian Magazine*, 27 (1906), 499-501.

Lighthall, W. D. *Songs of the Great Dominion*. London: Walter Scott, 1889.

MacCallum, F. L. "Agnes Maule Machar." *The Canadian Magazine*, 62 (1924), 354-56.

McManus, Emily. "*Lays of the 'True North' and Other Canadian Poems.*" *The Canadian Magazine*, 14 (Dec. 1899), 174-77.

Rev. of *For King and Country*. *The Canadian Monthly and National Review*, 6 (Dec. 1874), 571-72.

Rev. of *Marjorie's Canadian Winter: A Story of the Northern Lights*. *The Week*, 14 Oct. 1892, pp. 731-32.

Rev. of *Stories of New France*. *The Week*, 21 Feb. 1890, p. 188.

Rev. of *The Heir of Fairmount Grange*. *The Week*, 15 March 1895, p. 375.

"*Roland Graeme: Knight.*" *The Week*, 25 Nov. 1892, pp. 826-27.

Vipond, Mary. "Blessed Are the Peacemakers: The Labour Question in Canadian Social Gospel Fiction." *Journal of Canadian Studies*, 10, No. 3 (Aug. 1975), 32-43.

Wetherald, Ethelwyn. "Some Canadian Literary Women — II. 'Fidelis.' " *The Week*, 5 April 1888, pp. 300-01.

Secondary Sources: *General*

Bentley, D. M. R., and Mary Lynn Wickens. *A Checklist of Literary Materials in* The Week. Ottawa: Golden Dog, 1978.

Brown, Mary Markham. *An Index to* The Literary Garland. Toronto: Bibliographical Society of Canada, 1962.

Egoff, Sheila. *The Republic of Childhood*. Toronto: Oxford Univ. Press, 1975.

Flitton, Marilyn. *An Index to* The Canadian Monthly and National Review *and* Rose-Belford's Canadian Monthly. Toronto: Bibliographical Society of Canada, 1976.

Frye, Northrop. *The Secular Scripture: A Study of the Structure of Romance*. Cambridge: Harvard Univ. Press, 1976.

Klinck, Carl F., gen. ed. and introd. *Literary History of Canada: Canadian Literature in English*. Toronto: Univ. of Toronto Press, 1967.

Logan, J. D. *The Highway of Canadian Literature.* Toronto: McClelland and Stewart, 1924.

MacMechan, Archibald. *Headwaters of Canadian Literature.* Toronto: McClelland and Stewart, 1924.

MacMurchy, Archibald. *Handbook of Canadian Literature.* Toronto: Briggs, 1906.

McKillop, A. B. *A Disciplined Intelligence: Critical Enquiry and Canadian Thought in the Victorian Era.* Montreal: McGill-Queen's Univ. Press, 1979.

Morgan, Henry J. *Sketches of Celebrated Canadians.* Quebec: Hunter, Rose, 1862.

————. *Bibliotheca Canadensis.* Ottawa: Desbarats, 1867.

————. *Canadian Men and Women of the Time.* Toronto: Briggs, 1898.

Pacey, Desmond. *Creative Writing in Canada.* 1952; rev. ed. Toronto: Ryerson, 1967.

Pierce, Lorne. *An Outline of Canadian Literature.* Toronto: Ryerson, 1927.